PELICAN BOOKS

A 380

EDUCATION

W. O. LESTER SMITH

W. O. Lester Smith was born in Montgomeryshire in 1888, and educated at the King's School, Chester, and Merton College, Oxford. After teaching in a Grammar and a Public School, he served as an assistant education officer in Warwickshire and Lancashire. He was for seven years Chief Education Officer for Essex, and from 1931 to 1949 Manchester's Chief Education Officer. He has served on several of the national councils and committees referred to in this book, and has been President of the Education Section of the British Association, the Association of Directors and Secretaries of Education, the College of Preceptors, and the School Library Association. From 1949 to 1953 he was Professor of the Sociology of Education in the University of London. Among his publications are *To Whom do Schools Belong?*, *The Impact of Education on Society*, *Education in Great Britain*, and *Compulsory Education in England*.

EDUCATION

AN INTRODUCTORY SURVEY

W. O. Lester Smith

PENGUIN BOOKS

Penguin Books Ltd, Harmondsworth, Middlesex, England
Penguin Books Inc., 3300 Clipper Mill Road, Baltimore 11, Md, U.S.A.
Penguin Books Pty Ltd, Ringwood, Victoria, Australia

—

Published in Penguin Books 1957
Reprinted 1958
Reprinted with revisions 1961, 1962, 1964, 1965

—

Copyright © W. O. Lester Smith, 1957

—

Made and printed in Great Britain
by Hunt, Barnard & Co. Ltd, Aylesbury
Set in Monotype Baskerville

CONTENTS

CHAPTER ONE

WHAT IS EDUCATION?

Can it be Defined?

Defining education has been likened to a parlour game, an innocent but useless way of passing the time. This comparison does less than justice to the many, including some of the truly great, who have striven to define it; but the comment is not altogether unfair. For education does not lend itself to definition, and certainly not to one that can endure as unalterably true. Gilbert Murray once said of religion that like 'most other living things' – he instanced poetry – it cannot be defined.[1] Education belongs to that category, but this does not warrant a complete disregard of the various definitions that have come down to us; we can learn much from them, even from their inadequacies. But it does suggest that it is idle to expect an authoritative, unequivocal answer to the question – What is education?; and it suggests, too, that when thinking about education we must not forget that it has the growing quality of a living organism. While it has permanent attributes, it is constantly changing, adapting itself to new demands and new circumstances. No one who has personally witnessed the remarkable development of education in this country during the last fifty years will deny that in that relatively short period it has undergone something like a transformation.

Education not only changes with the years; it is as sensitive to place as it is to time. It bears a different meaning in different countries, and it is never quite the same thing in rural surroundings as it is in a crowded industrialized area. And

1. Quoted by N. Micklem in *Religion* (Home University Library, 1948), p. 9.

certainly some bad mistakes can be made by interpreting it in the same way in an under-developed country as in one that has reached an advanced stage of what we are pleased to call civilization. Even countries with many affinities tend to differ considerably in the theory and practice of their education. There is a good illustration of this in Dr J. B. Conant's *Education and Liberty*. This great American wished to give his fellow-citizens the best advice he could about the future development of secondary education in the U.S.A. So he visited a number of English-speaking countries, assuming that their conception of secondary education would be close enough to that of his own country to yield some useful comparative data. His tour led him to this firm conclusion: 'I do not believe', he wrote, 'that educational practices are an exportable commodity. I fear the contrary assumption has been implied to some extent in our dealings with Germany and Japan since World War II. At times in our own history, attempts to import a British or European concept have done more harm than good.'[1] But the fact that interpretations of education differ does not imply that we cannot learn much from those current in countries other than our own. Indeed comparative education is a most valuable study from a practical standpoint, and a world-wide organization like UNESCO does good work by showing how education is interpreted in different countries. We can learn much from each other, but it is not unreasonable to assume that diversity of interpretation will continue however contracted or accustomed to the intercommunication of thought our world becomes.

We need not, however, look outside our own country for differences of opinion about the meaning of education. Wide variations of interpretation exist among ourselves, usually as a result of religious or political convictions or both. We thus bring to our discussions about education and its problems different attitudes which profoundly influence the meaning that we assign to it; and just as we often find the conflicting

1. *Education and Liberty* (Harvard Univ. Press, 1953), p. 2.

opinions of our friends a stimulus, so also can the various interpretations of the great thinkers of the past prove a spur to thought. None has had more influence on educational development in this country than John Stuart Mill's. He was trying to persuade his mid-Victorian contemporaries to adopt a more generous view than was then customary. His words had no great effect at the time, but, percolating slowly, they have had a considerable influence on modern educational thought both here and elsewhere. A significant feature of his interpretation is that he gives education much wider frontiers than many have done; it embraces in his judgement not only the deliberate processes of school and college but much more, including even indirect and incidental influences. 'Not only does education include', he claimed, 'whatever we do for ourselves and whatever is done for us by others for the express purpose of bringing us nearer to the perfection of our nature; it does more: in its largest acceptation it comprehends even the indirect effects produced on character, and on the human faculties, by things of which the direct purposes are quite different; by laws, by forms of government, by the industrial arts, by modes of social life, nay, even by physical facts not dependent on human will; by climate, soil, and local position.' But, summing up, he suggests as the core of education: 'the culture which each generation purposely gives to those who are to be its successors, in order to qualify them for at least keeping up, and if possible for raising, the level of improvement which has been attained.'[1]

In recent years John Milton's definition has had a considerable vogue: 'I call, therefore, a complete and generous education, that which fits a man to perform justly, skilfully, and magnanimously all the offices, both private and public, of peace and war.'[2] This owes some of its attraction to the magic of its phrasing, but its present popularity is probably more due to the fact that it was coined in and, in some

1. Inaugural address as Rector of St Andrew's University, 1867.
2. *Areopagitica and other Prose Works* (Everyman's Library), p. 46.

respects, seems particularly appropriate to a troublous and revolutionary era. Like Milton and his contemporaries we, too, have to be ready for anxious days and prepared for the changes and chances of an uneasy world, knowing not whether our lot is to be peace or war.[1]

When appraising definitions it is well to have regard to their context, and of the importance of this Milton's formula provides a good illustration. It forms part of a letter, generally known as *The Tractate on Education*, which he wrote in response to an urgent request by a Polish refugee, Samuel Hartlib, who was seeking support for a reform of education along lines advocated by Comenius, the famous Czech educator. At the time Milton was fully occupied with affairs of State: the Civil War was at a crucial stage and he was one of Cromwell's principal secretaries. *The Tractate* for all its noble idealism is not a particularly coherent document; it would not be rash to guess that it was written in haste, and it certainly contains traces of impatience. But when writing it, Milton found time to indicate what he had in mind as the method of providing the 'complete and generous education' that he recommends. His idea was that about 130 boys should be selected and that they should be boarded in a spacious mansion and there educated between the ages of 12 and 21 with Latin and Greek as the basis of instruction. While a system of rearing a *corps d'élite* in some such way would commend itself to some, it may be doubted whether it would be regarded by many, who quote his definition with approval, as particularly appropriate to education in a modern democracy. Most interpretations of education that have come down to us from the past reflect the political and social theory of their day, and it will not have escaped notice that Mill's interpretation, also, reflects the spirit of his age in its acceptance of Victorian perfectionism and confidence in progress.

Disraeli once said that he hated definitions, and many feel

1. For a word by word exposition of Milton's definition see Sir John Newsom, *The Child at School* (Penguin Books, 1950), pp. 15–22.

the same about them. They are in a study like education good servants but bad masters. On the other hand, no one can dispute the practical value of an honest effort by thought and study to arrive at one's own interpretation. For the knowledge thus gained is twice blest; it helps us to clear our own minds, and makes us more competent to help others. For whether as parents or teachers or members of an educational body or as citizens influencing opinion we can be much more effective if we have genuinely tried to sort out the basic issues. It is no easy task, but if at times we find it intolerably perplexing we can console ourselves with the thought that some of the great thinkers have found it difficult, too. 'The farther I sail,' says the wise Montaigne when in quest of the meaning of education, 'the more land I descry, and that so dimmed with fogs and overcast with clouds, that my sight is so weakened I cannot distinguish the same.'[1] Even Aristotle, one of the greatest of them all, found the task overwhelming as he searched for the answers some 2,500 years ago. 'We must not leave out of sight', he observes, 'the nature of education and the proper means of imparting it. For at present there is a practical dissension on this point; people do not agree on the subjects which the young should learn, whether they take virtue in the abstract or the best life as the end to be sought, and it is uncertain whether education should be properly directed rather to the cultivation of the intellect or the moral discipline. The question is complicated, too, if we look at the actual education of our own day; nobody knows whether the young should be trained at such studies as are merely useful as means of livelihood or in such as tend to the promotion of virtue or in the higher studies, all of which have received a certain number of suffrages. Nor again, if virtue be accepted as the end, is there any agreement as to the means of attaining it . . .'[2]

1. *Essays*, Florio's translation (Blackie), p. 31.
2. *Politics*, Book V, Chapter 3, p. 224. Welldon's translation (Macmillan, ed. 1888).

EDUCATION

A Continuous Process

It is impossible to arrive at a sensible interpretation of education without first settling the question of its span – when does it begin and when does it end? Opinion about this has fluctuated. Broadly speaking, there are two main views; one regards education as more or less co-terminous with school and college, while the other sees it as a process that continues through life.

The idea that education was an accomplishment that you acquired in school – or, if you were privileged, at college also, or from a private tutor – had a long reign in this country and in Europe. Throughout the eighteenth and much of the nineteenth century it was the normal belief that the public schools and the grammar schools supplied the kind of education 'necessary for a gentleman', while charity and other such schools provided all the education deemed appropriate for children of lower status. This conception of education as something almost confined to schools and colleges so embedded itself in our tradition that even to-day many, who would stoutly disown it, pay lip-service to it. Indeed most of us when talking about the education of our own or other people's children have specially in mind their schools and what happens to them there. When parents take out an insurance policy to cover the cost of their children's 'education', they are getting ready to pay the high fees of the exclusive schools for which they have entered them. Or, again, when careers are recorded in that massive reference book, *Who's Who*, those born with silver spoons enter as their 'education' Eton and Trinity or some similar combination, while those who have come up the hard way follow the example of Ramsay Macdonald, and give their 'education' as 'Board School' unless they are more specific like that beloved Minister of Education, George Tomlinson, who rejoiced to be able to give all the credit to Rishton Wesleyan.

The earlier Victorians had many virtues but their conventional attitude to education was not one of them. For they drew a sharp distinction between education and life, and their pedagogy was an affair of the class-room, harsh and joyless. The grammar schools still, as Charles Lamb described those of his day, revolved 'in a perpetual cycle of declensions, conjugations, syntaxes, and prosodies', while the elementary schools drilled their children in the 3 Rs with rod and regimentation. Bell and Lancaster, the rival exponents of the monitorial system, set the pattern of what their admirers were pleased to call 'education'. The basic aim of our first great education statute, the Elementary Education Act of 1870, was to get the children to school, and there was a strong tendency to assume that securing attendance at school was equivalent to education. This was the climate of opinion when Mill expounded his very different interpretation of it, as recorded in the preceding section; it was the utterance of a great prophet in revolt against a conception of education that seemed to him based on a false view of human rights and of human nature. It is worth noting here, incidentally, that Mill's Autobiography gives, perhaps, the best self-portrait in our literature of 'a life-long learner'. He got many of his ideas from his father, 'but he was perpetually bringing them into contact with fresh experience and new trains of thought, considering how they worked, and how they ought to be modified in order to maintain what was really sound and valuable in their content.'[1]

The Victorian era was an age of prophets, and most of them in different ways sounded the note of educational reform, and proclaimed the need for more vision and a much wider interpretation of scope and function. The seeds sown by them took a long time to germinate, and it was not until the twentieth century had got under way that education began to feel the impulse of radical change. Surveying the educational landscape as it appeared after the First World War one of the shrewdest of contemporary observers notes especially the changing attitude of the public towards educa-

1. L. T. Hobhouse, *Liberalism* (Home Univ. Library), p. 107.

tion and the growing influence of psychology within the school; 'the influence of psychological ideas on education', he notes, 'may be seen in the agitation for Nursery Schools, in the new methods of teaching young children, in the conception of definite stages of mental growth, in modern discipline, and in the concentration of efforts to deal with the turbulent period of adolescence.'[1] The publication of the first Hadow Report in 1926 gave a great impetus to this new outlook, and it stands out as a notable landmark. For in this constructive document the Consultative Committee, under the chairmanship of Sir Henry Hadow, embodied much new thought about education and gave their weighty official support to a much more generous interpretation of it. It dealt specifically with 'The Education of the Adolescent', but the same Committee followed it up with two further reports covering the junior and infant stages, in which they took full advantage of the new knowledge about child development that the study of physiology and psychology had made available. These reports, together with the Spens Report published in 1938, provided a solid basis for the reconstruction of education from the infant stage to the end of the secondary school period. It is not too much to claim that they gave education in the school sense a new meaning, which later found statutory expression in the Education Act of 1944. During the same period child study, the nursery school movement, and the influence of maternity and child welfare clinics transformed the attitude to the pre-school stage, and stimulated a new interest in the upbringing of very young children. The old conception of education as something that began when you first went to school ceased to be tenable; there can be few thoughtful people to-day who do not recognize the educative significance of the pre-school years.

There is also an increasing emphasis on the importance of the immediate post-school years, the education of the young worker. Not only is there a considerable literature about the

1. H. Ward, *Notes for the Study of English Education, 1860–1930* (Bell, 1937), p. 92.

special problems of adolescence but ever since the Lewis Committee reported in 1916 on the need for continuation schools we have as a nation been conscious that some such provision for universal part-time schooling for youth ought to be made. H. A. L. Fisher included such a project in his Act of 1918 but as a result of alleged economic difficulties it was still-born. Similarly County Colleges were an outstanding feature of the Act of 1944, but once again post-war economics stood in the way of fulfilment. The requirement that they shall be provided at a time to be determined is, however, still on the statute book and definitely the law of the land; and the acceptance by Parliament of the principle of their provision is additional evidence, if such is needed, of the modern view that the educative process should not be regarded as something that ceases when full-time schooling ends. Further evidence of this attitude is afforded by the Youth Service, the numerous apprenticeship schemes, and the notable increase in the schemes for the part-time education of young workers. The conversion of industry to a belief in continued education is, when one recalls the not-so-distant past, truly remarkable. In 1938 about 40,000 young employees were receiving systematic education during working hours. After the war this number 'went up by leaps and bounds. By 1947 it had grown to over 167,000 . . . by 1952, when the number of participating occupations had risen to over eighty, to almost 300,000';[1] and by 1962 to 500,000.

One reason for the growing belief in a continuing education is that we are realizing more and more that a Welfare State needs an educated democracy with a good sense of citizenship. Without that it can all too easily become drab, impersonal, lacking aims and ideals. This has led some of the best minds of our time to regard education at the adult stage as of supreme importance. We are now consciously and unconsciously shaping a new order of society, and so far, with our strong desire for social security, we have tended to give

1. H. C. Dent, *Growth of English Education, 1946–52* (Routledge and Kegan Paul, 1954), p. 133.

priority to the economic foundations. But as de Tocqueville warned America over a century ago you cannot have a decent democratic society without a good quality of citizenship. 'The first duty which is at this time imposed upon those who direct our affairs', he argued, 'is to educate the democracy; to warm its faith, if that be possible; to purify its morals; to direct its energies, to substitute a knowledge of business for its inexperience, and an acquaintance with its true interests for its blind propensities.'[1] Among leaders of opinion in this country there has been much advocacy along these lines, and this view largely accounts for the ready acceptance of the comprehensive and costly Education Act of 1944. And for the same reason a significant feature of our time has been a widening conception of adult education, for which much of the credit must go to institutions unknown in the early years of this century, such as the BBC, the Arts Council, the Community Centre, and to movements like the Army Bureau of Current Affairs that have helped to foster the habit of group discussion.

'Nothing moves in this world', said Sir Henry Maine, 'which is not Greek in origin'; and it is certainly noticeable that some of the best constructive thinking about education in our time has been done by men like William Temple, Sir Ernest Barker, and Sir Richard Livingstone, all steeped in the philosophy of Ancient Greece. It may seem odd that the Ancient World should thus contribute to an understanding of the needs of a twentieth-century society, but the issues which Plato and Aristotle thought about so clearly were in many respects the same as those which exercise us to-day. In that sense they are a good deal more modern than some thinkers of more recent date; 'modernity', as Sir Richard Livingstone observed, 'is a question, not of date, but of outlook.'[2]

One of the issues which these Greek philosophers regarded as of cardinal importance was the quality of citizenship. We

1. *Democracy in America*, Preface.
2. *Some Tasks for Education* (Oxford Univ. Press, 1946), p. 5.

tend to stress the material benefits of the welfare state; they reckoned the quality of society and its ideals as the paramount consideration. To secure quality they placed great emphasis on education at the adult stage, believing that it is then, and not before, that fundamental problems can profitably be studied. We are gradually moving to a somewhat similar conception of further education, and are beginning to appreciate that a welfare state, however well-planned in a material sense, does not become thereby a good society. While genuinely thankful for full employment and all the beneficent social legislation, we are now recognizing more than we did that there are other elements – spiritual, ethical, cultural – essential to the good life. And the more we think along these lines, the more shall we agree with the Greek conviction that, however sound the foundations laid in childhood and adolescence, education must not end there; but that, on the contrary, it is only in maturity that the citizen can pursue effectively certain essential studies and interests.

The importance of adult education has been recognized in this country by thoughtful people for at least a century. F. D. Maurice founded his Working Men's College in 1854, Professor Stuart and others launched the university extension movement in 1867. We owe a great debt to the founders of settlements and polytechnics, and we are justly proud of the fine service rendered by the W.E.A. since its inauguration in 1903. In that sense there is nothing new in our regard for adult education, but there is an important change of attitude to the adult stage. We are beginning to appreciate much more that education at that stage, whether in an organized course or by self-study or the cultivation of some worth-while interest, is not an 'extra' but a natural and necessary continuance of the educative process, a further stage to which studies and pursuits requiring study and experience necessarily belong. We are, also, as a result of the redistribution of income, the expansion of universities, and the provision of secondary education for all, moving rapidly away from the notion that adult education is a service specially concerned with the enlightenment of unprivileged classes. At the same time our conception of the scope and function of adult education is widening to embrace new features, such as good drama and music, designed to enrich the cultural life of the neighbourhood.

The case for a fuller recognition of the importance of the adult stage has been argued by no one more cogently than Sir Richard Livingstone. The pith of his contention was that the most pressing need in education to-day is for courses at residential colleges or otherwise that 'will include that study of human ideals and achievement which we call literature, history, and politics, and that study of the material universe which we call science.'[1] Such education, he believed, can best be given in maturity. 'After fifty years spent in receiving or giving education,' he added, 'I am convinced that for the studies in question the years after 18 are a better age, and those after 30 better still.' In a book written in his later years Sir Ernest Barker illustrated the case for adult study with a personal reminiscence recounted with characteristic modesty. He told how he had been associated with courses for the training of men of an average age of nearly forty, 'some of them men of affairs more versed and experienced than he can claim to be, and some of them scholars of an equipment equal at least to his own.' He concluded with the comment: 'It has been a moving experience. We all learned, both those who were nominally teachers and those who were nominally students. But above all, we all learned that we needed to learn, and that we still had the faculty of learning and a zest for the use of our faculty.'[2]

One further reason why the adult stage is important is that so many people develop late, and frequently children who put up a poor performance at the age of 11 or fail to shine in the class-room or in examinations during their schooldays respond eagerly, when they have left school, under the stimulus of new interests and environment. There are many

1. *The Future in Education* (Cambridge Univ. Press, 1941), Preface.
2. *Reflections on Government* (Oxford Univ. Press, 1942), p. 415 note.

instances of men and women who after doing none too well at school made their mark in the world of affairs or learning. Wellington and Napoleon, so it is said, were reckoned dull boys, and much the same has been said of men of such various eminence as Sir Isaac Newton, Dean Swift, Clive, Sir Walter Scott, and Sheridan.[1] In our time Sir Winston Churchill provides the best example of a powerful intellect that did not get into its stride until schooldays were over. The urge to read and think came to him when, as a young subaltern, he was stationed at Bangalore. 'It was not', he tells us in a graphic account of his unaided struggle to educate himself, 'until this winter of 1896 when I had almost completed my twenty-second year, that the desire for learning came upon me. I began to feel myself wanting in even the vaguest knowledge about many large spheres of thought.' And with that introduction he devotes a whole chapter to his studies at that period of his life in ethics, history, philosophy and religion, and it is doubtful whether the case for education at the adult stage has ever been stated so vividly or with such humanity.[2] In 1953, when Churchill was Prime Minister, the then Minister of Education proposed some economies in the national expenditure on adult education. Sir Winston, himself, perhaps mindful of days and nights of intensive study at Bangalore, made a vigorous protest, expressing in his own inimitable way a belief in education at the adult stage on grounds that Plato would have highly approved. 'I have no doubt', he said, 'that a man or woman earnestly seeking in grown-up life to be guided to wide and suggestive knowledge in its largest and most uplifted sphere will make the best of all pupils in this age of clatter and buzz, of gape and gloat. The appetite of adults to be shown the foundations and processes of thought will never be denied by a British Administration cherishing the continuity of our island life.'

In framing the Education Act of 1944 Mr Butler, Mr Chuter Ede, and their advisers discarded the traditional nar-

1. Lubbock, *The Use of Life* (Macmillan, ed. 1895), p. 106.
2. *My Early Life* (Butterworth, 1930), Chapter IX.

row conception of education, and decided that 'the system of public education will be organized as a continuous process conducted in three successive stages – primary, secondary, and further.'[1] Ever since, the doctrine of the continuous process has been the basis of our national policy, and in official literature there are now frequent references to the educative significance of the pre- and post-school years as well as of the years of school. In the White Paper, in which Mr Butler outlined the underlying principles of the legislation he was to propose, he made it abundantly clear that he conceived education as beginning in early childhood and continuing through the adult stage. And he specifically endorsed the view of those who, like the Greeks, regard education as reaching its highest quality in later life. 'It is only', he observed, 'when the pupil or student reaches maturer years that he will have served an apprenticeship in the affairs of life sufficient to enable him to fit himself for service to the community.' And there is an echo of de Tocqueville in his remark: 'It is thus within the wider sphere of adult education that an ultimate training in democratic citizenship must be sought.'[2] While there may be individual differences of opinion about the span of education, there is no doubt about our official policy; as a nation we have decided to assume that education is a life-long process.

Emphasis on Growth

Throughout this century education in this country has been on the march, and the impact of new ideas and new techniques has revolutionized the inner life of the schools. The rate of change has accelerated in recent years and much that was written about education in the nineteen-twenties and thirties has already a musty out-of-dateness; especially has there been a transformation in our conception of the teacher's task. Fifty years ago in most schools education was considered

1. *Education Bill. Explanatory Memorandum*, Cmd 6492 (H.M.S.O., 1943).
2. *Educational Reconstruction*, Cmd 6458 (H.M.S.O., 1943).

to be almost entirely an affair of the class-room, and although the iniquitous system of payment-by-results had been repealed it continued to cast its shadows. Some older teachers accustomed to its rigid requirements still concentrated on the practice of drilling young children in the detail of what they regarded as essential knowledge; for them education was literally a process of knocking facts into empty heads. Their class-room procedure was based on a belief that the child mind is a vacuum that has to be filled with knowledge, and that we are endowed with certain faculties, such as memory and observation, which to be effective subsequently must be constantly exercised in childhood.

By the nineteen-twenties there was a notable change in normal class-room procedure; the old rigidities were becoming unfashionable and most teachers by then had very different ideas about the make-up of children's minds and of their duty towards them. But the outworn creed of 'knocking it into their heads' still lingered in schools that were behind the times, and during that period one finds Aldous Huxley vigorously protesting. 'The mind', he observed, 'is not a receptacle that can be mechanically filled. It is alive and must be nourished. Nourishment is best absorbed by the organism that feeds with appetite. If we treat the stomach as though it were a bucket and pump food into it, it will in all probability reject the nourishment in a paroxysm of nausea. So will the mind.' To lend emphasis to his point, Huxley drew a grim picture of the child of that time in his class-room: 'Passively, with his forty or fifty dissimilar and unique companions, he sits at his desk while the teacher pumps and mechanically repumps information into his mental receptacle.'[1] And clinching his argument, he quoted:

> Ram it in, ram it in!
> Children's heads are hollow.
> Ram it in, ram it in!
> Still there's more to follow.

Although hardly fair to the majority of schools at that time,

1. *Proper Studies* (Chatto and Windus, ed. 1927), p. 97.

Mr Huxley's scathing words had positive and constructive value, for they helped to breach ramparts still stubbornly resisting the advance of new knowledge about child development; but to-day they are interesting only as a period piece. For we are all biologists now, and there are few schools in which his contention about growth, nurture, and appetite or interest is not fully appreciated and acted upon. As a result of the scientific study of children we have acquired new ideas about their development, their differences, and their normal characteristics at various stages of growth. Teachers, as part of their preparation for their vocation, are grounded in knowledge of this kind, and many thoughtful parents take advantage of the now abundant literature about child development. This sense of growth has led us to think much about children's physique; we regard it as part of the business of education to see that they have nourishing meals and to ensure their bodily well-being. Physical education has ceased to be just drill, and its stress is on growth and movement; and our dieticians keep a watchful eye on the menus for school meals to secure that they are well-balanced and provide the right sort of food for children at different stages of growth.

Our attitude to mental development is not unlike our attitude to physique. The modern teacher thinks of the child, not as a passive recipient of imparted knowledge, but as learning most readily when actively pursuing some problem or project; he watches the developing mind and does his best to help and guide it, and he thinks of it as requiring, like the body, the right environment and the right nourishment for the various stages of growth. Formal teaching there still is in plenty in the later stages of childhood and adolescence, but it is designed to quicken a desire to learn and stimulate mental growth, and not as in the past to fill empty mental spaces. 'The immaturity of the learner, far from being a void which needs to be filled, is a positive capacity or potentiality for growth.'[1] It would, however, be wholly wrong to convey

1. J. S. Brubacher, *Modern Philosophies of Education* (McGraw-Hill, ed. 1950), p. 50.

the impression that all teaching in the early part of this century was of poor quality; if the theory was mistaken, that did not prevent hundreds of able and devoted teachers from giving their pupils good measure and inspiring them by the influence of their personality. Whatever the prevailing theory, it is always true that: 'Education is essentially the influence of one person on another. . . . Always the influence is that of one mind, one personality, one character on another. That, at any rate, is how it all begins.'[1] Nor can it be claimed that the transition to the modern way of nurture came about easily or smoothly without mishap; there has been much study, much hard thinking, much research and experiment.

And there have inevitably been some bad miscarriages, especially when teachers experienced in the old ways have without conviction been called upon to apply the new. A good example of the difficulties that can arise from revolutionary change in educational theory is afforded by a series of misunderstandings that followed a recommendation in one of the Hadow reports. After considering much evidence from psychologists and others about ways in which children develop, the Hadow Committee decided to make a strong recommendation deprecating the amount of formal instruction at the junior stage then customary, and urging instead the adoption of methods better calculated to develop individuality and foster mental growth. They crystallized their advice in the following words: 'The curriculum is to be thought of in terms of activity and experience rather than of knowledge to be acquired and facts to be stored.'[2] Many zealous teachers, not having comprehended fully the tenor of this well-balanced report, interpreted this advice in ways that were clearly not intended, and there were some school inspectors, also, who misconstrued it. In some schools, therefore, 'activity' was given a very literal and physical meaning, and

1. Sir John Wolfenden in *Education in a Changing World*, edited by C. H. Dobinson (Oxford Univ. Press, 1951), p. 47.
2. Report of Consultative Committee on the Primary School (H.M.S.O., 1931, 1945 reprint), p. 93.

there was a tendency for this to become purposeless, and for very little attention to be paid to the acquisition of 'knowledge' and 'facts'. This was particularly unfortunate because juniors (7–12), leaving fantasy behind, dislike aimless activity and enjoy actual achievement. The curiosity characteristic of that age whets the appetite for knowledge and for gleaning useful information.

Too often, therefore, children found the so-called activity boring, and the general effect of this widespread misunderstanding was to create an unwarranted suspicion of the new doctrine and a call for a return to the ancient ways. Commenting on this passage in the Hadow report, a Consultative Committee of the National Union of Teachers made this wise observation: 'We consider that this judgement needs revision in the light of subsequent experience. In our view this antithesis has proved unintentionally misleading, conveying the impression that the acquisition of knowledge and facts is not important in the junior school. There is great value in activity and experience . . . but we wish to emphasize that activity under the influence of a good teacher provides valuable opportunities for the acquisition of knowledge and facts at a time when so many pupils . . . show the characteristics of later childhood.'[1]

Alongside this new emphasis on mental and physical growth, there came new attitudes to moral training and the development of character. Historically the modern stress on character-training dates back to the Public School revival in the nineteenth century, and owes much of its inspiration to some great headmasters of that period, of whom Arnold and Thring made, perhaps, the greatest stir. It was a long, sustained, powerful movement at work throughout the century – Arnold and Thring were not contemporaries – and as well as the headmasters some of the pioneer headmistresses like Miss Beale and Miss Buss made important contributions to it. As a result character-training is an outstanding and es-

1. *The Curriculum of the Secondary School* (Evans: for the National Union of Teachers, 1952), p. 11.

sential feature of what we sometimes call the public school tradition. The majority of schools were, however, untouched by this new influence until the early years of the present century; for the elementary schools had been held back by the payment-by-results and merit grant oppressions. In 1904, however, Sir Robert Morant, one of the most constructive of our line of educational administrators, determined as permanent secretary of the Board of Education to get them out of the narrow groove in which they had run so long and so unhappily. A new code was issued, for which Morant wrote a preface opening with the words: 'The purpose of the Public Elementary School is to form and strengthen the character and to develop the intelligence of the children entrusted to it. . . . ' Commenting on its remarkable influence, the Ministry of Education recently observed: 'As a statement of aims it is still largely valid, and it was repeated in every edition of the Code until 1926, and thereafter in the Board's "Handbook of Suggestions for Teachers."'[1] Gradually this strong emphasis on character-training, which began in the Public Schools, has become normal practice throughout our educational system, and is firmly rooted in our tradition of education which, as Sir Cyril Norwood has well said, is not 'the monopoly of any type of school, or of any class in the community.'[2]

Character-training, as we interpret it, is closely linked with the conception of school as a society; for we believe that the best way to train character is by enabling boys and girls to learn the art of living as members one of another in the fellowship of school. Once again the doctrine of growth comes into play; we think of the pupils growing up and gaining experience of leadership and service in a microcosm of the greater society in which they will subsequently live as citizens. Thus, when advocating the raising of the school-leaving age prior to the passing of the Education Act of 1944, William Temple based his case chiefly not on the intellectual

1. *Education 1900–50*, Cmd. 8244 (H.M.S.O., 1951), p. 36.
2. *The English Tradition in Education* (John Murray, 1929), p. 243.

benefits but on the character-training value of the school during years of adolescence. 'The main ground', he argued, 'is the necessity of providing a social life or community in which the individual may feel that he has a real share and for which he may feel some genuine responsibility. . . . He needs a society of people about his own age, in the activities of which he may take a share equal to that of any other member, so that it may reasonably claim his loyalty, and he may have the sense of being wanted in it. Nothing else will draw out from him the latent possibilities of his nature.'[1]

As one would expect, these new conceptions of the educational needs of the child have transformed the relationship between teacher and pupil. The authority of the teacher is still a vital factor in the educative process, but he has become much more a guide and friend and much less the stern disciplinarian and instructor. Teachers of an earlier generation attached first importance to the presentation of their lesson material, and to their techniques for securing its assimilation by the pupil. Such considerations still have their place, but to-day 'the motivation of the pupil, the compatibility or incompatibility of the social climate of the school and that of the community, and the *rapport* between teacher and taught are considered of more importance than method.'[2] Aubrey de Selincourt cleverly reflects the modern teacher's way in the class-room in this brief description: 'Knowing that children learn only what they like,' he observes, 'we do what we can to make them like what we think they ought to learn. It is a great step forward. Many of the modern Infant and Junior Schools are wholly admirable in this respect, the best of them being well-furnished and fascinating play-grounds where the medicine of knowledge is offered in a sugar plum so large and delicious that it is swallowed with delight; and the same principle, suitably modified, most good teachers continue with boys and girls throughout their

1. *William Temple and his Message* (Penguin Books, 1946), p. 228.
2. Dr W. D. Wall in lecture at University of London Institute of Education. *The Times Educational Supplement*, 3 December 1954.

schooldays. . . . There is no doubt at all that good teaching depends upon making the work acceptable to children, no matter what their age; but to make work acceptable is not the same thing as to make it easy – or if it is, it won't do. Sooner or later every pupil has got to get down to the hard core of his subject.'[1] It is scarcely necessary to add that the practice of making subject-matter acceptable is to-day almost as usual in the grown-up world; there are journalists who spend their lives at it, some BBC producers are masters of the art, and so often are those who lead discussion groups or chair brains-trusts.

In the period between the wars leading exponents of education put the stress on individuality; the teacher's task, as they saw it, was to help each individual child to grow to 'full stature', a favourite phrase of the time. Among those influencing educational thought at that time none carried more weight than Sir Percy Nunn and Sir Cyril Norwood. Nunn's *Education: its data and first principles* has deservedly become a classic in educational circles; it made a profound impression, its declared objective being 'to reassert the claim of Individuality to be regarded as the supreme educational ideal.'[2] Soon afterwards came Sir Cyril Norwood's *English Tradition of Education*, which lent strong support from another angle to Nunn's individualist creed. 'We must stress individuality in education,' he maintained, 'individuality of the pupil, of the teacher, of the school . . . for, indeed, it is the key position of all. If this principle is lost, all is lost.'[3]

In recent years there has been an important shift of emphasis. We are no less mindful of the needs of the individual child and the development of his own personality, but we are rather more alive than we were in pre-war days to the necessity for fostering a spirit of service and a sense of responsibility to the community, and we are certainly more

1. *The Schoolmaster* (Lehmann, 1951), p. 70.
2. Edward Arnold, 1st ed., 1920, p. vii.
3. Murray, 1929, p. 308.

conscious of social influences – the home, the group, the local environment – and their bearing on child development. We think of children not only as individuals with rights of their own but even more – to use the title of one of the best pamphlets issued by the Ministry of Education in recent years – as 'citizens growing up', getting accustomed to duties and responsibilities. Some indeed think that the study of society will in the years ahead be the dominant factor in shaping educational thought and practice. Commenting on this trend, Professor Niblett observes: 'The study of the influence of society upon the individual has made giant strides in the past quarter of the century. The many exciting contributions made by sociology to our knowledge of human limitation, of human possibility, and the mechanisms of social change, are bound to have their effects upon educational practice both inside and outside the school. Indeed the findings of sociology may be as seminal in their influence upon the study and organization of education in the next fifty years as the findings of psychology in the last fifty.'[1]

Aims

In the burst of enthusiasm after the passing of the Education Act of 1944 much was said and written about education, and many educationalists were tempted to air their views on the difficult theme of aim and purpose. Some were inclined to be dogmatic, asserting definitely 'the aims of education are . . . ' or 'the purpose of education is . . . '. Speech-day platforms were littered with their pronouncements. In a book written at the time Mr T. S. Eliot assembled a little assortment of these bold assertions, and made this comment: 'When writers attempt to state *the purpose* of education, they are doing one of two things: they are eliciting what they believe to have been the unconscious purpose always, and thereby giving their own meaning to the history of the subject; or they are formulating what may not have been, or

1. *Education and the Modern Mind* (Faber, 1954), p. 21.

may have been only fitfully, the real purpose in the past, but should in their opinion be the purpose directing development in the future.'[1]

Even if we confine ourselves to the immediate present, about which we can claim some personal knowledge, it is scarcely possible to say what our educational aims are: this is a free country in which each school society has its own ideals and the Ministry of Education never does more than suggest. Remember, too, Aristotle's observations about education in his time; this is not a question about which thoughtful people easily agree. But here there is an under-lying unity, and, while admitting variations, we can arrive at a broad conclusion about the aims that are normally pursued. In formulating them we shall not go far wrong if we remember Morant's two top priorities, the formation of character and the development of intelligence; and it is well to have regard, also, to Mill's aim of transmitting and, where possible, improving our cultural heritage. Mr Eliot has little good to say about the aims that he collected, but he does say that it was a relief to find one that presented 'the simple and intelligible notion that equipment to earn one's living is one of the purposes of education.' Here then are four important aims, and there can be few schools in this country which do not have regard to each one of them, though some hit the target more often and more effectively than others.

But whatever its aims a school does not function in isolation; as a miniature society set in a particular neighbourhood and one of many societies within the Great Society it is sensitive to extraneous influences. 'Hence,' it has been well said, 'any educational aims which are concrete enough to give definite guidance are correlative to ideals of life,'[2] and as in this revolutionary age there is much uncertainty and confusion about ideals schools have a difficult time in deciding and achieving their objectives. Aims only have significance

1. *Notes towards the Definition of Culture* (Faber, 1948), p. 96.
2. Sir P. Nunn, *Education: its Data and First Principles* (Edward Arnold, 3rd ed., 1945), p. 2.

when applied; and in practice their application is usually related to actual situations in which real people are involved, children, parents, teachers, committee members, officials and all the various human contacts of the school society. Within this society everything turns on the quality of the persons applying the aims, whatever these may be; hence the oft-repeated truism that the personality of the teacher is all-important. It is he, and especially the Head Teacher, who interprets and applies the aims to the situations as they arise; and therefore such merit as they possess derives largely from his wisdom, convictions, standards, and values. He has to have regard not only to the problems as they arise within the school, but also to the social and intellectual and moral back-ground. He is like the Consultant in Mr Eliot's *Cocktail Party*, who found that his patients were often 'only pieces of a total situation'.

This total situation, the ferment of our time, makes steering in education very difficult; the best of coxswains loses direc-tion in stormy water. It is not surprising, therefore, that critics of modern education find evidence of lack of clear purpose. Thus, to quote one of the more thoughtful of them: 'The most serious weakness in modern education is the un-certainty about its aims. A glance over history reminds us that the most vital and effective systems of education have envisaged their objectives quite definitely, in terms of per-sonal qualities and social situations. Spartan, Feudal, Jesuit, Nazi, Communist educations have had this in common, they knew what they wanted to do and believed in it. By contrast, education in the liberal democracies is distressingly nebulous in its aims.'[1] This charge of aimlessness is not confined to the newer types of education, schools like the secondary modern or comprehensive which have yet to establish a firm tradi-tion. A similar lament is to be heard in discussions about grammar schools and universities. Lord James of Rusholme, in an able diagnosis of the problems of the grammar

1. M. V. C. Jeffreys, *Glaucon. An Inquiry into the Aims of Education* (Pitman, 1950), p. 61.

school curriculum, pleads earnestly 'that more careful and precise thought should be devoted to the exact nature of what is to be taught in schools and universities.'[1] And for many years Sir Richard Livingstone kept urging us to think constructively about such vital questions as: 'What are we to teach? At what should education aim? What sort of human beings should it produce?'[2]

Such questionings are by no means confined to this country; they are to be heard across the Atlantic, where they are expressed sometimes even more forcibly but often with a shrewder appreciation of the impact of the 'total situation' on educational pilotage. The famous Harvard Report about education in the U.S.A. well describes the difficulties that confront liberal democracies, seeking to expand education in the midst of a social revolution: 'The unparalleled growth – one could almost say eruption – of our educational system, taking place as it has while our way of life was itself undergoing still vaster changes, is like a mathematical problem in which new unknowns are being constantly introduced or like a house under construction for which the specifications are for ever changing. . . . The wonder is not that our schools and colleges have in some ways failed; on the contrary, it is that they have succeeded as they have.'[3] That can be said, also, without hesitation of our own schools and colleges, but it may well be that both here and in the U.S.A. the complex problem of educating in this revolutionary age has been made more difficult by too close an adherence to theories of education conceived in less challenging days. But that is a debatable issue that must be closely examined in the next chapter.

1. Lord James of Rusholme, *Essay on the Content of Education* (Harrap, 1949), p. 10.
2. *Education for a World Adrift* (Cambridge Univ. Press, 1943), p. xi.
3. *General Education in a Free Society* (Harvard Univ. Press, 1945), pp. 5–6.

CHAPTER TWO

THEORIES THAT INFLUENCE EDUCATION TO-DAY

Our Distrust of Theory

It has often been said that in this country we do not like theory: we prefer to think of John Bull as very practical. That shrewd and witty Bishop of London of the end of the last century, Mandell Creighton, once remarked: 'An Englishman not only has no ideas, he hates an idea when he meets one.' In more recent times, under the duress of grave events, we have become much more responsive to new ideas. The City, the natural habitat of the practical man – if the appropriate page of the newspaper is any guide – is continually discussing conflicting theories about economics and finance. While the BBC seems always ready to allot philosophers a good share of broadcasting time to enable them to ventilate their ideas.

In education we are certainly much more receptive of new ideas than we used to be, but we continue to dissemble our interest in them by associating them with movements. 'The development of educational thought in this country', it has been aptly said, 'has been implicit in educational movements and in educational expansion rather than explicit in the development of educational theories or educational plans and policies.'[1] One glance at the list of educational societies in *Whitaker's Almanack* or at the annual programme of *the Conference of Education Associations* will provide convincing evidence of our tendency to sample, discuss and promote various theories by promoting groups for that purpose.

1. Address on 'The English Tradition in Education' by Sir Philip Morris in *Pioneers of English Education* (Faber, 1951), p. 59.

In the nineteenth century this vigorous group activity was concerned mainly with the building, equipment and maintenance of schools; there was in comparison with other leading countries very little interest here in educational theory. This seems the more remarkable when one recalls the stature of the great prophets of the Victorian Age – men like J. S. Mill, Newman, Herbert Spencer, Matthew Arnold, and T. H. Huxley – who expounded their educational doctrines with such compelling force. It can be explained partly by the pressing need for more schools; public attention in the sphere of education was perforce riveted on the urgent problem of school accommodation, and such thorny aspects of it as 'the religious question' and local administration. Thanks largely to Kay-Shuttleworth good work was done in the establishment of training colleges, a *sine qua non* of the rapid expansion of school provision; and in some of these training colleges students were made aware of the ferment of educational thought, so characteristic of nineteenth-century Europe. But in most of them the formalities of class-management were the normal stock-in-trade.

In his excellent survey of education during the period 1850–1950, Mr A. D. C. Peterson notes that in this country during the first half of this period an outstanding characteristic was our disregard of new ideas. 'Apart from "the Public School Code" (the unspoken principles on which the great private boarding schools were based . . .),' he observes, 'England contributed nothing to the newly arising art or science of education; and where she was ignorant herself she was extraordinarily slow to borrow. The true line of theoretical advance in this century derives from the work of Rousseau, Pestalozzi and Froebel; and the vast mass of English teachers or educationists were totally ignorant of it.' And he continues, 'It was in Germany that the theories of Pestalozzi, Froebel, and Herbart were put into practice and further developed. The Americans, with an enthusiasm for education, unmatched in Europe, borrowed and tried out each new idea, as it became known: but they soon abandoned the monitorial system of Bell and Lancaster and accepted Pestalozzi and Froebel as their masters. It is from America rather than Germany that the new theories of education have reached England.'[1]

It should be noted, however, that throughout this period there were enthusiasts in this country doing their utmost to propagate new doctrines. The Home and Colonial Society was founded in 1837 for the purpose of training teachers, especially Infant School teachers in the principles of Pestalozzi; and the influential Froebel Movement began in the eighteen fifties. Later the Froebel Society was formed, taking in 1875 as its title 'The Froebel Society for the Promotion of the Kindergarten System.'[2] Those nineteenth-century pioneers certainly had a considerable influence on education at the primary stage, but it was not until the twentieth century was well under way that schools in this country became responsive on a wide scale to 'the New Teaching', as it came to be called.

After World War I we moved rapidly into an era of educational change; and although in other spheres – social, economic, political – there were many bad years between the wars, it was within the schools – and particularly the Elementary Schools – a period of renaissance. To teachers weary of the customary formal routine the New Teaching came as a welcome release, and for young teachers eager to experiment it was a golden age:

> Bliss was it in that dawn to be alive,
> But to be young was very heaven.

Although slow to hearken to the many blasts of new doctrine, we certainly moved fast when the day of our renaissance dawned. By 1928 Sir Michael Sadler, with his unrivalled knowledge of comparative education, past and present, was able to say: 'Great Britain, and especially England,

1. *A Hundred Years of Education* (Duckworth, 1951), p. 72.
2. For an excellent account of the Froebel Movement, see *Friedrich Froebel and English Education*: edited by E. Lawrence (Univ. of London Press, 1952).

is at this time the world's greatest exporter of educational ideas, just as France is *par excellence* the centre from which now proceed the most stimulating influences in the art of painting. At one time the main source of the world's educational suggestions was France. Then Germany, especially Prussia. Then the United States. Then Germany and the United States, *pari passu*. Now the United States and Great Britain, but Great Britain easily first. . . . A greater change has come over the educational scene in England during the last thirty years than within any like period of time (save one) in the whole of our history.'[1]

Charles Lamb in a famous essay tells of the wide gulf between the old and new schoolmasters of his time (circa 1800). But in the nineteen twenties and thirties the gulf between the veteran teacher and the young teacher was much wider – at least as wide as that which in the sixteenth century separated the disciples of Colet and Erasmus from teachers adhering to medieval pedagogics. Since then we have travelled much farther along the new road; and, although the British tradition in education survives, a mighty chasm divides our modern education from education as conceived and practised before the twentieth century. C. S. Lewis, discussing our literary history, contended that a similar revolutionary change can be observed in our culture, 'the greatest change in the history of Western Man'. 'I have come to regard', he said, 'as the greatest of all divisions in the history of the West that which divides the present from, say, the age of Jane Austen and Scott. The dating of such things must of course be rather hazy and indefinite. No one could point to a year or a decade in which the change indisputably began, and it has probably not yet reached its peak. But somewhere between us and the Waverley Novels, somewhere between us and *Persuasion*, the chasm runs.'[2] We are certainly

1. Presidential Address to Conference of Educational Associations, 1928.
2. *De Descriptione Temporum*. An Inaugural Lecture (Cambridge Univ. Press, 1955), p. 11.

living in the midst of a profound revolution in education; but it would be as difficult to say when it began as to guess when or how it will end. Perhaps we shall not be very wide of the mark if we regard the principal Hadow Report (1926) as its first official milestone and, like C. S. Lewis, we can conjecture with some justification that 'it has probably not yet reached its peak.'

We are not by nature revolutionary; confronted with new ideas, we handle them with care, saying like A. H. Clough:

> Old things need not be therefore true,
> Oh, brother men! nor yet the new!

In this educational revolution, we had a few whole-hoggers, enthusiasts quick to scrap the old and exploit the new with maximum intensity.[1] But the great majority made their changes cautiously, seeking a synthesis of old and new. As Mr J. S. Ross has so well said: 'There are comparatively few schools in this country that can be labelled by names such as Montessori, Froebel, and Dalton. We are reluctant to believe, even when struck by a new idea, that everything we have done in the past has been on wrong lines, and we hesitate to scrap well-worn modes of educational practice. Rather it is our genius to allow the new ideas to permeate the old, to keep what has been found of value in the past, adding to it what seems of value in the new.'[2]

Rousseau's Influence

The major prophet of our educational revolution was Jean Jacques Rousseau (1712–78). This strange erratic genius is one of the most original thinkers of all time; his famous political treatise, the *Contrat Social*, has had an immense influence on democratic thought, and his *Émile* has had a profound effect upon education both in Europe and America. A born revolutionary, he had no respect for existing institu-

1. For examples, see A. S. Neill, *The Free Child* (Jenkins, 1953) and G. Holmes, *The Idiot Teacher* (Faber, 1952).
2. *Groundwork of Educational Theory* (Harrap, ed. 1952), pp. 34–5.

tions or conventions. 'He believed that it was necessary to start altogether afresh. And what makes him so singularly interesting a figure is that, in more than one sense, he was right. It *was* necessary to start afresh; and the new world which was to spring from the old one was to embody, in a multitude of ways, the visions of Rousseau.'[1] His influence on education flowed into the schools through many channels. For he had many followers who, if they did not always adhere strictly to his creed, were none the less satellites of his constellation. 'Each in his own way,' to quote M. L. Jacks, 'Pestalozzi, Herbart, Froebel, the McMillans, Montessori, Caldwell Cook, Dewey are his successors: and such devices as the Nursery School, the Dalton Plan, the Play Way, and the Project Method are the practical results of what they taught.'[2]

In *Émile* he 'starts afresh', thinking about education. He does not ignore the opinions of earlier thinkers – Plato, the Stoics, and our own John Locke were among those whom Rousseau had studied before he wrote *Émile* – but he takes nothing in the existing order for granted and considers education with a fresh mind, untrammelled by precedent or tradition. To understand his approach to educational problems – or any other problems – it helps if one remembers his love of hiking. He has been called 'the first hiker'; he loved tramping alone and, as he once said, uncumbered by 'duties, business, luggage, and the necessity for playing the gentleman.' 'This love of travelling on foot', writes a modern admirer, 'is so characteristic of Rousseau, it springs from such fundamental things in his mind, that it would be possible, without exaggeration, to show you its connection with almost the whole of his teaching and the whole of his influence upon the generations which came after him.'[3]

1. Lytton Strachey, *Landmarks in French Literature* (Home Univ. Library, ed. 1939), pp. 185–6.

2. *Modern Trends in Education* (Melrose, 1950), p. 116.

3. Leonard Woolf in *Some Makers of the Modern Spirit*, edited by John MacMurray (Methuen, 1933), p. 101.

In *Émile* he shows all the good hiker's dislike of formality, convention, and stuffy restrictions: and his purpose is to convince the world that education should be 'according to nature' and free from stupid artificialities. This book which in time changed the whole trend of educational thought is rather like a fairy story. 'It concerned a boy named Émile who was brought up in a generally delightful way by a thoughtful tutor who let him roam about the countryside absorbing beauty. Up to the age when our children now move on to the secondary school the tutor allowed his charge to discover the meaning of the physical world and the working of his own body and mind by contacts with things, especially natural objects, which were unobtrusively brought into the field of his attention at the appropriate stage of his physical development and were absorbed into the boy's extending mental vision without any very serious resort to mental effort.'[1]

Rousseau certainly influenced education here in the nineteenth century, especially at the Infant stage; Robert Owen, and the movements associated with Pestalozzi and Froebel in their different ways reflect his outlook. But not until this century did he become a dominant force in our schools. Although he had lived and thought so long ago, his ideas seemed suddenly to come to full fruition in this country in the nineteen twenties and thirties. Ever since, his impact on our schools and on the upbringing of children has been far-reaching; and the Education Act of 1944 contains much that derives from him. The famous White Paper, which heralded that Act, opens dramatically with the words: 'The Government's purpose in putting forward the reforms described in this paper is to secure for children a happier childhood. . . . '[2] It is interesting to speculate whether Mr Butler and his colleagues would have made this objective No. 1 if Rousseau had never lived to write *Émile*.

1. A. V. Judges, *Freedom: Froebel's Vision and our Reality* (National Froebel Foundation, 1953).
2. *Educational Reconstruction*, 6458.

It is interesting, too, to consider what characteristics of modern teaching are a consequence of what Rousseau thought and wrote some two hundred years ago. John Morley described *Émile* as 'The Charter of Youthful Deliverance', and certainly it was Rousseau who first thought about childhood and children much as we do to-day; among his famous sayings are: 'Nature would have children be children before being men,'[1] and 'Childhood has its own ways of seeing, thinking and feeling.'[2] It is also often said that by stressing the necessity of understanding child nature, he set us on the road which has led us to educational psychology. Others before him, Comenius, for example, had written about the stages of education: but Rousseau goes further and explores the normal characteristics of children at each stage, thus posing a problem which modern psychology has pursued to good purposes. He was a pioneer, too, in his emphasis on the importance of the study of adolescence, regarding it as 'the crisis which forms a bridge between the child and the man.'[3] And Rousseau can certainly claim some credit for the friendly character of teacher-pupil relationship to-day: teaching, he held, 'is a question of guidance rather than instruction.'[4]

For our modern methods at the primary stage we are certainly much indebted to Rousseau; and it is impossible to read the Hadow Committee's Report on the Primary School or the Scottish Advisory Council's Report on that stage of education without being constantly reminded of his *Émile*. He, for example, stressed like these reports the undesirability of a rigid curriculum; and he like them appreciated the value of activity and experience. 'The outstanding feature of the *Émile*', it has been well said, 'is the complete abandonment of the pre-determined curriculum. Émile was to be educated entirely through activities and by first-hand experience.'[5] In

1. *Émile* (Everyman's Library), p. 54.
2. *Émile*, p. 54.
3. *Émile*, p. 278.
4. *Émile*, p. 19.
5. R. R. Rusk, *Doctrines of the Great Educators* (Macmillan, 1954), p. 165.

many other respects this remarkable innovator set us along paths which are now well trodden. To-day 'learn by doing' is a commonplace of pedagogy, but it was a revolutionary idea when Rousseau suggested it, observing: 'Teach by doing whenever you can, and only fall back upon words when doing is out of the question.'[1] Émile was to be satisfied with one book – *Robinson Crusoe*!

The key-notes of Rousseau's educational creed are nature and freedom, but his ideas on these two great issues have not always been well understood by those who have acclaimed them. He certainly believed that children should develop 'according to nature' and enjoy freedom. But, to quote some wise words of Mr Rusk's, 'education according to nature is frequently interpreted to mean nothing more than the spontaneous development of the innate dispositions of the child, nothing more than what modern psychologists term "maturation". Education according to nature, nature in the sense of endowment, leads to the non-interventionist policy in education, a hands-off procedure for which, however, there is no warrant in the *Émile*.'[2] Nor should one overlook Rousseau's belief in guidance and in a 'well-regulated liberty':[3] for it governs his attitude both to development and to discipline. Discussing discipline, Sir Fred Clarke observes: 'Rousseau shows flashes of insight into the truths which have been either overlooked or widely misunderstood. He is emphatic that the child has to be "formed" by education; that neither instinct nor "development" alone can be trusted. Yet he can declare passionately concerning the child: "Never command him to do anything whatever, not the least thing in the world." The whole point here is missed unless we realize the full weight of meaning that Rousseau puts in the word "command".'[4]

It is also common to find Rousseau's attitude to religion misunderstood, some, because of his persecution by the

1. *Émile*, p. 144.
2. Rusk, *op. cit.*, p. 147.
3. *Émile*, p. 56.
4. *Freedom in the Educative Society* (Univ. of London Press, 1948), pp. 63–4.

Church, assuming him to be an atheist. No one who has read *Émile* could so regard him. 'In the middle of this book he inserted a famous and beautiful passage about religion. Rousseau was a believer in God. He was a deist, and he states with extraordinary sincerity and simplicity the reasons why he believed in the existence of God. But he added the reasons why he mistrusted the dogmas and authority of the Church.'[1] It is, however, important to note that Rousseau believed that 'man is by nature good'[2] and that he assumed the innate goodness of the child. This belief is, of course, in direct conflict with Christian tenets about original sin, and 'contrasts oddly with the modern psycho-analytic view of human nature.'[3] All the same Rousseau's view has had a considerable influence in modern education, and terms like sin and conscience that figured so prominently in Dr Arnold's vocabulary have lost their former significance. This tendency to disregard the frailty of human nature led Sir Fred Clarke after much thought to the opinion that 'of all the needs of democracy, some abiding sense of the reality of Original Sin may yet prove to be the greatest.'[4]

If Rousseau was the prophet of naturalism in education, Wordsworth was its poet; and his influence upon teachers, especially in the North of England, has been and still is considerable. In pre-war days he almost monopolized the hours devoted to poetry in some Training Colleges, and one distinguished Professor of Education in a well-known course of lectures to student teachers on 'Poetry and Teaching' directed the attention of his audience to Wordsworth alone, evidently regarding this great poet as of supreme significance for those entering the teaching vocation. Many teachers found in Wordsworth the most satisfying religious sanction for the naturalism characteristic of Rousseau's educational theory; Dean Inge once described him as 'the greatest prophet' of

1. Leonard Woolf in *Some Makers of the Modern Spirit*, p. 109.
2. *Émile*, p. 198.
3. Rusk, *op. cit.*, p. 159.
4. *Freedom in the Educative Society*, p. 97.

nature-mysticism, and his creed was reflected in the teaching given in many schools.[1] In the series of lectures just referred to, the young audience was advised to take Wordsworth as its guide: 'He was simple, orderly, disciplined, so he came to see in the simplicity, the order, the discipline of Nature, in the wide sense which he would have given to the word, not merely the Unity of Law and Principle, but another Personality, answering to his own, a Mighty Being, awake, breathing, listening, speaking to him – a personality not less real than that of human friends, vast and yet not vague.'[2]

There are some important points of difference between Wordsworth's views on education and those of Rousseau but it has been well said that 'at times both men seem to speak the same language.'[3] His picture of ideal childhood would certainly have appealed to Rousseau:

> A race of real children; not too wise,
> Too learned, or too good; but wanton, fresh,
> And bandied up and down by love and hate;
> Not unresentful where self-justified;
> Fierce, moody, patient, venturous, modest, shy;
> Though doing wrong and suffering, and full oft
> Bending beneath our life's mysterious weight
> Of pain, and doubt, and fear, yet yielding not
> In happiness to the happiest upon earth.
> Simplicity in habit, truth in speech,
> Be these the daily strengtheners of their minds;
> May books and Nature be their early joy!
> And knowledge, rightly honoured with that name –
> Knowledge not purchased with the loss of power.[4]

Rousseau would not have agreed with his reference to books, but their difference on this point is not a very real one. For while Wordsworth found room for books, his preference was the Book of Nature:

1. *Christian Mysticism* (Methuen, 1899), p. 305.
2. E. T. Campagnac, *Poetry and Teaching* (Constable, 1910), pp. 34–5.
3. Curtis & Boultwood, *A Short History of Educational Ideas* (Univ. Tutorial Press, 1953), p. 301. (See pp. 285–302 for an excellent discussion of Wordsworth's views on education.)
4. *The Prelude* V, ll. 411–425.

One impulse from a vernal wood
May teach you more of man,
Of moral evil and of good
Than all the sages can.[1]

And like Rousseau, he appears to have believed in innate goodness; for though a life-long and loyal member of the Church of England, he dismissed the doctrine of original sin with those now famous words:

But trailing clouds of glory, do we come
From God, who is our home:
Heaven lies about us in our infancy.[2]

The Influence of Psychology

Between the wars there were signs of a fundamental change in the attitude to children; many teachers were showing a scientific interest in childhood and child development. Having accepted the Rousseau creed that children should be educated according to their nature, they realized that this involved a more than ordinary knowledge of children and their ways. 'Childhood', Sir John Adams had said – and what he said carried weight in the teaching profession, 'has a meaning and a value in itself apart from its value as a step on the way to maturity. The better the child, that is the truer he is to his child nature as such, the better man will he make when the proper time comes.'[3] So child nature became a study that hundreds of teachers actively pursued with psychology as their principal guide.

Characteristically, movements were set on foot for this purpose, and even as far back as 1893, James Sully – sometimes called the father of child psychology – sought to harness psychology to education by founding the British Association for Child Study.[4] But in these earlier years teachers often

1. *The Tables Turned.*
2. *Ode on Intimations of Immortality*, stanza 5.
3. *Evolution of Educational Theory* (Macmillan, 1912), p. 94.
4. For a definition of Psychology, see J. Drever, *A Dictionary of Psychology* (Penguin Books, 1952), pp. 227–8.

43

found psychology an unprofitable study, so usual was it to present it in a drab, unimaginative manner, making it seem remote from the actual problems that arise in school. Margaret Weddell, later to become a distinguished Principal of a Training College, has in reminiscences of her student days described her introduction to this new science at the beginning of this century. 'The psychology', she observes, outlining the course that she was required to pursue, 'was a dull subject, consisting of talk of concepts, images, and percepts. Children did not enter into it at all.'[1]

So it might have continued but for a few sympathetic interpreters of psychology who were able to show its relevance to the daily business of school. Much of the credit for rescuing it from the dull and dismal slough into which it had fallen should be given to Sir John Adams, Principal of the London Day Training College, 1902–22. He had a gift for extracting from contemporary thought new knowledge relevant to the practice of education. His *Herbartian Psychology Applied to Education* has been described as 'the first attempt in this country to put the new psychological theories into a form that would be useful to the practical teacher.'[2]

Herbart (1776–1841) was a German philosopher whose principles as expounded by Adams had at the time a considerable influence on teaching technique, but of more enduring significance is the fact that, thanks to Adams, we learned from Herbart to appreciate that psychology had important contributions to make in the field of education.[3]

Soon after World War I it was noticeable that many new words were creeping into teachers' vocabularies; the cacophonous jargon of psychology had reached the common

1. *Journal of the Institute of Education of Durham University* (January 1955), p. 26.

2. A. D. C. Peterson, *A Hundred Years of Education*, p. 71.

3. See Adams, *Herbartian Psychology Applied to Education* (Heath, 1907); and for recent opinion of Herbart, Peterson, *op. cit.*, pp. 77–82, Pantin, *Modern Teaching and Technique* (Longmans, 1944), pp. 95–8, and Curtis and Boultwood, *Short History of Educational Ideas*, pp. 343–56.

room. 'The teacher found himself', says M. L. Jacks, 'confronted with a mysterious and unexplored world of complexes and inhibitions, of propensities and dispositions, of interests and sentiments, of instincts and sublimations – terms which were as indefinite in meaning to him as they sometimes seemed to be to the psychologists who used them. . . . Faced by these puzzles, and by the necessity of mastering a new subject, the teacher found his task infinitely more difficult – more difficult, but infinitely more fascinating: for this was a new world upon which he had entered.'[1] The study of individual children, their characteristics and circumstances, became a normal part of the keen teacher's technique: obsessions, complexes, neuroses were noted, and the causes traced.

The psycho-analysts had a considerable vogue: Freud, Jung, and Adler had their devoted disciples. 'The teaching of Freud', Mr J. S. Ross observes, 'was a godsend to the postwar apostles of naturalism, both in the educational sphere and outside of it; it was believed to have proved the soundness of their case for untrammelled self-expression and for entire freedom from restraint. Books on psycho-analysis applied to education flooded the market and found many eager readers. Educational systems informed by psycho-analysis aim at free, natural development through the prevention of repression and its resulting state of unconscious conflict and neurosis.' And he makes this comment, which is significant coming from so wise and thoughtful an observer of the contemporary educational scene: 'Although there have been many extravagances and one-sided views, this educational movement has been on the whole a healthy one. It has fostered a sane attitude towards sex and towards authority; it has warned educators against the dangers of undue prudery, authoritarian methods, corporal punishment, in short, against any bottling up of the child's energies. Perhaps most valuable of all has been its contribution to the understanding of delinquency in childhood and adolescence and, even more,

1. *Modern Trends in Education* (Melrose, 1950), p. 32.

its determined effort to avoid the causes of such delinquency.'[1]

At first there was a tendency in some quarters to over-estimate the contribution that psychology can make to education, and there were psychologists who made claims that they would have found difficult to justify. Thus in juvenile courts while there were magistrates who were scept-ical of the value of the psychologist's report, there were others who assigned to it more authority than it deserved; and similarly while some psychologists expressed their opinions for the guidance of magistrates cautiously, there were others who couched their reports in language more assured than their study of the case or their knowledge warranted. Our leading educational psychologists, however, have always maintained the highest scientific standards of investigation, and it is a characteristic of the best of them not to overstate the value of their findings.

Here, for example, is Professor P. E. Vernon's estimate of the place of psychology in education. 'Educational psy-chology', he observes, 'is in many respects an advanced and highly technical form of applied science. Owing to the nature of the material with which it deals, it is more com-parable to medicine than, say, to physical engineering. Hence also its present status in education is a humble one; it cannot by itself give answers to definite questions about the art of teaching. Still less can it affirm the soundness of educational policies or ideals; perhaps it is more often useful in a negative way, that is in indicating what principles are unsound. Though it has established a number of important conclusions regarding mental qualities and attainments, their measurement, inter-relations, their distributions, etc., about selection, guidance, teaching materials and methods, these conclusions are essentially actuarial. Their application to any individual child or educational problem depends on other things being equal, and therefore usually necessitates non-scientific or clinical judgements. The psychologist, when asked for the answer to any educational problem, should

1. *Groundwork of Educational Theory* (Harrap, 1942), pp. 99–100.

admit this, and should realize that his own judgement is often no better or even poorer than that of the parent, the teacher, or the administrator who have consulted him.'[1]

It can, however, be claimed, without forgetting its limitations, that modern psychology has made an immense contribution to education. It has been a principal factor in transforming teaching at the primary stage; and the child of to-day owes much to the work of pioneers like Susan Isaacs, who first at the Malting House School in Cambridge and later at the Institute of Education in London devoted her life to the study of childhood, awakening in many teachers an interest in problems of mental growth, and the social and emotional development of young children. 'Thousands', said Sir Fred Clarke, 'will be the happier for what she has done.' Psychologists at work in this field have done and are doing experimental work of great value, usually in co-operation with teachers in nursery, infant or junior schools.

Notable advances have also been made in discovering new methods of assessing and classifying individual children; and there has been an increasing use of intelligence, attainment, and aptitude tests. France and America have a fine record of experimental work in this field, but this country has also achieved much. Indeed we may fairly claim to have initiated this branch of psychology; for it was Sir Francis Galton who first recognized the importance of anthropometric research and is often referred to as the father of mental testing.[2] And it has been justly claimed that 'four British psychologists – Ballard, Burt, Spearman, and Thomson – have done at least as much as any others to establish the principles on which such tests must be constructed and standardized.'[3] Although research of the highest quality has been done in this field, it has not won for itself the

1. *Modern Educational Psychology as a Science* (Evans Brothers for University of London Institute of Education, 1950), pp. 29–30.

2. F. Galton, *Inquiries into Human Faculty and its Development* (first published in 1883: reprinted in Everyman's Library).

3. Rex Knight in *Education in a Changing World*, edited by C. H. Dobinson (Oxford Univ. Press, 1951), p. 96.

appreciation that it deserves, and in fact has evoked a good deal of criticism. Two factors largely account for this: (1) a principal use of the tests has been in that storm-centre of modern education, selection for secondary education; (2) when the tests first came into general use, some advocates in their enthusiasm made exaggerated claims for their predictive value.

On the first point, it has been well said that 'so crucial has the selection procedure become to so many people that it has evoked an enormous amount of controversy and criticism – often ill-informed.'[1] It is doubtful whether, when intelligence tests were first launched for general use by local authorities, those who framed them sufficiently appreciated the importance of stressing their limitations. I.Q. was allowed to become an idol, with attributes of infallibility and constancy that it does not possess. When the tests became an influential feature in a public service, the public relations aspect at once assumed importance, and it may well be that public relations is not the psychologist's strongest point. 'Unfortunately,' writes a contemporary psychologist, who has appreciated the value of a supporting public opinion, 'psychologists, for various reasons, have usually fought shy of writing for anyone but other psychologists; they have preferred to leave the popular exposition of their achievements to people without the scientific background necessary in order to stay on firm ground, and without the ability to say "We don't know" instead of "It is certain". Thus popularization of psychology has usually been of a kind to encourage over-optimistic attitudes in some, and exaggerated scepticism in others.'[2] In assessing the pros and cons of intelligence testing, the optimists had a good run in the nineteen-thirties; but to-day the sceptics are more prominent, especially among those who favour the Comprehensive School as

1. P. E. Vernon in foreword to *Selection for Secondary Education* by J. J. B. Dempster (Methuen, 1954).
2. H. J. Eysenck, *Uses and Abuses of Psychology* (Penguin Books, 1953), p. 10.

the best method of providing secondary education for all.

There are several other aspects of modern education in which psychology is exerting a strong influence; here it is possible to make only a brief and inadequate reference to some of them. The solid work done by psychologists in child study largely accounts for the important advances made in recent years in the education of handicapped children, and this has also stimulated the provision of Child Guidance Clinics, of which there are now some 300. Some of our leading psychologists have given much time and thought to problems of adolescence, and it is to be hoped that when County Colleges are established full advantage will be taken of their investigations. Much consideration has been given, also, to the question of incentives, and to that of punishment. Questions asked in Parliament about corporal punishment led to a full scale investigation of punishments and rewards under the auspices of the National Foundation for Educational Research, and the resulting volume provides a good example of the valuable service the National Foundation is able to render by enlisting the services of trained psychologists to study difficult problems, assisted by evidence furnished by teachers and others with special knowledge and experience.[1] To-day there is more interest than ever in the intricacies of the art of living together, and it is recognized that it is an important aspect of education. This brings the social psychologist into the educational scene, and explains why so many teachers find the writings of social anthropologists like Margaret Mead and Ruth Benedict interesting and instructive.

It may well be asked how does the teacher find time to assimilate the new knowledge psychology has to offer? Clearly much of it has to be studied second-hand in textbooks, and at refresher courses. But to quote one of the wisest and shrewdest of guides: 'No text-book, or indeed any book whatever, can take the place of personal observation, and an

1. M. E. Highfield and A. Pinsent, *A survey of Rewards and Punishments in Schools* (George Newnes, 1952).

important part of every teacher's work is the systematic study of children, both as individuals and groups. ... All that psychologists can do for us teachers, and indeed it is an enormous debt we owe them, is to suggest wise lines of thinking about children and so help us to understand them.'[1]

American Influence

All who were teaching in this country in the years after World War I will remember the sudden arrival here from the U.S.A. of the Dalton Plan, and the astonishing vogue that it had. This teaching method, initiated at Dalton, Massachusetts, was first described in detail in this country in *The Times Educational Supplement*, the account being serialized in six separate issues; and then came a book by the originator of the Plan which immediately had in educational circles all the popularity of a best-seller.[2] The purpose of this Plan was to provide a method of teaching children as individuals instead of as a class. The pupils entered into a monthly 'contract' with their teacher to carry out a syllabus or course of study but were free to distribute their time within the month as each thought fit. Class-rooms ceased to be classrooms, and instead were called subject-laboratories; the pupils had free access to them, and in each was a teacher to offer guidance on the particular subject, and the pupil would find there also suitable books and illustrative material.

Commenting on the Plan at the time, Dame Olive Wheeler observed: 'The advantages gained by doing away with the rigid class time-table are obvious. Each pupil can work at his own rate and can work as a free agent.' And she made this shrewd criticism: 'It may possibly be true that this plan puts an exaggerated emphasis on the continual need for individual work and fails to recognize the full value of the training that

1. Nancy Catty, *The Theory and Practice of Education* (Methuen, ed. 1954), p. xi.
2. *The Times Educational Supplement*, 2, 9, 16, 23, 30 July, and 6 August 1921; Helen Parkhurst, *Education on the Dalton Plan* (Bell, 1923).

comes from the performance of tasks in common with other members of a social group. Perhaps a mean between herd teaching and the Dalton plan will prove to be what is required for most pupils.'[1] And most of the schools which had adopted the Plan gradually came to some such conclusion. Its popularity waned; 'it has not, however, been without very considerable influence upon the development of a number of enlightened methods in our schools'.[2]

Another, and earlier, project of American origin also aroused great interest; and, although transient, exercised like the Dalton Plan a continuing influence. This was an experiment conducted on a farm in Dorset by an American psychologist, Homer Lane. Here he maintained a small community of boy and girl delinquents; and, calling it 'The Little Commonwealth', he applied principles which, it was said, had proved successful with delinquents at the George Junior Republic in the U.S.A. The essential feature of the experiment was that Lane allowed his young citizens to govern themselves in complete freedom. His aim was to show 'that freedom with social responsibility has power to regenerate individuals who have previously been at variance with society and with their own higher selves.'[3] This idea of self-government appealed at the time to a good many teachers in search of new ways of maintaining discipline, and in *An Adventure in Education* J. H. Simpson described a valuable experiment conducted by him at Rugby, in which self-government was tried out with the 'form' for which he was responsible.

The readiness with which so many teachers embraced schemes that reached us from across the Atlantic showed how eager they were to find alternatives to the rigid formalities

1. *Bergson and Education* (Manchester Univ. Press, 1922), p. 102.

2. J. H. Panton, *Modern Teaching Practice and Technique* (Longmans, 1944), p. 222 note.

3. O. Wheeler, *Bergson and Education* (Manchester Univ. Press, 1922), p. 76. For an excellent full account of this experiment see E. T. Bazeley, *Homer Lane and the Little Commonwealth* (Allen and Unwin, 1928, second edition 1948). See also W. D. Wills, *Homer Lane* (Allen and Unwin, 1964).

of the traditional technique. Not only did the theories of Rousseau and his followers now reach us afresh and with great force via the U.S.A., but that country also furnished from its own stock a great contemporary thinker whose influence on education in this country in our time has been profound and far-reaching. From the nineteen twenties onwards the educational creed of John Dewey (1859–1952), the great American philosopher, has been dominant in British Education. When, in 1918, Mr Rusk wrote his now famous book on *The Doctrines of the Great Educators*, there were twelve stars in his constellation – Plato, Quintillian, Elyot, Loyola, Comenius, Milton, Locke, Rousseau, Pestalozzi, Herbart, Froebel, and Montessori. Reprinted over and over again, another edition was called for in 1954, and the author felt obliged on this occasion to add John Dewey to this select company. By sheer quality he had definitely played himself into this team of immortals. 'We have to return to Pestalozzi', said Mr Rusk, 'to find an educationist who so dominated the educational stage as John Dewey did throughout the first half of the twentieth century, and he played his part by virtue of the fact that in him were concentrated in a special degree the progressive tendencies of his age and country.'[1]

Dewey's influence can also be attributed in part to his noble and attractive personality. He was sincere in all that he said and did; when he lectured, his words came slowly, and with the hesitation of one desperately anxious to express exactly what was in his mind.[2] He also had the advantage of being not only pre-eminent in the educational world but also pre-eminent in academic circles as a great philosopher. So often in universities education tends as a department to stand separate, somewhat isolated and often not too highly regarded by other faculties. Commenting on this weakness and seeking a remedy, Dr J. B. Conant recalls John Dewey and the prestige that he gave to education in academic circles,

1. Rusk, *op. cit.*, p. 284.
2. For a description of Dewey as a lecturer see Gilbert Highet, *The Art of Teaching* (Methuen, 1951), p. 210.

and remarks: 'Barring the advent in the educational world of another great figure like John Dewey, who was both an academic philosopher and a leader of professors of education and school teachers, this building of a bridge between certain scientific disciplines and the schools of education seems the most likely way to improve the training of teachers.'[1]

As a philosopher, Dewey was a pragmatist deriving much of his thought from C. S. Peirce and William James, though on certain points he differed from both of them.[2] As a pragmatist he was more concerned with immediate issues that have a practical bearing on human interests than with long-term considerations of purpose and value. The essence of his thought about education is contained in his famous saying: 'The educational process has no end beyond itself; it is its own end.'[3] He regarded education as growth, and its purpose therefore was, in his view, to encourage growth, mental, moral, and physical. Of his books on education, probably the most influential have been *Democracy and Education* (1916) and *School and Society* (1899). But to quote one of his most ardent disciples, 'Dewey did not write in a style that was easy to read. . . . A colleague of his at Teachers College of Columbia University, William H. Kilpatrick, had the gift of simple, interesting writing and great skill as a speaker. It was Kilpatrick who made Dewey's ideas (plus his own which were in harmony with Dewey's) widely known.'[4] In that way Deweyism became a popular movement, and the Progressive Education Association was launched to promote his doctrines.

For a just appraisal of Dewey's influence it is important to read at least the two books named; for many excesses have been committed in his name for which his theories offer no justification. But for those who desire, however, nothing more

1. *Education in a Divided World* (Oxford Univ. Press, 1948), pp. 147–8.
2. See W. B. Gallie, *Peirce and Pragmatism*, and Margaret Knight, *William James* (both Penguin Books, 1952 and 1950 respectively).
3. *Democracy and Education* (Macmillan Coy., New York, 1916), p. 59.
4. Carleton Washbourne, *Schools aren't what they were* (Heinemann, 1953), p. 77.

than a general picture of the kind of education that he advocated, his own *Schools of Tomorrow* can be commended; for there he gives a simple, straightforward account of a few schools 'trying to work out definite educational ideas', and in a running commentary discusses 'theoretical aspects in order to point out some of the needs of modern education and the way in which they are being met.'[1] This book shows how greatly Dewey was influenced by Rousseau – the first chapter on 'Education as Natural Development' consisting largely of quotations from *Émile*; and it also enables one to realize how many of our own schools have assimilated Dewey's ideas, for his 'Schools of Tomorrow' are very like many of our own schools to-day, especially those for the primary stage. As Professor J. W. Tibble observes in commenting on the extent of our adoption of 'progressive' methods: 'A survey of the use of these and similar methods in English Education shows a very varied picture. They are almost standard methods in Nursery and Infant Schools, are not uncommon in Junior Schools, are used for certain types of work in some Secondary Modern Schools, are almost unknown in most Grammar Schools and Independent Schools, but may be fully used in those Independent Schools which call themselves "progressive".'[2] Certainly Dewey's influence is at work in the great majority of our schools; and when we see children busily active at their various crafts, or carrying out an elaborate project, they are being educated as this great pragmatist intended. So also are we following Dewey when we aim at an 'integrated curriculum', and when in other ways we attempt to break down the barriers between school and the world outside. And the single or 'common school' for all is an idea that comes from Dewey, and those who by the establishment of comprehensive schools seek to break down social barriers are, consciously or unconsciously, putting his creed into practice.

1. John and Evelyn Dewey, *Schools of Tomorrow* (Dent, 1915).
2. In Preface (p. 10) to Carleton Washbourne, *op. cit.*

The Swing of the Pendulum

We are familiar with the swing of the pendulum in the political arena. Much the same process operates in education as in all human affairs, and often it is difficult to account for the behaviour of the pendulum and still more difficult to predict forthcoming changes, even when they are imminent. On the one hand there is always the desire for stability, and on the other there is the urge for reform and reconstruction; sometimes one is in the ascendant, and sometimes the other. Two thousand years ago Polybius noted these competing elements in human nature, observing that it was the mark of a statesman to be able to discern how, why, and whence new movements come.[1] We can now see that the emancipating movement in education that began with Rousseau, and was stimulated by Pestalozzi, Froebel, Dewey, and others was welcomed only when opinion became profoundly dissatisfied with the rigid formalism and rigorous discipline that had long prevailed. But while we can attempt to interpret the past it is doubtful whether even Polybius's statesman could tell us what shape the next phase in education is going to assume. All that we can be pretty sure about is that sooner or later further fundamental changes in educational thought and practice will come. Are there any signs apparent now to guide us in guessing the shape of things to come?

Most observers of the educational scene during the past thirty years or so will agree that it is remarkable how the Rousseau creed has been assimilated without shedding some of the best elements in our educational tradition. We have somehow gradually achieved a synthesis of old and new, and a similar synthetic process has been at work in America where the impact of Dewey was more potent and immediate. 'Few adults,' says an observer of the American landscape, 'now out of school for twenty years can grasp the revolution that has taken place in school teaching. Methods, texts,

1. *History* III, 6.

subjects are different, and the end is not yet. Progressivism is imbedded in America to-day. On the other hand, progressivism is itself quite different and chastened since its scudding days when theory was untrammelled by experience. The fine progressive schools have been tempered by practice and conflict, and the starry-eyed parent who still dreams of fitting a child for society by unlimited self-expression, who holds that sweetness and light are entirely adequate substitutions for hard work and thoroughness may have a difficult time finding a school dedicated to such pleasant and irresponsible theories. . . . The fact is that the good progressive schools to-day are remarkably conservative and the good conservative schools are remarkably progressive. They are still different, and that is a social good, but the points of difference are more marginal than central.'[1]

In searching for signs it is worth noting the recent change of attitude to examinations. Less than twenty years ago it was fashionable to condemn them, especially those organized by external bodies; they were held to be an anachronism outdated by the emancipating process. 'The time is past', said the Norwood Report of 1941, 'when such guidance and direction as teachers need can be given by means of an external examination. To retain a profession in leading strings is to deny it the chance of growing up into responsibility.' It was recommended that certificate examinations for grammar schools should after a period be abolished; and it was considered one of the strongest assets of the new secondary schools established by the Act of 1944 that they would be completely unfettered by syllabuses set by external examining bodies. 'But during the past few years examinations have been making a come-back. The antithesis is being propounded with greater and greater force against the original thesis of the Norwood Report, and it is interesting that the strongest contributions to this movement are coming from

1. Frank D. Ashburn, *New York Times Magazine*, 23 September 1945. Quoted in F. J. Brown, *Educational Sociology* (Technical Press, 1947), p. 288.

the secondary modern schools themselves.'[1] The motive behind this demand is a belief that pupils of secondary school age need the incentive, stimulus, and discipline that working for a definite objective provides. The scheme of awards initiated by H.R.H. the Duke of Edinburgh is further evidence of this growing belief in the educative value of a stimulating objective.

This search for incentives is but one symptom of contemporary discontent with the aimlessness which sometimes results from the application of the Dewey doctrine that the education process 'is its own end'. We have gained much from the revolution that gave us a child-centred education instead of the rigid, strictly disciplined formalism of the old-time class-room. But have we attached too much importance to growth and development, making those almost our sole aim? And have we in our zeal for projects, topics, centres of interest and other media of individual and group activity been too ready to assume that they provide all that education should offer? Such are the questionings often heard to-day; and to quote one of Dewey's own countrymen: 'In such, the chief indictment of growth as the ultimate aim of education is that it appears to fail to specify what is a desirable or right direction for growth to take.'[2]

This lack of decisiveness, it is alleged, also tends to invalidate our efforts to train character. There was one point in which Dewey's view coincided with that of Thomas Arnold: both believed strongly in bringing up children to be good and useful members of society. But their interpretation of this task was widely different: 'where Arnold believed that the good society for which boys were being fitted was already established as the Church of Christ, the progressive thinks that the good society will be some new form of social organization,

1. *The Times Educational Supplement*, 25 March 1955, in Leading Article entitled 'Pendulum Swing'. See also *Secondary School Examinations other than the G.C.E.*, a report of the Committee of the Secondary Schools Examinations Council (H.M.S.O., 1960), the Beloe report.
2. J. S. Brubacher, *Modern Philosophies of Education*, p. 109.

better than the present one, more Christian perhaps, but which the pupils themselves, as they grow to maturity, will create.'[1] Arnold was clear about the type he wanted to produce; we are not so sure and, remembering how Hitler misused character-training to produce a particular type, we tend to avoid any certain objective. Indeed some, following Dewey, take the line 'that there are certain modes of democratic society which, if boys practise as boys, they will find easy and attractive as men'.[2]

So the critics of modern education bring us back to the question with which we concluded the last chapter: is our child-centred education, with its strong impress of Rousseau and Dewey, the right way to bring up children in these challenging days? To such a question there will be many answers, but it is possible to discern two distinct points of view. On the one hand, there are those who, like Dewey, consider the educative process all important and have great faith in natural goodness if children are brought up under wholesome, intelligent influences. This view is widely held: 'we have a tendency', says one critic, 'to believe in the myth of natural goodness, if left to develop.'[3] The other standpoint is that, while growth and development are certainly most important, so also are aim and purpose. Most of those who are of this opinion consider that there are certain values to which all others are subordinate; and that these values should determine the aim of education. They should also, in their view, profoundly influence its content, and while teachers should continue to be free to determine the curriculum, 'it should be the freedom to choose within a framework laid down by higher authority.'[4] This belief in a recognized basic education is also gaining ground in America and finds a place in the reports of both Harvard and Columbia.

1. A. D. C. Peterson, *A Hundred Years of Education*, p. 114.
2. A. D. C. Peterson, *A Hundred Years of Education*, p. 115.
3. Professor L. A. Reid in *Education in a Changing World*, p. 114.
4. Lord James of Rusholme, *An Essay on the Content of Education*, p. 113. (In a chapter on 'Liberty and Education' the author discusses at length what 'the higher authority' should be.)

There are other signposts, also, which suggest that our route now lies along a road which will lead us, not back to the Locke-ian view that strict obedience is all-important or to the rigidities of the Victorian school-room, but forward to a new philosophy of education in which authority will count for rather more than it has done since the nineteen twenties when we were, perhaps, too ready to say good-bye to all that. We are acquiring a regard for the Victorian prophets, especially Matthew Arnold; and we are prepared to admit that Herbert Spencer was not just being pompous when he urged us, in framing the curriculum, to consider 'What knowledge is of most worth?' There is also a growing tendency in the education of older pupils to encourage, as in the U.S.S.R., a positive attitude to work as a vital contribution to the well-being of the community, and it is notable that an important report of King George's Jubilee Trust makes a strong plea that our schools should 'foster in their pupils a responsible attitude to work . . . as a contribution to the health, wealth, and happiness of the community.'[1]

1. *Citizens of Tomorrow. A Study of the Influences affecting the Upbringing of Young People* (King George's Jubilee Trust, 1955), p. 14.

CHAPTER THREE

THE HOME AND THE LOCAL COMMUNITY

Has Family Life Deteriorated?

It is often said that family life in this country has deteriorated, and that home is no longer the wholesome influence that it used to be. It is difficult to accept this vague generalization if you think of the housing conditions that were normal in populous industrial centres a century, or even half-a-century ago. In spite of slum clearance there are still some grim reminders of the squalid, miserable circumstances in which many children were brought up in comparatively recent times. For the majority of workers then there could have been little family life, and those children who escaped infant mortality must often have had a bleak introduction to this world.

The physique, high spirits, and charming responsiveness of modern children brought up in happier environment are ample evidence that for the great majority home is a much happier place than it used to be. Much re-housing remains to be done, but the transformation so far achieved has made a vast difference to home life. In one of his earlier essays Mr J. B. Priestley recalls some of the houses in the West Riding towns of his boyhood, where the conditions were of a kind that blunt the senses and make existence a misery. 'In the West Riding town that I used to live in', he writes, ' – and there are hundreds like it in the industrial North and Midlands – there were districts known as "back o' the mill", and in these districts there were rows and rows of what are called "passage houses".' In the nineteen twenties when this essay was written these houses were still there, and similar conditions then prevailed in most populous areas. Mr Priestley notes the contrast between the home life of the children and the education they received in school: 'The children who attend the Council Schools, where they are taught to sing or even to read the poetry of Shelley, live in such houses. When they leave school they continue to live in them. Only a few are able to escape. One of the objects of primary education, I believe, is to refine its small pupils, to make them more sensitive. This seems rather a dirty trick when we consider that the children have to return to those houses.'[1]

The vast housing programmes of recent times have ensured for the great majority of children much pleasanter homes than those in which their parents or grandparents spent their childhood. And it is also true that parents as a whole are to-day much more interested in their children's well-being, and in their education. Contrast, for example, present-day relations between Home and School with those which A. P. Graves, the father of Robert Graves, the poet, describes in a sketch of a visit that he paid as a school inspector to a school in Southwark in the 1890s: 'As we pass a turning where a group of women are engaged in noisy dispute interlarded with much gross language we come upon an apparently brand-new Board School. . . . Let us enter it and have a chat with the headmaster, as true a missionary as ever sailed from our shores to spend his life among savages. When he first took charge of the school years ago, he tells us, all was opposition . . . and teachers were frequently jeered at and insulted on their way to and from their duties. They were at first so liable to these mobbings that they found it necessary to leave the school in a body, and even then had often to invoke police protection to escape molestation.'[2] There are still living retired teachers and school attendance officers who will tell you of similar experiences in days when the open hostility of parents was not unusual in certain areas of our big cities.

Such contrasts of then and now show how little there is in the romantic theory that there was once a golden age of

1. Essay on 'Houses' in *Self-Selected Essays* (Heinemann, 1932).
2. *To Return to all That* (Cape, 1930), p. 252.

family life when parents took their responsibilities seriously and there was no problem of home and school relationships; this false view, even if loosely held, obscures the real issue, namely that the social and technological revolution of our time has created new and serious problems for both home and school, which need to be studied with all the thoroughness their gravity demands. Our revolution is bringing us many advantages, especially in material well-being, but it is also presenting us with new issues of great complexity affecting the spiritual and ethical life of the Good Society. Some of the issues can be stated and measured but others, including the more formidable, do not lend themselves to analysis. To quote that excellent Ministry of Education publication, *Citizens Growing Up*: 'Admittedly conditions are not easy for a family living in the modern world. The "climate of opinion" is unstable, impatient, and cynical. Cheap and easy pleasures, some relatively harmless in themselves, others unwholesome and corrosive, occupy an undue share of some parents' time – and some children's and young people's too.'[1]

But whether the problems are measurable or not, our only hope of coming to grips with them is to study and discuss them with a more enlightened attitude towards them as our aim. It is idle, as some correspondents in the Press suggest from time to time, to think of solving them by putting the clock back; we cannot expect, even if we wish, to see in twentieth-century England the self-contained, secluded family life of the Trollopian country house. We can be sure, however, that the character of modern society will be immensely influenced by the quality of its family life; for home is a principal – some will say *the* principal – educator, and when children first come to school, they have already in and around the home acquired many of the social patterns, conventions, attitudes that become part and parcel of their personality. Clearly, therefore, the future of the family as a key social institution is of transcendent importance.

Viscount Samuel believed that two contrasted views about

1. H.M.S.O., 1949, p. 8.

family life will develop. 'The one', he suggested, 'will lay stress upon freedom, self-satisfaction, enjoyment; will treat sexual relationships lightly; will regard a marriage as experimental, separation or divorce as merely an incident in life; will prefer to be childless, or to have only one child or two, and in any case will look upon the children's interests as secondary. The other school will lay stress upon lasting affection, stability, the home; upon children; upon the social value of the family system. . . . They will not expose their own children to the fate of the children of broken marriages, with half a home in one place and half a home in another, and missing something always.' The first of these two 'schools', he notes, has the support of many brilliant minds in literature and the other arts; nevertheless he believes that the second 'school' will prevail because (1) its adherents find it, as a rule, a more satisfying way of life, (2) it is to the interest of society to maintain the family as an institution and when it is threatened, forces will be mobilized to fight for it, and (3) adherents of the first 'school' have few progeny, and so the tendencies of one generation are likely to weaken in the next and succeeding generations.[1] All concerned with education will hope that Lord Samuel's forecast proves right.

The Changing Role of the Family

In a primitive society family and tribe provide all the education that the young receive, and are the sole transmitters of culture. But when language characters develop and an alphabet and number system have reached a certain stage, there comes a demand for some formal teaching and so schools are established for a select few – prospective rulers and priests – to supplement the education given by family and tribe. When society becomes modern and complex, school does not lose its supplementary character; for however wide its scope and curriculum, it still remains true that the family is the first educator and a life-long influence. But in our

1. *Belief and Action* (Penguin Books, 1939), pp. 130-1.

modern way of life, the functions of the family tend to diminish, some to be assumed by school and still more by other agencies. Indeed one of the principal dangers of modern society is that by the usurpation of its functions the family's natural role will so diminish that it will cease to be an effective stabilizing force. While this danger can be exaggerated, it is certainly not one to ignore.

Home plays many parts in the life of the growing child; it is the natural source of affection, the place where he can live with a sense of security, it clothes him and, apart from the milk and meal that he gets at school, it feeds him, it educates him in all sorts of ways, provides him with his opportunities of recreation, it affects his status in society, and it influences his attitude to religion. If we consider briefly these various functions of the home, we shall see in what respects family life has changed in recent times. But before we analyse the significance of the family in that way, it is proper to note that Plato, perhaps the noblest of all the great educators, did not share the view, that seems axiomatic to us, that the family is of paramount importance to society and, in particular, to education. His communism, which exalted the State, led him to believe that the family was a hindrance to civic loyalty and devotion. To Plato the "home", which is so precious to us, was anathema. "Every Englishman's house is his castle" we say. "Pull down the walls," Plato replies, "they shelter at best a restricted family feeling." [1] In the early period after the revolution the U.S.S.R., for similar reasons, discounted the value of the family in the upbringing of the young, but it is significant that in the light of experience it completely reversed this policy, recognizing the importance of the family as a foundation of society.

Children Need Affection

Of all the functions of the family that of providing an affectionate background for childhood and adolescence has

1. Ernest Barker, *The Political Thought of Plato and Aristotle* (Methuen, 1906), p. 143.

never been more important than it is to-day. On the one hand, some of the other traditional functions have, as we shall note, become less significant, and this has had the effect of giving the affectional function a new precedence. While on the other hand, child study has enabled us to see how necessary affection is in ensuring proper emotional development; and the stresses and strains of growing up in modern urban society have the effect of intensifying the yearning for parental regard. 'We may', says an American sociologist, 'expect the family's affectional function to continue to be of major importance and even to grow in significance. As life becomes more regimented and disciplined outside the home – indications point in this direction – the home will have an even greater responsibility for emotional release and expression.'[1]

Another characteristic of our time is the increasing mobility of the population; new houses and the shift and expansion of industry lead to families changing their place of residence more frequently than ever before. A survey of one large American city showed that families there move on the average every two years, and there must be places in this country where the incidence of house-change approximates to that. As a result children are suddenly deprived of their friends, both those who visit their homes and those in the immediate neighbourhood; and for those of school age change of residence involves change of school. One has to experience this in childhood to know how upsetting it can be, involving readjustments that at the time seem almost unendurable. During the crisis the one stable factor is the family, and much depends on the affection and understanding shown by one's parents.

The many studies and surveys of juvenile delinquency that have appeared in recent years show how unwise it is to generalize about the reasons why boys and girls go wrong.

1. Jessie Bernard, *American Family Behaviour* (Harper, New York, 1942); p. 550. Quoted by F. J. Brown, *Educational Sociology* (Technical Press, 1947).

But there seems to be wide agreement with the conclusion, based on much evidence, that a disturbed or otherwise unsatisfactory home atmosphere is the most frequent of the various causes.[1] And as against the relative few who become wrongdoers, there must be hundreds permanently soured and embittered as a result of a childhood spent with heartless, indifferent, or quarrelsome parents or in homes broken as the result of the breakdown of the marriage tie. One can get glimpses of what bitter memories absence of affection in childhood bequeathes when some gifted person, who so suffered, writes about it in later life, as Samuel Butler did and Edmund Gosse in *Father and Son*. Teachers do much to help children who have to endure the misery of a loveless home, but nothing compensates adequately for lack of parental affection.

Children reflect the family atmosphere. Where there is affection, they show it by their responsive friendliness; and when the home is a loveless one, sometimes the children are impersonal, and even hostile. But often children neglected at home like to be noticed. 'Love', says one writer, 'is necessary food for the young; one has only to watch the efforts of children who are starved of love to gain attention somehow by *any* method, to realize how desperate is their need, for starved affections are as much a tragedy as starved bodies. The simple truth is that no one can grow fully as a person without this basic nourishment.'[2]

Parents, seeking to provide this essential affectionate background, have no easy task; for there are many pitfalls. Over-anxiety is one; and it sometimes arises from a smattering of psychological information about obsessions, complexes, and other abnormalities. Over-protection is another; and a good many parents, impressed by what they have read

1. See, for example, Carr Saunders, H. Mannheim and Rhodes, *Young Offenders* (Cambridge Univ. Press, 1943); and J. Gittins, *Approved School Boys*, a Home Office publication (H.M.S.O., 1952).

2. Marjorie Reeves, *Growing up in a Modern Society* (Univ. of London Press, 1946), p. 52.

or heard about the virtues of self-expression, tend, with the best of motives but an imperfect study of the self-expression creed, to indulge or spoil their children. It cannot therefore be too strongly emphasized that children like law and order, and to spoil or indulge them is no mark of genuine affection. Indeed it is the reverse, for it can be the cause of much unhappiness. 'There is ample evidence', wrote a psychologist of great experience, 'that lax discipline is a main cause in producing problem children. At the Birmingham University Remedial Centre, out of seventy-eight children referred only 12 per cent had suffered from too severe discipline in the home; but in 25 per cent of the cases discipline had been too lenient, and in 20 per cent the mother had been too protective. Various reports from other Child Guidance Clinics show similarly the bad effect of lax discipline.'[1]

Family Life To-day

One cannot generalize about family life to-day: it is too various, too kaleidoscopic. 'In the past,' it has been well said, 'societies have been characterized quite generally by a single prevailing type of family organization. But at present many different types of family organization exist, a situation which may be expected to continue in the future. Mowrer lists in the city to-day the paternal family; the maternal family; the equalitarian family, conventional and unconventional; and the filio-centric family. The rural family is quite different from the urban family, and the village family is somewhat different from both, though it tends to resemble the urban family more than the rural family. Broken families and families without children differ greatly from unbroken families and those with children. Thus continued diversification of family life is to be expected in our complex, rapidly changing society.'[2]

1. C. W. Valentine, *Parents and Children* (Methuen, 1953), p. 74.
2. Ogburn and Nimkoff, *A Handbook of Sociology* (Routledge & Kegan Paul, 1946), p. 485. The reference is to E. R. Mowrer's *The Family*, p. 96.

But some usual characteristics of modern family life may be noted, most of which have a close bearing upon problems of education. Parents have to do much less for their children to-day than they used to do, and home has become much less of a workshop. Clothes can be bought ready made, washing can go to the laundry, food can be bought cooked, canned or preserved, bread is baked and delivered by the baker, milk arrives on the doorstep, meals can be had at the restaurant, the works' canteen, and the school dining-room.

It is unusual now for father to pursue his trade or other employment at home, and his children rarely, if ever, see him at his place of work. Boys are therefore seldom trained to follow their father's occupation, and in many towns they have a fairly wide choice of employment and so do girls. The young wage-earner often earns good money, and soon acquires a feeling of economic independence. In textile areas it has long been customary for mothers to go out to work, but this practice has become so widespread that the working mother is now a not unusual factor in a child's home life, the number of married women in employment having more than doubled in the last twenty-five years. With mother earning and his older children drawing substantial wages father is seldom the dominant figure that he still was at the beginning of the century. When mother works economic advantages accrue, but children lose something of great value if mother's employment prevents her from being home to greet them when they return from school.

Our ways of spending our leisure hours have changed. Fifty years ago members of the family sought their recreation within the home or, when young, playing games in the street or on some near-by croft. To-day there is much more passive recreation, and much of it involves absence from home watching football or sitting in a cinema. The many active pursuits of to-day also take us away from home, motoring, cycling, hiking, camping. Public Libraries are well used and some publishers' statistics show that books of all kinds are widely read; but it is a rather different sort of reading from the fireside reading of other days. Much of it is done in trains and tubes, and it is quite usual to see someone reading a serious book while 'strap-hanging' on the journey to and from work. 'I like large still books,' Tennyson is reported to have said, and the saying once found much favour. To-day it sounds an impracticable kind of recreation: there is neither time nor room for the large, still book. All the same there is a big demand for good reading. One of the paradoxes of this hustling age is that there is more serious reading done in comparatively humble homes than in the homes of our parliamentary leaders, and higher executives in the civil service and industry. Addressing the annual meeting of the London Library Sir William Haley, the Editor of *The Times*, referred to this decline in serious and recreative reading among men of affairs. 'While documents were studied,' he said, 'books are skipped.' And he continued: 'I can remember that a former Cabinet Minister told me at Christmas time that he had managed to read one and a half books that year. I have seen the bulging brief cases of the senior officials and business men as they go home each evening and at week-ends. And each year the position grows worse; no one knows how to put an end to it.'[1]

The truth is that in most walks of life home has ceased to be lived in as it used to be; it may still be the Englishman's castle, but one in which he spends less and less of his time. Will some new magnet draw us back to our homes, and make the family a more closely-knit unit? It has been claimed that television will do it. 'It seems very probable', say two leading American sociologists, 'that electricity may keep much re-creation in the home. . . . The wireless, the gramophone, television, and facsimile transmission all may make the home a very attractive recreation centre. Also, electricity brings many convenient devices for the yard, the kitchen, library, dining-room, and bedroom. These developments, while quite material, are not without social influence.'[2] A renais-

1. *The Times*, 20 August 1955.
2. Ogburn and Nimkoff, *A Handbook of Sociology*, p. 485.

sance of family life by such means is not a prospect that will rouse much enthusiasm in educational circles.

Another remarkable change is that the family no longer has to act as a welfare service for its members in times of sickness and trouble. Social legislation from 1907 onwards, culminating in the Welfare State of to-day, has relieved the family of many heart-breaking anxieties. Ill-health, old age, unemployment are no longer the grisly spectres that they used to be, with the workhouse as the penalty for not providing for such misfortunes out of wages not much above subsistence level For all except the families of the well-to-do the provision of social security has come as a great blessing; and the young father to-day, assisted by various benefits – children's allowances, housing subsidies, school meals, maternity services – can if so minded concentrate on one of the most rewarding of all tasks:

> To make a happy fireside clime
> To weans and wife:
> That's the true pathos and sublime
> Of human life.

The Home as Educator

In the years just after World War II there were some who feared that the family would not survive as an effective institution. Not only was the State assuming much of the family's former responsibilities, but evacuation, the absence of men and women in H.M. Forces, the increasing mobility of labour, and above all the acute housing shortage had, so some thought, dealt it such shattering blows that it would never recover from them. This pessimistic view found expression in other countries also; 'many', to quote an American sociologist, 'predicted that World War II and its aftermath would bring the decay of the family, perhaps its total disappearance as a unit of social interaction.'[1] Fortunately this

1. F. J. Brown, *Educational Sociology*, p. 216.

calamity has not come about, but it is undoubtedly true that the family as a social unit is passing through an unsettled and unsettling phase.

At this point it may be convenient to hark back to the issue raised at the very beginning of this chapter, and attempt a more specific answer to the question, has family life deteriorated? Opinions will differ, but the following diagnosis may serve as a basis for discussion. What is happening, let us suggest, is a revolution in the family as an institution. It is in effect contracting in size, and losing its sense of responsibility for grandparents, uncles, aunts, or more distant relations. Often in this mobile age the big family unit has scattered far and wide: and, the State having taken over so many of the customary obligations, young parents do not have, to the extent they did in the past, to contribute to the maintenance and care of older or invalid relations. So it is as a smaller unit – parents and children – that the modern family becomes an effective social group, a closely knit companionship with a limited but important range of duties. This companionship type of family, if well ordered, concentrates on three main functions: the giving and receiving of affection, the bearing and rearing of the children, the upbringing or education of the children. If this diagnosis is anywhere near the mark, then for those concerned with education as teachers or otherwise, there is ground not for pessimism but for a genuine hope that the new family will be more keen and better informed about education than the old. Indeed there are abundant signs of an ever-increasing interest in education on the part of young parents. It follows also that the relationship between school and home assumes a new importance; only by close co-operation between teacher and parent can the latter adequately fulfil his or her educative function. It is also true that if parents are making a sincere effort to bring up their children well, it is desirable that the teacher should know something of the principles and methods they are following and thus be able to offer apposite advice.

Parents' Associations are sometimes criticized on the ground that only the 'good parents' attend the meetings. 'What is the use of preaching to the converted?' says the sceptic; but surely it is a misguided comment, for good parents urgently need and appreciate all the expert help in child education that can be given, and it should be our aim to increase their number by open days and other kinds of healthy propaganda. In the past many parents assumed that education was a function only of the school and not of the home, and it may well be that in our education policy from 1870 onwards we did much to foster this excessive reliance on school as the sole source of education. If that be so, we can rejoice that in many post-war official publications the educative function of the home is fully recognized. Thus we find the responsibility of the parent as educator emphasized in the English Central Advisory Council's report on *School and Life*, in the Scottish Advisory Council's report on *Primary Education* and in the Welsh Department's pamphlet on *Education in Rural Wales*. The last of these publications opens with these words: 'The first school of every child is his home, and his mother is his first teacher. The education which he received on his own hearth remains with him for the rest of his life, because early influences, as a rule, make the most permanent of all impressions.'

Wordsworth expresses similar thoughts in the language of poetry:

> . . . those first affections,
> Those shadowy recollections,
> Which, be they what they may,
> Are yet the fountain-light of all our day,
> Are yet a master-light of all our seeing.

As little children we each gain our first experience in the intimate group of our own family; gradually we attune ourselves to its standards and values; we learn to talk its language with its own particular intonation and accent; we copy its mannerisms and are affected by the range of its vocabulary – one family may have but 1,000 words vocabulary, while another may use a multiplicity of words; we assimilate its attitudes and its prejudices; and we grow up in its religion or without one.

Soon our contacts widen. We get to know neighbours, and assume our family's assessment of them; according to the usage of the household we become neighbourly or aloof. As the years pass we are half conscious of certain tensions: such as, perhaps, the different standards or culture of school and home or of other groups which we join. And, especially when adolescence comes, we may find ourselves involved in conflicts with the pattern of our home life or the wishes of our parents over such questions as friendships with the other sex, staying out late, money or dress. 'The paradox of education', it has been said, 'lies in the fact that the process of growing up is at once intensely personal, yet essentially social.'[1] From early childhood onwards we are adjusting our individual selves to the complex little world around us, and on the anvil of these various experiences our character is hammered out. We are blessed beyond measure if during these critical years we enjoy the advantage of a good home and wise and loving parents. 'Whether the professional educator wishes it or not,' wrote Dame Olive Wheeler, 'the fact remains that the home is the chief training ground of the emotions and consequently of character. This is particularly true in early years, when sentiments are being formed and emotional attitudes are being set; it is also true of adolescence, when new emotions make their appearance and conflicts between loyalties have to be solved. The love of parents and brothers and sisters, the give and take of a happy family life, the intimacies only possible in a small natural group, life in an atmosphere of consideration for others and respect for truth, beauty, and goodness, these are what are needed for the education of an individual's emotions.'[2]

1. Marjorie Reeves, *Growing Up in a Modern Society*, p. 9. For a revealing picture of childhood and home life see Richard Church, *Over the Bridge: an autobiography* (Heinemann, 1955).
2. *The Adventure of Youth* (Univ. of London Press, 1945), pp. 159–160.

The Widening Circle

We are born into a physical, material world of things, and a social world of persons and groups. The development of our personality depends largely on the contacts we make, and especially those with other persons individually or in groups. As children leave infancy behind, they begin to make their own contacts apart from and outside the family. While some are able to satisfy many of their social needs within the in-group of the family, others are by nature extravert and like to 'gang-up' with others. When they reach this phase it is important that it should be catered for appropriately; in school much trouble is taken to stimulate suitable group activities, but it is no less necessary to provide wholesome out-of-school interests.[1] Failure on the part of the adult community to provide such interests or, where they exist, failure on the part of the parents to introduce their children to them, can have unhappy consequences; and children are fortunate if they grow up in a neighbourhood where such organizations as boy scouts or girl guides have well-led units or junior clubs are available with suitable accommodation for the pursuits of hobbies. Voluntary services of this kind, so valuable in the upbringing of children, are often seriously handicapped by lack of funds and shortage of leaders, and this is partly due to the fact that those who shape our educational policy have not yet appreciated the significance of the group as a factor in education. Or it may be that our tradition of leaving the finance of such undertakings largely to private philanthropy is so strong that our rulers, while aware of the importance of such provision, do not think it necessary for the State to spend much in fostering services that provide group activities.

Remarkably little has been done as yet by central or local government to assist in the recruitment and training

1. See *Out of School*, Central Advisory Council for Education (England), 2nd Report (H.M.S.O., 1948).

of group leaders. One helpful practice is for the school, whether junior or secondary, to have an extra member of staff with the specific function of fostering out-of-school activities, and keeping a watchful eye on the kind of 'ganging' that leads to delinquency. Critics of organized out-of-school activities sometimes contend that in modern society life is already over-regimented, and that it is much better to leave children to find their own interests. There is something to be said for this view, but it ignores the fact that many children grow up in a built-up artificial environment and, if not well occupied, are a prey to the various temptations of their urbanized neighbourhood. This is not to suggest that children do not want clubs in a rural district, or that Arcadia is temptation free. As A. E. Housman reminds us:

> And lads knew trouble at Knighton
> When I was a Knighton lad.

But the greatest need for recreative outlets is in the urban areas, and one has only to see a play centre or adventure type of playground to realize how much children appreciate scope for their activities. And one cannot too strongly stress the importance of providing as an essential feature of every large block of flats adequate recreative facilities to offset the serious handicap of growing up in such a confined environment.

Religious Influences

Needless to say, the parents' attitude to religion is an important factor in a child's upbringing. In a truly Christian household he soon senses that there is a world beyond this in which the grown-ups are intensely interested and, taught to pray, he learns to think of God as an almighty Father and to love Jesus as a very real person and ever-present friend. And the parents in ordering the life of the family have regard not only to the natural order, changing and variable, but also to a supernatural order with immutable laws. Similarly Jewish households, true to their religion, observe standards and uphold values which they count fixed and absolute; and in no section of the community is family life stronger than in orthodox Jewry. For children brought up in homes in which religion is a potent force, membership of a Church or other religious institution often provides the most valuable early group contacts; and as religion can be a divisive, as well as an integrating, social influence these early alignments sometimes separate them from children who are not from homes of the same religion. But as they grow older they usually make wider contacts, for in this country to-day there is a spirit of tolerance which makes it easy for children as well as grown-ups to combine without regard to religious differences. But it remains true that membership of a church often provides the more valuable group contacts in childhood and youth; and the services or liturgy of the church, which children attend, are a source of words and sayings that so impress themselves on the memory that they become guides and directives throughout life's journey. When the late Dean Inge wrote or spoke about religious education, he seldom failed to observe that religion is something that is 'caught' rather than taught; and whether this be so or not it is certainly true that throughout the centuries many of our finest citizens have come from homes in which religious observance has been a strong feature of the family life.

But throughout this century there has been a gradual decline in church membership, and only a small proportion of parents are now regular church-goers. The decline is perhaps more marked in England than it is in Scotland and Wales. A census taken in York in 1948 showed that only about 13 per cent of the adult population attended church in that city of strong religious traditions, while in High Wycombe in 1947, only about 10.5 per cent attended.[1] In 1954 Dr John Highet, lecturer in sociology in Glasgow University, conducted a census in which authorities of eight denominations co-operated; and this showed that 20.1 per cent of the adult

1. See Rowntree and Lavers, *Life and Leisure To-day* (Longmans, 1951).

population of Glasgow attended their respective churches. This census also revealed that Church membership statistics are not a guide to the number of actual church-goers: for only 37.2 per cent of the members of the eight denominations attended on the three Sundays on which Dr Highet held his census. A census taken a year later after a visit by Dr Billy Graham, American evangelist, showed some increase in Protestant church attendance.[1]

On the other hand there is a good deal of evidence to suggest that modern youth is taking an increased interest in religion, although this often does not lead to church-going; the BBC listening figures show that their religious services attract a considerable audience, and there is perhaps some significance in the fact that Sunday School attendance statistics in some areas show an increase. The Education Act of 1944 makes clear the official attitude with its requirement of the daily corporate act of worship and religious teaching in every state-aided school. It is difficult therefore to accept the view of those who speak of Britain as becoming 'a pagan' country: and as to the attitude of parents, with which we are here principally concerned, the opinion expressed by Mr Chuter Ede during the debates on the 1944 Act is still relevant, namely that the great majority 'desire that their children shall have a grounding in the principles of the Christian faith as it ought to be practised in this country.' It should also not be forgotten that half a century ago church-going was conventional practice, whereas to-day it is not: and this seems to justify the deduction that the churchgoer of to-day goes to church because he is whole-hearted in his faith. It may be, too, that some stay away from church because the language employed for communicating dogma, thought, and experience is often so different from modern usage. Those who speak of a return to paganism should not overlook the fact that anthropology and the study of society appear to indicate that man needs religion.

'Why', to quote a standard sociological textbook, 'human

1. See *The Times*, 11 October 1954 and 23 September 1955.

beings need religious experience is difficult to say. It is probably related somehow to the nature of adjustment of human nature to culture. The strain, the loneliness, the yielding to temptation, the worry, the mental conflict, all indicate an unsatisfactory adjustment of our emotional life to the demands of culture. Most observers of human behaviour recognize all these conditions as existing among the people. They seem to have resulted from social life all through history and in preliterate times. If religion brings peace to the soul, eases the almost intolerable strain, provides a helpful philosophy for the good way of life, or arouses us to a nobler aim of accomplishment, then it is apparent that there is great need for religion.'[1] Some may criticize this as 'a view of religion which is pragmatist and humanistic', to use the words that Professor Jeffreys employs in a chapter on 'English educational ideals', but it is of great relevance to the interaction of home and school at the present time.[2] It is for such reasons that many parents, vaguely recognizing this need, appreciate the efforts of teachers to introduce children to the Christian religion even though little is said about it in the home; and it is for such reasons too that many teachers to-day recognize that religious education is of paramount importance.

Thus the Headmistress of a Secondary Modern School on a new housing estate observes: 'It is problems such as these which had convinced me before I became a headmistress that our work as teachers would be largely wasted unless Christian living became our ideal and Christian principles the model of our school life.' And she adds, 'It is encouraging to find how grateful many parents are to the school because it stands for high ideals'; and concludes: 'we realize fully how often we fail in our efforts, when outside influences are so strong that we appear to achieve nothing, or just through our own inadequacy; but in spite of its disappointments and frustrations, I believe that ours is a unique opportunity to

1. Ogburn and Nimkoff, *Handbook of Sociology*, p. 448.
2. *Education, Christian or Pagan* (Univ. of London Press, 1945), p. 23.

make Christian teaching a living reality.'[1] As a supplement to such work within the school, it is important that in their group activities out of school children should have the opportunity of joining social, cultural, and recreational clubs under Christian leadership. Too often because of their connexion with a Church, it is considered inappropriate to aid such clubs from public funds, but this is a policy difficult to justify, and in a recent report issued by King George's Jubilee Trust there is this comment: 'There should be no withholding of public funds from youth organizations providing recreative facilities of the kind contemplated by the Social and Physical Training Grant Regulations, 1939, solely because they are part of, or linked with, the work or activities of a denomination.'[2]

The Young Worker

Every year over 600,000 boys and girls in Great Britain leave school and enter employment; for each one that first day at work is a memorable event and an abrupt change from the child-centred life of school. Conditions of employment differ widely, and the youngster who gets a careful initiation and is well looked after is fortunate. 'Variety of type among industrial communities', it has been well said, 'is as great as anything that has been reported in families or in schools. . . . The reactions of adolescents to these communities also vary as widely as did their responses to differing types of handling at home or in school. Under dictatorial control they work submissively enough while they are watched; but they show little initiative. They react by noisiness, bullying or destructiveness when supervision is slackened; and their manner and gestures show apathy or boredom. Under *laissez-faire* discipline they are restless and lacking in any understanding of the purpose of their work. When, however, intelligent

1. *The School as a Christian Community.* A symposium (S.C.M. Press, 1954), pp. 64, 73, 77.
2. *Citizens of Tomorrow. A Study of the Influences affecting the Upbringing of Young People* (King George's Jubilee Trust, 1955), p. 45.

co-operation is expected and democratic tuition is given, the same adolescents have been reported to rise to quite unexpected heights of social maturity and purposeful activity.'[1] Criticisms of young workers are common enough, but it cannot be too strongly emphasized that their attitude to work and their general behaviour are greatly influenced by the treatment that they receive from their elders. Employers who write letters to the Press criticizing their young employees are often by implication criticizing themselves.

In recent years juvenile labour has been in strong demand, and youngsters can, if they live in an area with several alternative employments, pick and choose. The Youth Employment Bureau provides vocational guidance, and takes trouble in placing its young clients; but even so many change their jobs during their first years. In a recent investigation it was found that slightly less than half the boys stayed in their first jobs, and the girls did even more changing.[2] Many change employment two or three times during their first three post-school years. Of several reasons that can be given for this initial restlessness, an important one is that the strains and stresses involved in adjusting oneself to the new life of employment are formidable. Indeed adolescence is a problem period in an individual's life history, and one in which it is all too easy to take the wrong turning. 'One of the major adjustments of the individual to society in the period of youth', said Dame Olive Wheeler, 'is the finding and holding down of a job; and with this the other life adjustments – the finding of a mate, the acceptance of the responsibilities of citizenship and the finding of a working philosophy of life or a religion – are intimately interwoven.'[3]

It has long been recognized that young people greatly need

1. C. M. Fleming, *Adolescence* (Routledge and Kegan Paul, 1948), p. 198.

2. *Citizens of Tomorrow. A Study of the Influences affecting the Upbringing of Young People*, p. 72. For a good official account of the Youth Employment Service: see *Report of National Youth Employment Council on work of Youth Employment Service, 1956–59* (H.M.S.O., 1959).

3. *The Adventure of Youth*, p. 124.

education and guidance during this crucial period. Early in this century Haldane, Sir Michael Sadler, and others campaigned for the establishment of Day Continuation Schools, and at the close of World War I a government committee, presided over by Sir Herbert Lewis, outlined specific proposals and urged that in the interests of the nation prompt action should be taken. H. A. L. Fisher, then President of the Board of Education, therefore included a scheme for part-time compulsory continuation schools in his Education Act of 1918, after going to 'immense pains' – to quote his own words – to gain the support of employers to compulsory part-time education of this character. 'Hundreds of employers were interviewed and their opinions, which were carefully recorded, would fill a substantial volume.'[1] But the great venture perished in the gloom of post-war depression. 'When we achieved,' said Lawrence of Arabia, of those years of disillusionment, 'and the new world dawned, the old men came out again and took from us our victory, and remade it in the likeness of the former world we knew.' As World War II drew towards its close, Mr Butler revived Fisher's plan, and, rechristened County Colleges, these vital institutions are once again on the Statute book, awaiting the declaration by government of an appointed day for their universal provision. But a further long delay seems likely, For the Central Advisory Council for Education (England), under the chairmanship of Sir Geoffrey Crowther, in its report on the educational needs of boys and girls aged 15 to 18 recommended that priority should be given to the raising of the school leaving age to 16, and this important reform is now planned to take place in 1970. As for County Colleges the Crowther council advised that their full introduction should be postponed to some date in the 1970's.[2]

It would be unjust to lay the blame for this persistent inaction on the successive governments concerned, for there

1. H. A. L. Fisher, *An Unfinished Autobiography* (Oxford Univ. Press, 1940), p. 107.
2. *15 to 18*, Vol. I (H.M.S.O., 1959).

have been serious economic difficulties and other important educational needs with strong claims for priority. Pressure for this vital reform has also been weakened by a division of opinion; for in the Act there are these two unfulfilled major projects for the education of youth, the County College and the raising of the leaving age to sixteen, and there have been strong differences of opinion as to which is the more urgent need. But the stark truth is that this neglect of youth during the crucial age of 15–18 is a serious weakness of our modern Welfare State. 'So long as the young generation is, and continues to be, well brought-up, our ship of state will have a fair voyage; otherwise the consequences are better left unspoken.'[1]

In 1961 the Central Advisory Council (England) was asked to advise on the education of pupils aged 13 to 16 of average and less than average ability. It grappled with this difficult problem under the chairmanship of Sir John Newsom and two years later produced its report, arranging it in three parts.[2] The first part does not call for legislation or big administrative reforms, but it is most important, its aim being to promote 'a change of attitude'. It has been well said that 'it ought to be read and re-read by all who in any capacity have dealings with young people in school, home, church, youth organization or employment'.[3] The second part discusses problems that particularly concern teachers, while the third summarizes conclusions based on a survey of several modern and comprehensive schools. The Report's account of 'education in the slums' should stir the public conscience, and its suggestions about religious education should lead to a better understanding of the spiritual needs of adolescent boys and girls. This Central Advisory Council is now engaged under the chairmanship of Lady Plowden on a report about 'Primary Education'.

1. Plato, *Laws*, 813.
2. *Half our Future* (H.M.S.O., 1963).
3. Church of England Board of Education, *The Church and the Newsom and Robbins Reports*, p. 2.

Social and Recreative Influences

It was noted in the first chapter that a principal feature of John Stuart Mill's conception of education was 'the culture that each generation purposely gives to those who are to be its successors', and he added that 'it comprehends even the indirect effects produced on character.' Needless to say, in addition to the culture that we purposely transmit in home and school, there is much that we elders pass on to our young people without any educational motive. Indeed Mr T. S. Eliot has reminded those educationists who make too bold claims about the influence of schools on culture that there are many other sources from which our youth derives its culture. 'For the schools', he observes, 'can transmit only a part, and they can only transmit this effectively, if the outside influences, not only of family and environment, but of work and play, of newsprint and spectacles, and entertainment and sport, are in harmony with them.'[1]

The 'outside influences' that affect the outlook and character of young people are too numerous to specify, but it is true of nearly all that the grown-up members, and not the youth, of our society are responsible for them. The conduct of the Press, the quality of the cinema, sound broadcasting and television, relationships in factories and workshops, the organization of sport, advertising, pools, dance-halls, amusement arcades, in fact the whole gamut of human activities are in the hands of grown-up people; and the standards and values, the example they set, are a potent force in shaping the character of the younger generation. 'They', as so many young people call this adult community, set a pattern which invites imitation. Much depends, too, on the preferences of those with whom the young are in daily contact – parents, foremen, neighbours: the latter choose their newspapers, films, and interests on adult grounds and youths who come in contact with them 'catch' their particular kind of culture. It is important to note that this adult responsibility is personal

1. *Notes towards the Definition of Culture* (Faber, 1948), p. 106.

as well as collective; we are all individually involved in it and cannot contract out of it. What we each value and how we behave affects the younger generation profoundly. 'There is a danger', to quote the King George's Jubilee Trust Report, 'that even if this responsibility is theoretically accepted, it may not be personally recognized and realized by adult individuals as falling upon them individually. We are all so accustomed to leaving things to the State or to organized bodies that the personal responsibility of the individual is lost in a vague anonymity.'[1]

Beset by influences of many kinds, good and bad, the modern boy or girl needs considerable native shrewdness and common sense to make the right choices; and one of the best aids is membership of a stable social group under mature leadership. One characteristic of this century has been the growth of voluntary organizations instituted for the purpose of developing groups of this kind. The largest and most influential of these organizations co-operate through the medium of a Standing Conference of National Youth Organizations; the twenty-four organizations who are members of this body have a total of over 2,000,000 young people on their books. When we were faced with the prospect of a long world war in 1939 the government realized that adolescent boys or girls would more than ever need support if they were to come through that unsettling period physically and spiritually strong. So they decided to buttress the efforts of the voluntary organizations by making regular grants to them from the Exchequer and through the local education authorities. Though a wartime measure it was designed as a permanent contribution for the well-being of youth, and to operate the grant system and stimulate the provision of social and recreative facilities the government instituted in the same year a statutory Youth Service.

The essence of this Youth Service is a partnership between local education authorities and voluntary organizations, and as a result much was done both by the authorities and the

1. *Citizens of Tomorrow*, p. 94.

organizations to provide clubs and salaried leaders and instructors. Unfortunately during the post-war years the Youth Service lost much of the force and drive that characterized it during its initial period. For this the public conscience must take some of the blame; we of the older generation are quick to criticize youth, but slow to grasp the significance of that axiom which the report of King George's Jubilee Trust so strongly emphasizes – 'it is on the adult community that the responsibility for the well-being of young people depends.'[1] Thus in the Ministry of Education's Annual Report for 1952 under the head of Youth Service, we read: 'The further restrictions on financial expenditure and on building work virtually called a halt to all new developments in the Youth Service. There was evidence, too, that local education authorities' expenditure on the Youth Service was reduced during the year. . . . In order to eliminate less essential expenditure all branches of the service were subjected to very careful scrutiny and, as a result of this, some useful but not essential work had to be given up.'[2] Such parsimony is just bleak tragedy, and the crabbing of the 'non-essential' one of its worst features. For it is the experimental, the adventurous, the imaginative enterprises that appeal to some of the brightest spirits among our young people. There is now a more enlightened policy. For the Government, conscious of growing dissatisfaction, appointed a Committee under the chairmanship of the Countess of Albemarle to review the Youth Service. It reported in 1959, and there have since been several developments including the establishment of a Youth Service Development Council and the provision at Leicester of a national college for the training of full-time youth leaders.

The Educating Neighbourhood

Villages differ widely in the scope of their social and cultural

1. *Citizens of Tomorrow*, p. 94.
2. *Education in 1952* (H.M.S.O., 1953), p. 21.

life; in some the village hall is a hive of activities, while others have no meeting-place and the residents no great desire to meet. In towns and cities one finds similar differences: one area in a city is most neighbourly, churches, clubs, and fellowships are active and the community centre a hub of social and cultural pursuits, while other areas are socially dead and have no cultural life whatsoever. It is never easy to account for these differences, and as a rule several factors contribute to them; but the personal factor is a chief determinant. Some localities have had the good fortune in the past to have had residents with a flair for social leadership, and a neighbourly tradition has grown up and is still maintained by persons with social gifts to-day. Others are new localities which have gone right socially from the start, thanks to some wise initial leadership. The unsociable neighbourhoods have had no such luck, and social surveys are sometimes able to show not only absence of leadership now but a record of misguided leadership and quarrels in the past.

The cultural quality of a neighbourhood is one of the most potent factors in education; and a boy or girl is fortunate if he grows up in a locality which has a good tradition and persons capable of maintaining and enriching it. This was especially true in days when secondary education was less accessible than it is to-day; the abler boys of that period, particularly those born in rural areas, often owed their chance of a useful and satisfying career to the education that they received and the encouragement given to them by good neighbours. John Buchan used to illustrate this point on occasion by telling the story of the English visitor to Scotland who, looking at a wide expanse of bleak moor and bog, turned to a Highland shepherd beside him and said, 'In God's name, what does this country produce?' The shepherd solemnly removed his cap and said, 'Sir, in God's name it produces educated men.'[1]

Victorian England, as Samuel Smiles liked to show, had its large quota of men who with little formal schooling rose to be captains of industry and made their mark on their

1. *Canadian Occasions* (Hodder & Stoughton, 1940), p. 105.

generation; often the stimulus and such education as they received came mainly from the home or good neighbours. The classic Welsh example is that of Lloyd George, who owed little to his village school and a very great deal to his uncle, Richard Lloyd, and the intellectual stimulus of the chapel. A particularly interesting illustration of the value of an educative neighbourhood is afforded by the life story of Sir Henry Jones who, without any help from his local school in a Welsh village, contrived to lead a life of intellectual distinction, becoming Professor of Moral Philosophy in the University of Glasgow. He wrote and spoke much about citizenship and, bearing always in mind his debt to his own little neighbourhood, he never ceased to stress the importance of good social influences in character training and in intellectual and spiritual growth. Nor did he ever forget the stimulus that he derived from the debates and discussions that he had listened to as a boy when, as an apprentice, he worked with his father in the latter's shoemaker's shed. 'While the little workshop and my working companions', he recalled, 'exercised more influence and did more to form my mind and character than anything else, there were other forces in operation. After all the workshop was only an item in the wider and more varied life of the community, in which perforce I shared. For "social influences" were at their silent and restless play. And social influences, in my opinion, are powers whose extent has never been adequately realized. They are so constant, and they are so universal, and they are so intangible. . . . From their silent working came the uniqueness of the villagers of Llangernyw, making them distinguishable from the inhabitants of the neighbouring villages of Llanfair and Gwytherin.'[1]

It would not be far wrong to claim that on the quality of these social influences in our different neighbourhoods the character of our Welfare State depends. So far the emphasis has been on its material aspects, but we cannot continue with impunity to neglect its social, cultural, and recreative needs.

1. *Old Memories* (Hodder & Stoughton, 1922), pp. 45–6.

The Exchequer does very little to help the National Council of Social Service in its efforts to promote the erection of buildings in which the social life of the neighbourhood can develop under wholesome auspices. In the past Village Halls and Community Centres have had to stand at the back of the grant queue to receive the crumbs that fall from the Treasury table. The following extract from one of the Ministry of Education's annual reports illustrates this discouraging attitude: 'Under the Physical Training and Recreation Act, 1937, the Minister has power to give grants in aid of the capital cost of village hall and community centre schemes, whether sponsored by voluntary bodies or by statutory authorities. Since the war, restrictions have been placed on such provision from time to time because of the shortage of building resources, and early in 1952 still more severe measures had to be taken. Offers of grant were restricted to schemes which could be carried out by voluntary labour without the use of controlled materials, and to schemes which were necessary either to secure the continuance of existing facilities or to adapt newly purchased premises and put them into use, subject to the work costing less than £1,000. The rate of the Ministry's grant remained at approximately one-third of the total cost of each scheme. The National Council of Social Service continued to administer the arrangements for making loans towards the provision of village halls in rural areas, but during the year it was decided that it was no longer possible to make interest-free loans, and that interest would be charged at rates varying up to four per cent according to the period of the loan.'[1] There will come no doubt fluctuations in the degree of assistance given, but the Welfare State will lack an essential foundation unless there is whole-hearted recognition of the importance of the social and cultural life of the neighbourhood.

Many teachers have a flair for social leadership. Robertson Scott, founder of that excellent magazine *The Countryman*, commenting on village life, once observed: 'In hamlets I

1. *Education in 1952*, p. 21.

know best the standard-bearers of progress, civilization, evolution, well-doing, the high life, better living, true religion – call it what you like – have been without doubt teachers in our schools.' Some of the teachers in the Cambridgeshire Village Colleges have done heroic work in raising the cultural standards in their neighbourhood. Leadership in an urban area is a different proposition, but an impressive feature of evacuation during World War II was the confidence which parents had in the teachers under whose charge their children set off to their various destinations. One felt at the time that when peace once again reigned this teacher-parent relationship might greatly help in reshaping our shattered society. And undoubtedly teachers with a strong social conscience are to-day foremost in many areas, and perhaps especially in the new housing estates, in creating a community spirit and fostering those cultural and recreative developments that so help to raise the standards and values of a community.

Such leadership by teachers is of inestimable value in the kind of neighbourhood which many schools serve to-day. Stressing the modern teacher's obligation to society, the Advisory Council on Education in Scotland observes: 'What makes it so necessary to stress this new responsibility falling on the School is the profound change that has come over our national life in the last half century. Urbanization, limitation of families and the passing away of the unified family life, the immense scale and high specialization of industry, and the ceaseless movement of the population have transformed the relatively simple and stable community life of earlier times into a vast, incoherent complex in which the adolescent is lost. To speak of "detribalized youth" in Scotland, as many are doing, is no mere rhetorical exaggeration.'[1] And it is not only youth that is detribalized; around many schools is a teeming population of adults without any roots in the locality. Here indeed is Mr T. S. Eliot's waste land in its more

1. *Secondary Education.* Report of the Advisory Council for Education in Scotland (H.M.S.O., 1947), p. 11.

devastating state, and for those who can give social leadership and fail to do so, his criticism is not too severe:

> You neglect and belittle the desert,
> The desert is not only round the corner
> The desert is in the heart of your brother.

The development of an active community life in every neighbourhood is also important as a bulwark of democracy and an antidote to excessive centralization. During a period like ours of rapid transition in the direction of positive government, we are in grave danger, as Professor John McMurray has said, of 'losing democracy'.[1] The more there is direction and control from the centre, whether it be London or the County or Town Hall, the more important it becomes to ensure active local participation in the government of education and in the social services. Our tendency to-day in recruiting persons for service on various official administrative committees and boards is to select more and more those who are active in party politics, and to take little account of those who render valuable but unobtrusive service in their own neighbourhood. On this growing practice of preferring the politically active, Lady Wootton has some shrewd comments which deserve much more attention than they have so far received: 'Among them', she says, 'are found many persons of exceptional public spirit and unusual intellectual ability; but they include also a number of the maladjusted who gladly take refuge from the concrete problems on their doorsteps by escape into the cloudier world of abstractions and generalities. And they certainly exclude many of the public-spirited whose abilities are practical and constructive. Experience of war – and particularly of air-raids – has proved that sense of public responsibility, as well as qualities of leadership, imagination, and organizing ability are to be found amongst many of the (in the conventional sense) politically indifferent.'[2]

1. *Constructive Democracy* (Faber, 1943), p. 25.
2. *Freedom under Planning* (Allen & Unwin, 1944), pp. 153–4.

CHAPTER FOUR

ECONOMIC AND SOCIAL FACTORS

The Finance of Education

Lloyd George, during World War I, persuaded H. A. L. Fisher to quit for a time the calm of the academic world to become President of the Board of Education in his famous Cabinet. Although the war was at a critical phase, Lloyd George was confident that the time was ripe to prepare for a vigorous programme of educational reform. Fisher, when he took up Office, spent a few days surveying the nature of his task, and soon came firmly to the conclusion that there could be no advance without a sound foundation of education finance. 'Finance', he tells us, 'was at the heart of the problem. The cause which had been arresting educational progress in the country was lack of financial support. The engine was reasonably well built, but there was lack of petrol.'[1] Fortunately there was in the Board's pigeon-holes a first-class report on the whole question of public finance – the Kempe Report, published in 1914 but inevitably set aside because of the outbreak of war in that year. Fisher took this report as his guide, and made its recommendations on education finance the basis of his financial policy.

The principles outlined in the Kempe Report have governed practice in education finance until recently. 'It constitutes a landmark in the history of the finance of education, for it led to a new conception of education grants and of the relationship between the central and local authorities which should be implicit in their administration.'[2] The two main principles advocated in the report were (1) that the rate burden should be as equal as possible and, (2) that the system

1. *Unfinished Autobiography* (Oxford Univ. Press, 1940), p. 104.
2. *Education 1900–1950*, p. 24.

should 'provide' for an automatic expansion of the government grant concurrently with an increase of the local expenditure which it is intended to aid.' To give effect to these principles the Report suggested a formula for the computation of grant which took account of the rateable value of each area, and the amount of the local authority's net expenditure on education. An essential feature of the Kempe proposals was that the grant should be a percentage one. This vital principle of percentage grant has been challenged more than once by economy committees: e.g. the Geddes Axe Committee argued that the percentage system encouraged expenditure and was impossible to control. Experience has shown, however, that by grant regulations local expenditure can easily be controlled from the centre, and the percentage system survived until an entirely new system of financing educational expenditure was introduced by the Local Government Act, 1958.

Adhering to the principles of the Kempe Report, Fisher effected a complete reform of the system of grants to local education authorities. For the fifty-seven separate grants then payable by the Board of Education he substituted a system of annual substantive grant, making it dependent by grant regulations upon the maintenance of an effective system of education by the local authority. Unfortunately there had to be two substantive grants, one for elementary and one for higher education, because of the existence, as a result of the 1902 Act's compromise, of several separate authorities for elementary education only. The grant for elementary education was calculated on a formula, taking into account the number of children in each area and having regard to each area's assessable value. The grant for higher education was calculated at a flat rate of 50 per cent of the net local expenditure.

Up to 1958, except for certain services, such as School Meals, Training of Teachers, and some courses in advanced technology, the grant payable to local education authorities was based on a formula similar to that applied by Fisher to elementary education. The principle followed was that of relating the grant – to quote words used by Mr Butler in 1944 – 'to the number of children in the area and the capacity of the area to pay for their education'.

The percentage system fostered a sense of partnership between the central department and local education authorities, and this was one of the reasons why many educationists opposed its replacement by the grant arrangements authorized by the Local Government Act, 1958. Under this Act specific education grant to local education authorities was discontinued – the grant for school milk and meals is an important exception – and education was included among the services covered by the general grant paid to local authorities by the Ministry of Housing and Local Government. When this drastic change in the grant system was made, some feared that education would receive less generous treatment and that in some areas there might be a decline in the standard of provision for education. Happily there is, so far, no evidence to suggest that either of these forebodings was justified. There has been additional local expenditure on education, and an increase in the general grant to meet new expenditure. New regulations prescribing standards have been made under powers conferred on the Minister of Education by the Local Government Act. The Act also provides that the general grant payable to an authority may be reduced if the authority fails to maintain reasonable standards. One of the aims of the new system is to reduce the amount of control over the administration of local authorities, and in education several changes in administrative practice have been introduced with this objective in view. It is, however, too early to judge whether the new grant system will prove more or less satisfactory for education than the one it has replaced.

It is often complained that expenditure on education has increased excessively since the passing of the 1944 Act. There has however been little change, having regard to the difference in the value of money, in the expenditure on the central feature of the educational service – primary and secondary schools. In a paper read to the Manchester Statistical Society in 1955 Mr Norman Fisher showed convincingly that in real terms 'the total amount of money spent on primary and secondary education is now about the same as before the war when the increased number of children is taken into account'.[1] Four years later the Crowther Council, after a close study of relevant facts and figures, reckoned that 'in the last twenty years expenditure on the central purposes of education in schools, as distinct from health services on the one side and higher education on the other, has been doing little more than keep up with the general expansion of the national income.' The services that have, in varying proportions, cost more have been school meals and milk, technical education, university awards, administration, conveyance of school children, training of teachers, and schools for handicapped children. Of these the first three items account for more than half of the additional expenditure.

While the rising cost of education often provokes criticism, we spend but about five per cent of our national income on it.[2] Comparison with other countries is difficult because of different interpretations of 'educational expenditure', and for the same reason there are various estimates of our percentage.[3] While it seems formidable to say, as in truth one can, that we spend over a million a day on education, the statement sounds less imposing if one adds, as one can with equal truth, that this is roughly a daily charge of 5d per head of the population. How much more we spend on tobacco or drink! It was estimated in 1953 that Education consumed no more than 14 per cent of the social services budget. Commenting on such figures, Professor Judges observes: 'Comparison with pre-war

1. *Is Education Possible?* (Manchester Statistical Society, 1954), p. 14.

2. See chapter by Professor A. V. Judges in *Looking Forward in Education* (Faber, 1955), pp. 13–37; see also *15 to 18* (Crowther Report), Vol. I, pp. 56–60, and John Vaisey, *The Costs of Education* (Allen & Unwin, 1958).

3. See *Public Expenditure on Education* (UNESCO, 1953); *Education*, 29 Sept. 1961, pp. 456, 469.

figures is difficult, but it is evident enough that education, which at one time had the distinction of being the largest element in the social budget, apart from the Dole, has dropped to fourth or fifth place.'[1]

While in our national budget we classify education with the other social services, it should be noted that it has a security value at least as important as some items that figure as defence; and it is also economically productive to an extent that no other social service can claim. 'Industrialism no less than political democracy seems to carry with it inescapably the theory and practice of universal education. Industrialism creates a vast educational appetite; for clerks who can read, write and count, for lawyers, accountants, and administrators, for mechanics, tool users, and machine minders, for scientific researchers, technologists, inventors, and statisticians.'[2] For such reasons one might reasonably expect education to receive more sympathetic consideration at times of financial crisis than it normally does. It is, however, noticeable that statesmen in search of economies are much less ready to inflict severe 'cuts' in education than they were thirty years ago. Some may attribute this to more enlightened statesmanship, while others will regard it as evidence of an increasing public regard for education which the shrewd politician, when bent on economy, is obliged to respect.

Planning, Programmes, and Priorities

An old and effective planning procedure is the preparation of the annual estimates of expenditure. It occupies local education authorities for several months and is of fundamental importance. For it settles almost irrevocably the amount of money that will be available for each item of the education service in the ensuing year. Unforeseeable circumstances may justify and sometimes make imperative a supplementary estimate out of season, but once the local rate

1. *Looking Forward in Education*, p. 33.
2. *Is Education Possible?* p. 5.

95

for the year has been fixed it becomes difficult to meet the cost of such unexpected demands. When an individual makes an estimate of his personal spending, he is guided by the amount of money that he will be able to spend – that is to say, his probable income. A public authority on the other hand has, when fixing its estimate, to consider first and foremost the services that it has to fulfil, and until it has done that it cannot forecast its probable expenditure. In other words, an individual begins with a more or less definite figure, while a public authority ends with one.

As provider of a many-sided public service, a local education authority has first to consider every single aspect of that service in detail, and decide what it will cost to maintain it during the year. It is under a legal obligation to provide some of its services, irrespective of its own views, and it has also to have regard to minimum standards laid down in various statutory regulations. Some of its spending is, however, permissive or optional, and it is here that there is scope for parsimony and its opposite. Before the estimates can be submitted to the education committee there has to be an immense amount of meticulous staff work, and detailed consideration by the various sub-committees concerned. As a result there is each year a thorough review of the whole field of the local education authority's responsibilities and activities, and a careful survey of what each section of the service will do during the ensuing year. When an education committee has agreed its estimates, these are subject to further checks. They are, for example, closely scrutinized by the finance committee of the council and by officials of the Ministry of Education. And the way in which the money is subsequently spent is examined by government auditors – the modern Mr Cockertons – who spend weeks of each year in education offices assuring themselves that the innumerable government regulations have been observed and that there has been no 'irregularity'.

When the estimate of gross expenditure has been converted into a net figure by deducting government grant and income from fees, rents, etc., it becomes possible to forecast the rate that will have to be levied, and if an increase in the rate charge is involved there is soon forceful evidence of another effective check on expenditure, namely that of ratepayer opinion. While some increases may be unavoidable – for example, those that are a consequence of national salary or wages awards – others are debatable, especially those which provide for development. In times of austerity developments are few, but there are exceptions to this rule; for example, during the bleak years after the two world wars hundreds of schools were built in certain areas to accommodate the children in the new housing estates so characteristic of those periods.

Whenever there has been development in education there has been some measure of planning. Churchmen in pre-reformation days when building their cathedrals and monasteries no doubt discussed when and where the school should be built. The voluntary societies in the eighteenth and nineteenth centuries had to plan and programme in order to make good use of their limited resources. The school boards had to plan when 'filling the gaps' in school accommodation after 1870, and so had the local authorities after 1902 when expanding grammar school education. But planning to-day is on a vastly different scale, and is actuated by motives of a different kind.

Political thought has moved far away from the *laissez-faire* outlook dominant in the nineteenth century, and it would be almost true to say that we are all planners now, and none of us wholly unfamiliar with the techniques and jargon of twentieth-century planning. Two world wars have accustomed us to it, and our own personal experience of scarcities and short supplies has made us accept the necessity of planning as a method of making good use of restricted resources. It was partly for such reasons that parliament and the nation so readily accepted in 1944 the concept of a Minister of Education able to act as a chief planner in education and able also to speak authoritatively on behalf of education when priorities were being decided at the highest level.

Hence, too, the dissatisfaction felt when the Minister of Education was left out of the Cabinet during a long period in the early nineteen-fifties.

A somewhat ineffective attempt was made after World War I to apply modern planning methods to education. The 1918 Act made it the duty of every local education authority 'to contribute to the progressive development and comprehensive organization of education in its area,' and to secure this every authority was required to prepare and submit to the Board of Education a scheme or programme of development. Much time and thought were devoted to the preparation of programmes designed to secure a better education for the older pupils in elementary schools, but the Geddes Axe nullified much of this work although the surveys then made and the conclusions reached had later some influence on the Hadow Committee when it was considering its report on *The Education of the Adolescent*.

The Education Act of 1944 is by contrast a strong planning measure; the Minister is armed with authority to enforce his views, and the Act provides two effective planning devices – the development plan for primary and secondary education, and the scheme for further education. Clause 11 of the Act goes into elaborate detail, expressly stating the steps that local authorities should take to 'estimate the immediate and prospective needs of their area . . . in such form as the Minister may direct, showing the action which the authority proposes should be taken for securing that there shall be sufficient primary and secondary schools for their area and the successive measures by which it is proposed to accomplish that purpose.' When the Minister approved these elaborate plans, he made in accordance with clause 12 of the Act an Order making the plan obligatory, subject to amendment by him whenever he deems it expedient 'by reason of any change or proposed change of circumstances.' The preparation of these development plans was a formidable task involving detailed surveys of every school and much consultation with interested parties, and the same is true of the schemes for further education. As a result there is now in existence a detailed masterplan for the organization of education in England and Wales, indicating developments for many years ahead; and the Minister is empowered to secure its implementation stage by stage as he may decide.

Clearly there is much to be said for planning of this elaborate, purposive character. It compels local authorities to survey the educational needs of their area, and take careful stock of all shortcomings. It stimulates development and ensures that it is orderly and well considered. It educates all those concerned in the preparation of the plan, and also the various bodies and individuals who are consulted. It prevents the promotion of hasty and ill-conceived projects, and is an antidote to the pressure often exerted in the past by well-intentioned persons with influence or by local bodies to secure priority for favourite schemes without strong claims. If well publicized, it has a useful public relations value, and if well presented it enlists a supporting body of opinion. It compels advance consultation with interests affected, and with other departments of the council concerned. It ensures co-ordination with the general county or civic plan, and helps to secure that new schools are well-sited in relation to anticipated developments in housing, roads, parks, libraries, and other services. And one of its main purposes is, of course, to help the Minister, when determining annual programmes in the light of his knowledge of the resources available, to judge what projects should receive priority.

Of the dangers of planning for education much has been said and written in recent years, of which a great deal is irrelevant to its practice in this country. For although our Ministers of Education, as planners-in-chief, are by the Act of 1944 vested with vast power, all have exercised it with conspicuous moderation, and a similar spirit has been usual in the planning done by local education authorities. But it has been well said that, 'all the old clichés are just as true as ever they were – power still corrupts, absolute power still corrupts absolutely, and eternal vigilance is just as much the price of liberty as ever it was.'[1] One of the perplexities that besets the planner is to know where to stop; if planning could be confined to means, the danger to freedom would be much less, but in education means and ends are often inextricably mixed. While economic planning for education is one thing, and educational planning is another the relationship can be very close. The school dinner may on first thoughts seem to have no educational implications, and indeed some teachers have regarded it in that way, expressing a desire to have nothing to do with it. But the communal meal, properly arranged, can be, and should be, an important educative occasion. The planning and erection of a secondary school involves many economic considerations, but it also closely affects the character of the education to be given and when the planner decides the type of school he is making a decision of great educational significance.

Another important point is that continuity is essential in educational planning, and sometimes party politics make this difficult to attain. There can be more continuity of policy in the BBC, or in a nationalized industry, than in a Ministry or Local Authority too responsive to electoral change. Planning of education is impracticable without a wide measure of agreement about aim and purpose, and this is not easy to achieve in a free democracy. 'Planned society', it has been said, 'needs a unifying purpose. This can be achieved either by the extermination or internment of those who do not agree, or by a spiritual integration of the members of society.'[2] On the other hand, it is possible for planning to be too rigid and fixed; it can lead to drab uniformity, stereotyping of approved patterns, and adherence to them when they have become out of date or after their defects are evident.

One of the dangers inherent in the development plans and schemes of further education, prepared so conscientiously

1. Barbara Wootton, *Freedom under Planning* (Allen & Unwin, 1945), p. 140.

2. Karl Mannheim, *Diagnosis of our Time* (Kegan Paul, 1943), p. 103.

during the immediate post-war years, is that they may 'fix' our educational landscape to the patterns then deemed desirable. It was not altogether a good time for making plans intended to revolutionize our educational system, for those responsible for making the plans locally and scrutinizing them at the centre could not have been at their brightest and best so soon after the strains and stresses of war. Reviewing, towards the end of the war, two books about planning, one for and the other against, Mr T. S. Eliot made this interesting comment: 'I regard it as unfortunate that we shall have the need, the opportunity, and the enthusiasm for a great deal of rebuilding and town planning, at a period in which there exists no great architectural style in which to build; similarly, as a consideration at least recommending caution, that we should have the need, the opportunity, and the enthusiasm for extensive social replanning at a time when values are so confused, and when popular approval is so easily obtained for both the untried and discredited, for both the callow and the jejune.'[1]

Planning can also have the effect of preventing experiment and curbing enterprise. In the past many of our educational advances have been the result of individual enterprise and imaginative leadership or of sustained experience in various localities. We owe much to pioneers like Thomas Arnold, Frances Mary Buss, Baden Powell, and Margaret Mc-Millan – to name but a few of a great company; and we owe much also to pioneering by local authorities and voluntary societies in many fields: e.g. school health, handicapped children, school broadcasts, county libraries, adult education, and school journeys. Nor – and this is specially true in a changing society – is the planner necessarily a good interpreter of future needs: he can only like the rest of us speculate and conjecture:

> But what was before us we know not
> And we know not what shall succeed.

1. *Theology*, May 1943, Review of Karl Mannheim's *Diagnosis of our Time*, and Christopher Dawson's *The Judgment of the Nations*.

It is important therefore that there should be diversity and encouragement of pioneering and experiment by local authorities, voluntary bodies, and individual teachers. 'The plan that does not leave the way open to change is scarcely less disorderly than the aimless empiricism that rejects plan. Renewal: flexibility: adjustment: these are essential attributes of all organic plans.'[1]

Equality of Opportunity

An essential aim of the Welfare State is to provide each citizen with the basic minimum requirements for leading a useful and satisfying life. Forward-looking statesmen were beginning to think along these lines in the nineteenth century, and our Elementary Education Act of 1870 and the subsequent adoption of compulsory education came at a time when one of the major prophets of the Welfare State, T. H. Green, was contending that 'the true function of statesmanship is to produce a community in which all the individuals shall, so far as is possible, be capable of living and free to live, a good life'. This conception of the State continued to gain ground; the Webbs pressed for a guaranteed 'national minimum of the requisites for efficient parenthood and citizenship', and this doctrine was implicit in the social legislation of the Liberals after they came into power in 1906. Writing to a friend in 1907, Sir Winston Churchill, then a Liberal, observed: 'Minimum standards of wages and comfort, insurance in some effective form or another against sickness, unemployment, old age – these are the questions, and the only questions, by which parties are going to live in the future.'[2]

The Education Act 1944 is an attempt to provide the Welfare State with the kind of educational system that it

1. Lewis Mumford, *The Culture of Cities* (Secker & Warburg, ed. 1940), pp. 380–1.
2. For an excellent short account of the rise of the Welfare State, see Bureau of Current Affairs pamphlet No. 124 by Dr Mark Abrams.

should have; and the basic minimum that it seeks to guar-
antee for every prospective citizen is education 'appropriate
to his age, aptitude, and ability' throughout the period of
full-time compulsory schooling. During the primary stage
we normally give this education in one type of school, according to the age of the child: that is to say, all except the
relatively few who go to independent or private schools,
attend county or voluntary infant and, then, junior schools.
But how best to provide 'appropriate' education at the
secondary level has proved to be one of the most difficult of
the administrative problems posed by the Act. The essence of
the problem is how to organize secondary education for all in
such a way as to secure that each child has, as far as possible,
an equal chance, aptitude and ability being the only important differentiating factors.

Of the advocates of secondary education for all in the
nineteen thirties and forties, the most effective by far was
R. H. Tawney, and in a passage often quoted he pleaded
especially for an educational system that would enable us
'to forget the tedious vulgarities of income and social position, in a common affection for the qualities which belong,
not to any class or profession of men, but to man himself.'[1]
By abolishing fees in all schools associated with the State,
except the direct grant schools, the Act of 1944 has helped us
'to forget the tedious vulgarities of income', and even in the
direct grant schools only about 50 per cent of the parents now
pay fees. But we have yet a long way to go before it can be
said that secondary education is unaffected by considerations
of income and social class.

Of all the reforms embodied in the Act of 1944 none has so
far received half as much attention or aroused more controversy than this requirement that every child shall receive
a secondary education appropriate to his ability and aptitude. Its complete fulfilment is obviously beyond human
reach, and it will be a formidable task to establish a system
for which we can honestly claim that it provides for all child-

1. *Equality* (Allen and Unwin, 1929), p. 200.

ren an education that approximately meets their individual needs. As a result of the experience gained since the passing of the Act we now have a better grasp of the problems that have to be resolved to secure an effective system of that kind; they are many and various – administrative, educational, economic, and social. So far we have tended to concentrate on the administrative and educational aspects, and the earnest consideration given to them by the Ministry, the local authorities, and teachers has been of great constructive value. We know a great deal more than we did in 1944 about the problem of organizing secondary education for all, and within the schools there have been many developments affecting both the curriculum and methods of teaching. Intensive consideration has been given by many teachers to the educational needs of pupils throughout the range of ability, from the truly gifted to those who are educationally sub-normal. By placing emphasis on the individual child – 'appropriate to his age, aptitude, and ability' – the Act has deliberately encouraged the child-centred approach, an interesting contrast to the approach in some other countries where the stress is on service to the State and the needs of the national economy.

Organizing Secondary Education for All

Before 1944 our policy was secondary education for the fortunate few; since 1944 it has been secondary education for all – as radical and revolutionary a change as our educational system is ever likely to experience. The transformation began with a change of nomenclature overnight, elementary schools by the hundred being rechristened 'secondary'; but problems of gravity and substance soon arose when local authorities got to work on their development plans and found themselves obliged to attempt a long-term forecast of the shape of things to come. They had to make up their minds in the course of a few months how they would organize secondary education throughout their respective areas.

When the authorities were embarking on this formidable task, the Ministry came out with a strong lead; they issued a booklet, *The Nation's Schools*, which left no room for doubt that the Ministry, like the Norwood Committee, desired, wherever practicable, a pattern of three alternatives – grammar, technical, and modern. In 1946 the Labour Party at their annual conference revolted against this tripartite policy; and Ellen Wilkinson as Minister, herself a staunch egalitarian, had to defend this booklet and the organization that it advocated. She did her best to convince her audience that tripartism was good democracy; and she tried to win its support by contending that there would be 'parity', a blessed word popularized by the Spens Committee which makes fourteen references to it. 'If the teachers get the same pay,' she argued, 'if the holidays are the same, and if as far as possible the buildings are good in each case, then you get in practice parity.' She apparently assumed that parity of conditions would quickly bring parity of esteem.

The Conference, however, was not convinced, and by resolution urged the fiery little Minister 'to reshape educational policy in accordance with socialist principles.' It is now more generally appreciated that parity is not only a question of conditions but even more one of status and esteem.[1] Our 1,400 grammar schools are heirs of a great tradition, for the grammar school as an institution has a thousand years of history behind it: their standards of education to-day are high; and they have for centuries been the normal gateway to the universities and the professions. So in post-war discussions about the organization of secondary education 'prestige' has figured as prominently as the ambiguous term 'parity'. Parents to-day clamour for the admission of their children to the grammar school not only because of the quality of education it offers but also because its academic education secures access to the leading pro-

1. For a full exposition of the implications of parity see Olive Banks, *Parity and Prestige in English Secondary Education* (Routledge & Kegan Paul, 1955).

fessions; and such a school is thought to confer on its pupils higher social status than the new secondary schools.

It is natural, and indeed creditable, that parents should without much thought about aptitude and ability prefer the grammar school in areas where the other schools do not yet offer a good standard of education. But in many localities secondary modern and technical schools have now matured, are proving their worth, and gaining the confidence of parents. It is, however, important to remember that this great educational revolution, so full of promise for the future, is still in the pioneer stage, and subject to all the growing pains of a new venture. Eight years after the passing of the Act Mr Butler, as its author, assessed the progress that had been made, and said that he had two 'anxieties'. 'I am not satisfied', he remarked, 'that we have found the best ways to choose pupils for the various types of secondary education'; and discussing his other 'anxiety', he observed: 'We have clearly not yet ensured that all our technical and modern schools provide a genuine, distinctive, and full education.'[1]

There has been some healthy development since then, but much remains to be done in regard to the two crucial points which Mr Butler specified, methods of allocation and the creation of genuine alternatives to the grammar school. When we have made a good job of these two essentials and not before, the revolution will have passed out of its running-in stage. A prodigious amount of thought has been given by psychologists and administrators to problems of allocation, and the utmost ingenuity has been shown in devising ways of testing aptitude and ability.[2] Much research during these post-war years has been devoted to ways of assessing a child's intelligence quotient, commonly called his I.Q.; and for a time I.Q. was widely accepted as a safe determinant and exalted to a pedestal of infallibility. But such idols have their

1. *Jubilee Lectures* (Evans for the Univ. of London Institute of Education, 1952), pp. 51, 52.
2. For an admirable survey see J. J. B. Dempster, *Selection for Secondary Education* (Methuen, 1954).

day, and after a Humpty-Dumpty-like fall intelligence testing is now valued in allocation more appropriately for use as a check on the school record, and within the school as a valuable diagnostic aid. 'One must admit', says a leading psychologist, 'that the more we adhere to objective techniques of mental measurement and prediction, the less we learn about the particular case.'[1]

Opinion about methods of allocation to secondary schools seems to be veering back to the view expressed in the White Paper presented to Parliament prior to its consideration of the Bill that became the Act of 1944. It suggested that the allocation of children to secondary schools should be decided 'not on the results of a competitive test, but on an assessment of their individual aptitudes largely by such means as school records, supplemented, if necessary, by intelligence tests, due regard being had to their parents' wishes and the careers they have in mind.'[2] We should worry more than we do about the distorting influence of selection tests and competitive examinations on the junior school curriculum, and assign to the Junior School the role cast for it by the Spens Report of acting as a recording angel, using its routine records of individual children as the main determinant for purposes of allocation. Surely the time has come when, for the sake of the sensitive child as well as in the interests of the Junior School, competitive tests should cease to be employed as a method of allocation. Several authorities have reached this conclusion and there is an increasing tendency to rely on other methods of dealing with the problem.

Much thought has been given to ways of organizing the system of universal secondary education. After the controversy over *The Nation's Schools* the Ministry made it clear that it did not want to press the tripartite solution unduly, and in a new booklet, *The New Secondary Education*, it stressed the value of diversity. 'There is, indeed,' it

1. P. E. Vernon, Lecture on *Modern Educational Psychology as a Science* (Evans for Univ. of London Institute of Education, 1950), p. 22.
2. *Educational Reconstruction*, p. 9.

declared, 'no end to the possible variations of organization; the system must be flexible and experiments of many kinds are to be welcomed.'[1] The Development Plans contained a variety of proposals: for some localities three schools (grammar, technical, modern) were proposed, for others two schools, and for others one comprehensive school was preferred. This diversified and experimental approach was in harmony with our tradition of embarking on new ventures empirically without too much regard for theory or precise pattern. And it was in accord with the view that had been expressed in the White Paper, which had stated: 'It would be wrong to suppose that they (i.e. grammar, technical, and modern schools) will necessarily remain separate and apart. Different types may be combined in one building or on one site as considerations of convenience or efficiency may suggest.'[2]

Nineteen years after the passing of the 1944 Act the statistical picture of grant-aided secondary education in England and Wales was as follows: Modern 3,906, Grammar 1,295, Direct Grant Grammar 179, Technical 204, Bi- and Multi-lateral 66, Comprehensive 175, Other Secondary 245. The number of all-age schools had dropped to 604, and the type should soon disappear.[3] There has been a good deal of unpleasant controversy about comprehensive schools which soon got involved in the rough and tumble of party politics. This was most unfortunate because it is important that their merits and demerits should be assessed without prejudice. The pattern of secondary education is certainly changing, and there is a growing tendency to blur the edges between the different types of school. It is doubtful whether we have enough experience of comprehensive schools in this country to be able to judge whether they are a good way of providing secondary education here, but their

1. P. 24.
2. *Educational Reconstruction*, p. 10.
3. *Statistics of Education, 1963*, Part One (H.M.S.O., 1964).

number is steadily increasing, and our knowledge of them grows.

At the beginning of this book reference is made to an opinion expressed by Dr J. B. Conant that 'educational practices are not an exportable commodity.' He wrote this after visiting a number of English-speaking countries to examine their system of secondary education; he had undertaken this tour in order to help him in forming a judgement on what secondary school organization would be best for the U.S.A. He came to the conclusion that for the U.S.A. a system of comprehensive high schools was best, largely because that type of school was well rooted there and, in spite of certain shortcomings, capable of improvement and development. But he was careful to suggest that what was good for the U.S.A. was not necessarily good elsewhere. 'It is', he observed, with characteristic wisdom, 'extremely difficult to say what is a good educational procedure except in terms of a particular society; a school cannot be separated from the context of the families that it serves nor from the over-all social framework in which the pupils will probably function as adults.'[1]

Experience will help us to solve the problems of school organization here. For such reasons it is fortunate that several local authorities in this country have established Comprehensive Schools, and that they are well distributed in areas very different in character. It is not proposed to discuss their merits or demerits, for it seems more sensible to suspend judgement until they have had more opportunity of proving their worth. We have, however, already an interesting interim survey written by Dr Robin Pedley after visiting new Comprehensive Schools in such different areas as London, Middlesex, Walsall, Anglesey, Westmorland, and the Isle of Man. The value of the survey is enhanced because it is followed by commentaries by Dr Pedley himself, Professor H. C. Dent, Lord James of Rusholme, Mr Harold Shearman, and Sir William Alexander. The latter in a final chapter supported

1. *Education and Liberty*, p. 2.

EDUCATION

the view that it was premature then to formulate conclusions.

'The theoretical arguments', Sir William observes, 'which have for the last twenty years been advocated with a good deal of fervour have suffered from the absence of factual evidence. The advocates of the comprehensive school have been able to claim potential virtues for it and the opponents have been able to point to serious disadvantages, neither being able to strengthen their argument with experience. We have known what grammar schools could do and do well; increasingly we have recognized that secondary modern schools were capable of achieving standards higher than had been expected; but the comprehensive school was an unknown quantity in this country.'

'It is, therefore,' he continues, 'of particular value that Dr Pedley should have made a survey of some fourteen schools, some of which have been running long enough to provide some useful factual information. It is, I think, clear that the survey must be examined for a few pointers rather than conclusive evidence; it is much too early for that. But these pointers are important. They tend to support neither those who favour the comprehensive school nor those who insist on a tripartite system.'[1] It is desirable, however, while the evidence of experience accumulates, to study the views of those who genuinely believe in these schools. A valuable exposition of the theory and practice of the Comprehensive School will be found in Chapter VIII of Dr A. G. Hughes's *Education and the Democratic Ideal.*[2]

Of official literature on the subject a report adopted by the London County Council in 1953 on the organization of these schools is well worth reading. The L.C.C. are as alive as are their critics to the problems caused by the size of their comprehensive schools: 2,000 for a three-form entry school, 1,200–1,500 for a two-form entry. And their report suggests

1. *Comprehensive Schools Today* (Councils & Education Press 1955), p. 52.
2. Longmans, 1951. See also *Inside the Comprehensive School* (N.U.T., 1958), R. Pedley, *The Comprehensive School* (Penguin Books, 1963), and *The Comprehensive School* (National Association of Schoolmasters, 1964).

various measures for counteracting the disadvantages of such large numbers – e.g. a system of houses and tutorial groups, and the L.C.C. evidently believe that in spite of the vast size of the building and the large roll-call the individual boy or girl will, as a result of the methods they propose, soon acquire a sense of 'belonging'. What of the headmaster or headmistress set in authority over that considerable kingdom? The report gives its answer: 'The headmaster will need to be an outstanding person. He will need to have not only great organizing ability, first-rate teaching power, vision, and originality, but also a personality congenial alike to staff and pupils. If he is to be able to devote himself to the things that are of first importance, he will need to delegate to others, and notably to his deputy and senior administrative officer, whole spheres of work ordinarily covered by the headmaster himself in a small secondary school.' What Bacon says of princes will be no less true of rulers of these schools: they 'are like to heavenly bodies, which cause good or evil times, and which have much veneration but no rest.'

The Social Ladder

Advocates of the comprehensive school usually claim that by educating all the children of a neighbourhood in one secondary school we shall produce a more democratic society. Social barriers will be broken down, they believe, and class distinctions will tend to disappear. 'The tripartite system, it is claimed, not only rests upon but perpetuates those class distinctions which many in the Labour Movement have pledged themselves to destroy. The aim of the comprehensive school has accordingly been envisaged as the promotion of social unity, at least between those pupils educated within the State system of secondary education. Its advocates within the political sphere are equalitarians. They are opposed alike to the social prestige of the grammar and to the prestige of the occupations for which the grammar school prepares. They hope that the creation of the common school will help to promote equality within the social as well as the educational system, and so prevent the new aristocracy of brains which, so the London County Council has argued, threatens to supersede the aristocracies of wealth and birth. Although educational considerations clearly enter into the advocacy of the comprehensive school within the Labour Party, they are motivated by something more than the inadequacy of selection techniques and the difficulty of transfers. Their case rests essentially upon the social effects of tripartitism and the social advantages of the common school'.[1]

It is possible to sympathize with these democratic aspirations, and yet doubt whether the comprehensive school will have the effect of breaking down class barriers. We have not yet enough experience to guide us on this point, and it is significant that Dr Pedley's interim survey 'provides no evidence on the question of the effect of these schools on creating a sense of unity.'[2]

Schools of every type from the Junior School onwards do in fact unintentionally encourage social stratification. For in order to give children the appropriate education that the law requires they 'stream' and classify them; and when they do this they are, as Professor T. H. Marshall has pointed out, influencing their occupational range and in the public mind social prestige is closely related to occupation. By requiring an education appropriate to each child's ability and aptitude the Act's intention is to promote equality of opportunity, but the processes of streaming and selecting which it entails make education have other consequences. 'Its aim is to eliminate hereditary privilege. In essence it is the equal right to display and develop differences, or inequalities; the equal right to be recognized as unequal. In the early stages of the establishment of such a system the major effect is, of course, to reveal hidden equalities – to enable the poor boy to show that he is

1. Olive Banks, *Parity and Prestige in English Secondary Education*, pp. 135–6.
2. *Comprehensive Schools Today*, p. 54.

as good as the rich boy. But the final outcome is a structure of unequal status fairly apportioned to unequal abilities.'[1]

Social class is a tenacious and pervasive influence in education as in some other spheres of life, and those who hope to eliminate it by means of educational organization are likely to be disappointed. It affects the admission of children to school, it affects them while they are there, it affects the length of their stay at school, and it affects their transfer from school to working life. One reason for this is, as suggested in the previous chapter, the paramount importance of the home; and it is still true that educative homes are more usual in some social classes than in others. A child from a good home with parents who care about education has advantages in the determination of his I.Q., his streaming, and his occupational prospect. No amount of legislation can prevent this differentiation nor any kind of school planning. The social benefits of the Welfare State, its better housing, full employment and the spread of education should in time minimize class (or home) differences, but meanwhile their existence as an important influence in opportunity must be recognized.[2]

It is often said that the British, and particularly the English, are intensely class conscious, and much of our humour is certainly based on the foibles due to class attitudes. But class plays a significant part in education in other countries also, including some that are professedly egalitarian. It will be found in education in the U.S.S.R., and it abounds in the U.S.A. in spite of the famous assertion in the Declaration of Independence, 'That all men are created equal.' 'There is,' to quote from a well-known American study of equal opportunities, 'a strong relationship between social status and rank in schools.' And it gives several illustrations of this, of which the following analysis of the 'streaming' of 103 girls

1. *Citizenship and Social Class* (Cambridge Univ. Press, 1950), pp. 65, 66.
2. See Mrs J. Floud's illuminating chapter on 'Education and Social Class' in *Looking Forward in Education*; and Professor Vernon's *The Bearing of Recent Advances in Psychology on Educational Problems* (1955).

in a Comprehensive High School, whose social background had been investigated, is typical:

1. Of the ten upper-class girls eight were in section A, one in B, and one in C.
2. Of the seven upper-middle class girls, six were in section A and one in B.
3. Of the thirty-three girls from lower-middle and indeterminate middle class, twenty-one were in section A, ten in section B, and two in section C.
4. Of the fifty-three lower-class, only six were in section A, twenty-eight in section B, and nineteen in section C.[1]

There can be little doubt that our educational procedures do less than justice to children whose background is unfavourable to their early development. Their I.Q. is not a reliable guide to their natural ability, they have less chance than other children to develop wholesome interests and aptitudes, they sometimes travel up the school in a 'stream' below their potential capacity, and they tend because of, parental attitudes to leave school earlier than their more fortunate fellow pupils. The handicaps of these early years would not, however, be so serious if they had not long-term consequences for the individuals concerned and also for the national economy. 'But,' to quote Professor Marshall again, 'as we all know, education to-day is closely linked with occupation, and one, at least, of the values the pupil expects to get from it is a qualification for employment at an appropriate level.'[2]

Occupation is now more and more closely associated with examinations; they are a gateway not only, as in the past, to the universities and older professions but also to an ever-increasing range of vocations. Nor is this only true of innumerable black-coated occupations; the City and Guilds of London and great regional examining bodies, like the Union of Lancashire and Cheshire Institutes, provide a range of

1. Warner, Havighurst & Loeb, *Who shall be educated?* (Kegan Paul, 1946), p. 73.
2. *Citizenship and Social Class*, p. 64.

examinations for mechanics and craftsmen the results of which often influence promotion. For many manual workers, therefore, a good secondary education is now essential as a basis for studying for examinations at the further education stage, and for training in the techniques of their employment.

As regards entry to the grammar school we have since 1944 made great strides along the egalitarian road. Among children born in 1920–9 over a half of higher middle class boys and over a quarter of lower middle class boys received education of the grammar school type against only one-tenth of working class boys. Now skilled manual workers' children are fairly adequately represented proportionately in our grammar schools. But the children of the unskilled worker still have a raw deal, and are not finding their way into the grammar school in substantially greater numbers than they were before 1944. While there are many excellent parents among the unskilled, it is unfortunately true that this class is often ill-housed and unable for various reasons to provide a good upbringing for children. With their restricted social background the latter find it difficult to reveal their potential abilities when confronted with a selection test and they are handicapped also in making the best of themselves in the class-room.

We cannot hope to get near to equality of educational opportunity until we achieve something like a basic minimum in standards of home life and housing. But within the sphere of education we can help by remembering that our classifying procedures profoundly affect life chances. 'Whilst it is true that "the limits set by inheritance always operate", the overlying effects of emotional and social factors are so considerable that no child should be written off as of low ability in any given direction until the best conditions and most effective stimuli for that particular child's success have been provided.'[1]

1. *The Curriculum of the Secondary School* (Evans, for the National Union of Teachers, 1952), p. 14. The quotation within this passage is from Dr C. M. Fleming's *Adolescence*, p. 231.

But the more one reflects on these problems of equality of opportunity and the social ladder,[1] the more surely does one return to those considerations of the decisive influence of home and family referred to in the last chapter. For the home is a much more potent factor in determining life chances than the school. When the Central Advisory Council for Education in England investigated the reasons why so many pupils leave prematurely those secondary schools which provide courses beyond the statutory age, they came to certain conclusions that are fundamental to any study of educational opportunity. Their first three conclusions are of paramount importance:

1. 'We have been impressed above all with the far-reaching influence of a child's home background. We have traced the school records of children in different social groups and we have found that from the children of parents in professional or managerial occupations at one extreme to the children of unskilled workers at the other there is a steady and marked decline in performance at the grammar school, in the length of school life, and in academic promise at the time of leaving. This is not a mere development of the better performance at the age of 11 of children in certain groups; it reflects a widespread changing of places in academic order between 11 and 16 or 18.'

2. 'The reasons must be very complex. Two important considerations are serious over-crowding in the home, which must handicap especially the children of many semi-skilled and unskilled workers, and the different social assumptions which affect not only a child's parents but the whole society in which he is brought up.'

3. 'There is need here for a great deal of research, which is beyond our means. The influence of the home on children at

1. For an important and illuminating study of various aspects of the social ladder, see *Social Mobility in Britain*, edited by Professor D. V. Glass (Routledge and Kegan Paul, 1955).

different ages is so profound that its consideration is of the highest importance, particularly in a period of rapid social change. It has not yet received adequate attention and urgently needs prolonged and thorough investigation.'[1]

1. *Early Leaving* (H.M.S.O., 1954), p. 56.

CHAPTER FIVE

THE GOVERNMENT OF EDUCATION

Who Should Control Education?

This is a historic issue, the cause of many wordy battles in this country in the past, and some bloodshed. But in the world at large, if not in this country, it is also a live contemporary question, one to which the nations give widely different answers.[1] To some it may seem odd that so homely, human, and child-loving an activity as education should cause dissension in high places, but the reason for so much controversy becomes plain if we recall the poet's saying that 'The child is father of the man'.

For it is the man that interests the eminences, who argue about control – what the child, grown to manhood, will believe, what his loyalties, attitudes, and conduct as citizen will be. If they are statesmen or politicians, they want the child to grow up to be a good member of the kind of society that they champion. If they are ecclesiastics they want him to be a loyal supporter of their church and its doctrine. But, of course, these eminent people are not alone in their concern about what the child will become; the parent is interested in that, too, and so is the teacher. But their interest is more intimate and personal, and not, as a rule, provocative; it is the statesmen and the high ecclesiastics who fan the controversial flames.

Happily in this country we have almost ceased to quarrel about this issue, and that helps us to consider its various implications with a detachment that would have been impossible at the beginning of this century. It is significant

1. For a fuller examination of this question, see W. O. Lester Smith, *To Whom do Schools belong?* (Blackwell, ed. 1945).

that in 1918 H. A. L. Fisher decided that if he introduced questions of religious education or local government into his Bill, there would be such a row in Parliament and the Country that it would never become law. But in 1944 Mr Butler was able to grasp the two nettles that Fisher decided to leave alone; and there was no controversy about the religious clauses, while the opposition to his local government provisions, of which the chief was the abolition of Part III authorities, was, though stubborn, a relatively mild and ineffective protest.

Discussing the various claims to a controlling voice in education, Bertrand Russell once summed up the position in this characteristic way. 'Authority,' he said, 'if it is to govern education, must rest upon one or several of the powers we have considered, the State, the Church, the schoolmaster, and the parent. We have seen that no one of them can be trusted to care adequately for the child's welfare, since each wishes the child to minister to some end which has nothing to do with its own well-being. . . . Unfortunately, the child lacks the experience required for the guidance of its own life, and is therefore a prey to the sinister interests that batten on its own innocence. That is what makes the difficulty of education as a political problem.'[1] When Lord Russell wrote these words about thirty years ago, we did not appreciate as we do to-day how important these issues of control are. Since then the world has seen education flagrantly and blatantly exploited by dictators to further their selfish aims and we are familiar with its use by rulers as a weapon in ideological warfare. Words like 'indoctrination', 'conditioning' and, since the Korean War, even that hideous expression, 'brain-washing', have found a place in popular vocabulary. Anyone old enough to remember the days when Hitler and Mussolini were building up a supporting public opinion will recall how freely they used the schools and national youth movements to further their ambitions.

No aspect of education escaped the attention of their propagandists. German teachers and youth leaders were

1. *Sceptical Essays* (Allen and Unwin, 1928), pp. 190, 191.

called upon to pledge their whole-hearted support of the Nazi cause. The indoctrinating process in Mussolini's Italy was no less thorough: teachers who were not whole-hearted exponents of the Fascist creed were removed by the purification law of 1925; and, like the Hitler Youth Movement, the National Ballila was carefully organized to stimulate an unwavering allegiance to the state. 'In this extreme form,' wrote one wise observer, commenting at the time on such gross misuse of power, 'education becomes a kind of advertising medium; its purpose is to put across a system of ideas, values, emotional reactions; and even if the ideas were true, I should repudiate this conception of education as a treason against the integrity of the human mind.'[1]

Under a totalitarian régime the state is all-powerful and all-embracing; and the ruler or rulers control education with an absolute, unshared authority. There are procedures to ensure that teachers are wholly loyal to the régime; textbooks are written and compiled to support and propagate its doctrine; and technical education is planned to supply the skilled man-power necessary for the military and industrial requirements of the state. In short, education is strongly state-centred. The most striking contrast to this is the attitude to education under a *laissez-faire* policy such as obtained in Britain at the beginning of the last century. Under a régime of this kind, the state refrains from intervention in education, leaving its provision to voluntary and private enterprise with aims and principles unfettered and unguided. There is no compulsion of any kind, and it is left to parents to decide whether to arrange for their children to receive education or not.

Between these two opposites comes the kind of régime sometimes called constructive or positive democracy or the Welfare State. The principle of planning is accepted with the state as the arch-planner, but the state operates not as a dictator but rather as the big brother of other interests concerned with the task of education. The state does not

1. W. R. Matthews, Dean of St Paul's, in an article on 'Spiritual Objectives of Education', *Journal of Adult Education*, December, 1936.

dominate the way of life. For society is regarded as consisting of many associations and groups, of which the state is one, admittedly powerful. In a positive democracy there is planning in education and there are programmes of development with the state responsible for determining priorities. But other societies – local authorities, teacher associations, and voluntary bodies – have a prominent role, and there is something like a partnership between the state and the other principal parties engaged in education. As far as possible a distinction is drawn between means and ends; and while means come within the scope of the planning function of the state and the local authority, ends are determined by the interplay of diverse influences, the commerce of thought, and the free interchange of opinion in debate and group discussion.

While the prevailing political philosophy largely determines who controls education in any country, it is not the sole determinant. Of other influential factors history is, perhaps, the most important. Some countries, like our own or the U.S.A. have a long tradition of freedom, while others like Russia and Germany have a very different past. Although there have been great developments in education in Russia since its twentieth-century revolution, it has had a state system of education since the days of Catherine II in the later eighteenth century. And its present highly centralized administration bears a close resemblance to that of the Tsarist period: the revolution did not and could not obliterate the past. 'This fundamental fact of identity between historical Russia and the present international Marxist Soviet Union should', it has been well said, 'be borne in mind in order to understand the theory and practice of Soviet education.'[1]

In Germany also, long before Hitler, education was regarded as the obedient servant of the state; and its use as a means of moulding a desired type of citizenship was fully

1. Nicholas Hans, *Comparative Education* (Routledge & Kegan Paul, 1949), p. 308.

recognized. 'What you would put into the state, you must first put into the school,' Von Humboldt declared, when as part of her programme of national recovery Prussia re-organized her education after the crushing defeat by Napoleon at Jena in 1806. When the German Empire was being built up on a strong military foundation under the Hohenzollerns, a well-known German professor explained to a Cambridge audience with considerable pride how well education had served and was still serving the interests of the régime. 'The forces which the nation require,' he declared, 'were nourished in the schools; in them the weapons were forged with which the battle for progress was fought. The activity continues even at the present time; and since the re-establishment of the German Empire it bears a national imprint.' And later in the same address, he observed, answering the question where control should be: 'The school is a "politicum"; it must educate citizens of the State. Therefore it must have compulsory education. . . . Compulsory education is closely connected with compulsory military service and manhood suffrage. Though educational matters have an individual foundation, they are part of a social whole. . . . It is for this reason that, according to German views, the State, which embraces politically the social whole, is and must be master of the school.'[1] Hitler was, therefore, but following precedent when he used the schools and the youth movement to further his expansionist aims. Admittedly his methods were exceptionally crude, but in using education to serve the expansionist aims of the German state he was not an innovator.

Our Belief in Diversity

In this country our educational system cannot be understood without some knowledge of our history; for its compromises

1. *Education in the Nineteenth Century* (Lectures edited by R. D. Roberts). Lecture on 'The Development of Educational Ideas' by Professor W. Rein (Cambridge Univ. Press, 1901), pp. 246, 257.

bear the splinter marks of unhappy, far off things and battles
long ago. And it has also many good features that reflect our
past. Of these one is our belief in the virtues of diversity and
flexibility. With our strong regional and local traditions –
and a fine record of independence in asserting them – we look
askance at proposals that urge conformity to some uniform
pattern, and want proof that they are sound and sensible
before we think of accepting them. The fate of the Ministry's
pamphlet, *The Nation's Schools*, emphasizing the merits of
a tripartite secondary school organization, illustrates our
dislike of theoretical pattern-making; and so does the
resistance aroused when any local authority plumps with
exclusive ardour for the comprehensive school. Empiricism,
as well as a liking for diversity, is part of our make-
up.

Of our respect for distinctive tradition, Scotland provides
the outstanding example. For although England and Scotland have shared one parliament since the Union of 1707,
the Scots have fully maintained their separate educational
system and traditions, and the Secretary of State for Scotland
(and not the Secretary of State for Education and Science) is
responsible to Parliament for Scottish education, and for its
central administration. And although Scotland has often
followed the example of England in the government of her
education, she has done so at her own time and in her own way.

Like England she established elective school boards, but
under a separate Act of 1872, two years later. And like
England she abolished them, but 16 years after England had
done so. Then for many years she had a system of County
Education Committees and Education Committees in five of
her principal cities: and these were, like the school boards,
ad hoc bodies. Not until 1929 did she do what England had
done in 1902, namely, entrust her local administration of
education to County Councils and the Councils of her large
burghs.

Moreover, unlike England and Wales, Scotland has not
been faced with the complexities of a dual system. For her

religious history has been different, and bears the strong imprint of John Knox. For centuries Kirk and State have worked together for the advancement of education, and as a result the number of voluntary schools in Scotland is comparatively small. For this reason Scotland was able to solve its voluntary school problems in 1918 by transferring Roman Catholic, Episcopalian and other voluntary schools to the local authorities without diminishing their denominational character. The local authorities appoint the teachers to these schools and are responsible for all expenditure connected with the school. The teachers have, however, to be approved as regards their religious belief by representatives of the Churches concerned.

When Mr Butler was pressed in connexion with the 1944 Act by members of the Roman Catholic Church 'to adopt the arrangements which have worked so smoothly in Scotland', he answered by stressing the wide differences in the historical background of England and Scotland. 'Conditions, history, and tradition are', he said, 'wholly unlike north and south of the Tweed. In Scotland there has never, whereas in this country there has always, been a ban on denominational religious instruction in provided schools. Here non-provided schools outnumber the publicly provided schools; in Scotland in 1918 nine-tenths of the schools were publicly provided. Moreover very many of the Church of England Schools here, particularly those in rural parishes where no other school is available, have in course of time come to be attended by a high proportion of children of non-Anglican parents. It is felt to be a real grievance that these children can only receive Anglican religious instruction unless they are made conspicuous by being withdrawn therefrom. The application of the Scottish system to the many schools in which this difficulty is felt would be inappropriate and, instead of assuaging, would perpetuate a grievance which ought as far as possible to be mitigated. Similarly, the Scottish solution would do nothing to remove, and would indeed aggravate, a further objection to the dual system which is strongly felt here, that it involves denominational religious tests for teachers.'[1]

Largely because it had not had the complexities of a dual system, Scotland was able to organize its education in progressive stages. For all these reasons its legislative problem for the reconstruction of education after World War II was much simpler than that of England and Wales. The Education (Scotland) Act of 1945, the Scottish counterpart to Mr Butler's Act of 1944, is therefore a comparatively short and simple statute. Wales also has a distinctive educational tradition and a lively national culture. For over 30 per cent of her children Welsh is the language of the home; there is a considerable Welsh literature, and both in this century and the last there have been vigorous Welsh literary movements. Her religious history differs also in many respects from that of England, but her education, unlike that of Scotland, has been administered with that of England and in conformity with the general English pattern.

In the last century it was the practice of English administrators to frown upon the use of Welsh in schools, and among them was Matthew Arnold in spite of his interest in Celtic literature. A stupid Commission set up in 1846 to report on Education in Wales gave this attitude every possible encouragement, but towards the end of the century Parliament's attitude to Welsh education began to change, and ever since respect for her distinctive traditions and aspirations has gradually increased. In 1889 the Welsh Intermediate Education Act was passed, and as a result secondary schools were founded in many Welsh towns, supplementing the facilities offered by the few endowed grammar schools. And in 1893 the recently established Welsh University Colleges were incorporated in a University of Wales. In 1907 a separate Welsh Department was created within the Board of Education, and since that date there has been a complete reversal of the old practice of disparaging the Welsh Language and the culture of the Welsh people.

1. *Educational Reconstruction*, p. 15.

The White Paper that preceded the Education Act of 1944 dealt at length with the special educational problems of Wales. 'The Policy of the Board', it declared, 'has now been officially disassociated from the views about the Welsh language expressed by the Commission of Inquiry in 1846. It is now hoped that the encouragement of studies which are traditional in Wales will not be developed so as to form a barrier between Wales and its neighbours but will provide a livelier association in the world of thought and culture.'[1] Both Scotland and Wales now have their own Central Advisory Councils for Education, and no one studying their reports along with those of the English Council can fail to notice wide differences of approach and yet an underlying unity. While Scotland and Wales, because of their national background, may provide the best examples of our regard for separate traditions, it is no less true that the English Counties and County Boroughs, with their different characteristics, contribute substantially to the diversity of our educational landscape.

The Church in Control

There were two main reasons why the state was slow to intervene in education in England. One was the dominance of the *laissez-faire* philosophy in the nineteenth century, and the other was the complex issue of Church and State. To appreciate the significance of this issue it is necessary to take a rather long journey back into the past. For the Church began building schools more than 1,300 years ago – the first was probably at Canterbury in 598 when Ethelbert was King.

Throughout the middle ages, when western Christendom was undivided, the Church was responsible for education. Only those who by life-long study have grown familiar with the medieval way of life and thought can speak with authority of how the Church fulfilled this task. But there can be

1. *Educational Reconstruction*, p. 31.

little doubt that our ancestors of those distant times had a genius for founding schools and colleges, and there is ample evidence to suggest that they concerned themselves with elementary education no less than with the development of grammar schools and colleges at Oxford and Cambridge.

Like us, they appear to have had a three-tier system of administering education. We have the Department of Education and Science, the Local Authority, and Governing Bodies; they had the central government of the Church, an active diocesan organization, and a governing body of some sort associated with the school through abbey or guild or in some other way. Each one of these 'tiers', to use our modern jargon, could function with effect. Typical of government from the centre was the Council of Westminster of 1102, over which Anselm presided as Archbishop. It had a heavy agenda, but education figured prominently. One item of its business was how to ensure that no one taught who was not deemed suitable, and another was how to prevent the setting up of free lance schools, not conducted under approved auspices.

The diocesan organization has been likened by A. F. Leach, who made a long study of medieval education, to a regional inspectorate with the Bishop acting like a Chief Inspector and his Archdeacons and other emissaries as inspectors.[1] As for the third tier, the local administrators or governors, they fully shared the medieval fondness for rules and regulations, often going into meticulous detail to prescribe the conduct to be expected of the teachers and their pupils.

These school ordinances laid down the law about teachers' qualifications, their duties and behaviour, the text-books to be used, attendance at Church and religious observances. If the N.U.T. or the Joint Four had flourished in those days, their officials' desks would have been piled high with case files. To give one example, among the innumerable statutes of Westminster School is one that states: 'The masters shall

1. See A. F. Leach, *English Schools at the Reformation: Schools of Medieval England* and *Educational Charters*.

never, not even for a day, be away from home except for the most urgent cause, to be approved by the Dean or in his absence the sub-Dean and prebendaries at home, and then no longer than has been directed by the same.'

Those who sometimes speak as if schools to-day are in chains as never before and suggest that there was once a golden age of freedom will not find medieval administrative practice helpful to their argument. But it may well be that schools in those days were able to enjoy more freedom than some of their ordinances suggest. Except for episcopal controls and visitations – and bishops and archdeacons must have found travelling irksome – the school was subject only to its own ordinances, the law of its immediate governors. There is a sentence of A. J. Carlyle's about the medieval conception of freedom which helps to explain the sort of freedom a school can enjoy within an authoritarian framework. 'A free community', he says, 'was one which lived by its own laws, and under the terms of the supremacy of the community itself, not only in its own law, but in its control over all matters which concerned its life.'[1]

Such autonomy as medieval schools enjoyed was, however, always subject to the absolute authority of the Church. The most effective instrument of control was the Bishop's licence to teach, a device which was used to ensure that all who taught were loyal to the doctrine of the Church. It is interesting to note, in view of recent attempts by one local authority in this country to bar teachers because of their political opinion, that it was administered more strenuously during periods of intellectual and political ferment. There was a McCarthy touch about its operation in Lollard days, and indeed our forefathers could outdo Senator McCarthy when so inclined. For example, Eton masters had to take an oath not to 'favour the opinions, damned errors or heresies of John Wycliffe . . . under pain of perjury, and expulsion *ipso facto*.'

It has been estimated that in England and Wales before

1. *Political Liberty* (Oxford Univ. Press, 1941), p. 21.

the Reformation for a population of 2¼ million there were about 400 grammar schools, a striking contrast to the position revealed by the Schools Inquiry Commission in 1864 when it was calculated that there were only 830 secondary schools of all grades for a population of 19 millions. 'Grammar schools were not, as used to be thought,' Dr Trevelyan observes, 'the result of the Reformation: they were its cause.'[1] By educating a new middle class of laymen and clergy, they prepared the way for social and intellectual change.

The Reformation marks the end of an era in education and of a system of school government. 'The Renaissance and the Reformation', Sir Cyril Norwood notes, 'were both disintegrating influences. The Renaissance by itself might have been an inspiration, for it brought in a more living curriculum, and more valuable subjects of study. But it also brought with it much individualism, and questioned the old loyalties to Church and State. It was the Reformation which in this country dealt the hardest blow to education. It broke up the unity of the nation. The Catholics were outlawed and persecuted, and the Protestants broke into sects. Many schools were plundered and destroyed, and a spirit of self-seeking, of private profit to be made at the expense of the public benefit, was let loose. By the end of the reign of Elizabeth, many of the schools were refounded, but in a different spirit, with smaller resources and less opportunity. They were for one class – the sons of the members of the Established Church. There was no access for the sons of Catholics and Nonconformists.'[2]

The Great Conflict about Control

The control of education became, therefore, one of the great issues of our seventeenth-century revolution; and our present religious compromise is largely a consequence of the Civil War of that period and its ultimate effect on English opinion.

1. *English Social History* (Longmans, 1944), p. 75.
2. *The English Tradition of Education* (Murray, 1929), p. 12.

It is difficult to disentangle the strictly educational conflict from the social, economic, and religious controversies which so violently divided our forefathers and led them to take up arms against each other. But as regards education, there were two essential points; (1) both the Anglicans and Presbyterians believed that there should be but one religion – their own – for the whole nation, and (2) both used the schools as instruments of their policy and, to use our modern jargon, 'screened' teachers to ensure conformity with their respective orthodoxies. Under the vigorous leadership of Archbishop Laud the Anglicans enforced by every possible means 'the licence to teach', while the Presbyterians, when they in turn gained power, pursued relentlessly in both England and Wales the practice of 'approving' and purging teachers.

After referring to the first of these points, calling it after Hooker the doctrine of equivalence, Sir Ernest Barker summed up the contest with characteristic clarity in these words, at the same time introducing the vital third party to this historic dispute: 'Now in 1641', he observed, 'there were two schools of opinion which both accepted this doctrine (of equivalence), but none the less differed from one another. There were the Anglicans who believed that all England should be a single Anglican Church, episcopally governed, and following a modified form of the old medieval ritual. There were the Presbyterians or Calvinists, who believed that all England should be a single Presbyterian Church, governed by presbyteries and synods of presbyteries, and following the new ritual of Geneva.. . . But between both, or over and above them both, there remained a *tertium quid*. This was the Independents; in other words, the members of the Free Churches; in other words again, to mention their two great varieties – the Congregationalists and the Baptists. The essence of their position was that they denied what I have called the doctrine of equivalence. . . . They did not believe that a single political society was, or ought to be, a single religious society. They did *not* profess the doctrine of religious territorialism. They were essentially and literally Nonconformists. They believed that any voluntary society of Christian men and women, in any area or neighbourhood in which they were gathered together, should be free to form their own congregation and constitute their own Free Church.'[1]

That bogey of English education, 'the religious difficulty', dates from this Civil War period; and, in the language of photography, was 'fixed' by the renewal of persecution after the Restoration under the Clarendon Code. In education henceforward the nation was divided into two camps: Anglicanism and non-conforming Dissent. Unfortunately it became even more than a religious issue; for social class and party politics entered into it as well. For normally the landowners, their tenantry, and their many dependents supported the Church schools, while the middle classes, especially in the towns, favoured schools of the Dissenting tradition. This division affected secondary as well as elementary education; for the dissenters established highly successful academies that rivalled the grammar schools. 'The social character of English religious divisions', observes Dr Trevelyan, 'was stereotyped at the Restoration and continued with little change until the Victorian era.'[2] As for the political alignment, it was broadly true that the Tories backed the grammar schools and the church elementary schools, while the Whigs lent their support to the schools of the dissenters.

These unhappy divisions, as good Victorians euphemistically called them, have been a baneful influence in English education. Their impact is to be seen in various aspects of the charity school movement, and at the other end of the scale in the two universities which until the University Test Act of 1871 persisted in excluding all who were not members of the Established Church. And in the final phase of complete reliance on voluntaryism for the provision of elementary education, the old cleavage of Anglicanism and Dissent was

1. *Oliver Cromwell* (Cambridge Univ. Press, 1937), pp. 30–3.
2. *English Social History*, p. 255.

reflected in the dual character of voluntary organizations. If ever there was a time for concerted action by men and women of goodwill, it was at the beginning of the nineteenth century, when the rapid growth of population and the new urbanization, caused by the industrial revolution, had created an unparalleled and urgent demand for new schools and new sources of teacher supply. But Church and Dissent again found themselves at loggerheads, altogether unable to co-operate either in the erection of schools or the founding of training colleges. They went their separate ways. Two rival voluntary Societies were established. First, the dissenters set up the Royal Lancasterian Association (1810), later known as the British and Foreign School Society, and immediately afterwards the Church followed suit with 'The National Society for the Education of the Poor in the Principles of the Established Church' (1811), familiarly known until recently as the National Society.

Other religious societies then came into operation. At long last the Roman Catholics were enabled to provide schools for children of their faith, for in 1829 Parliament passed the Catholic Emancipation Act and in 1847 the Catholic Poor School Committee was constituted for the purpose of promoting elementary education. Education had been a central feature of John Wesley's evangelizing work in the eighteenth century: of the school that he himself established at Kingswood he said: 'I have spent more money, time, and care on this than on almost any design I ever had. . . . But it is worth all the labour.' So like the Anglicans, Dissenters, and Roman Catholics, we find the Methodists in the mid nineteenth century founding their own training colleges and schools and in 1838 they set up an Education Committee to promote and supervise their educational effort. The Jews, too, established several schools in the large towns, and they set up a Committee to organize their education.

One reason why these various religious bodies established central committees was to provide a channel for communication with the government department that distributed grant-in-aid. For in 1833 Parliament began the practice of voting an annual grant to assist voluntary bodies in their work of providing education. It was, however, all too clear that voluntary enterprise, even with state-aid, was proving lamentably unequal to the task of providing elementary education for all. When in 1870 Parliament at last tackled effectively the problem of legislating for a national system, the statistics submitted to them left no room for doubt that more positive intervention by the State was urgently necessary. Here, for example, are some figures of educational provision by voluntary agencies in four big cities, produced in the course of the protracted debates to convince those still reluctant to agree to active intervention by the State:

	Children of School Age	School Places Available
Birmingham	64,787	30,169
Manchester	66,591	36,612
Leeds	45,444	24,295
Liverpool	91,375	46,739

After thirty days of acrimonious debate, with 'the religious difficulty' the main source of controversy, the House of Commons succeeded in agreeing upon the measure, the Elementary Education Act of 1870, that laid the foundation of our national system of education. In due course with some amendment it was approved by the House of Lords and received the royal assent. The basis of the agreement was an ingenious compromise, cleverly designed to reconcile the conflicting opinions. England had obtained 'better later than never, a system of education without which she must soon have fallen to the rear among modern nations.'[1] The compromise has stood the test of time and experience. The dual system of local authority and voluntary schools, its main characteristic, was confirmed and buttressed by the Act of

1. G. M. Trevelyan, *English Social History*, p. 581.

1902; and although the Act of 1944 greatly modified it so that it could meet modern educational needs, it is still essentially the same concordat with the same tolerant respect for a parent's wishes about the religious education of his child.

The reasons which led the government to retain the dual system in 1944, in spite of its complexities, are clearly stated in the White Paper already referred to. 'Discussions carried on in recent months with the many interests concerned,' it explains, 'have satisfied the Government that there is a wide measure of agreement that voluntary schools should not be abolished but rather that they should be offered further financial assistance, accompanied by a corresponding extension of public control which will ensure the effective and economical organization and development of both primary and secondary education. It is believed that the view will generally be taken that in framing these proposals for such control the services of the churches to the community as pioneers in public education, as the protagonists of Chistian teaching in schools and as having for many generations voluntarily spent large sums on the provision and upkeep of premises for this purpose, cannot be justly disregarded.'[1]

Control in a Constructive Democracy

As the White Paper indicates, the modifications in the dual system in the 1944 Act were designed to give the voluntary schools 'further financial assistance' and, at the same time, bring them more under public control. Since 1902 they had, like the local authority schools, been maintained out of rates and taxes, but under the 1902 Act they had from their own voluntary funds to find the capital for building new schools and for structural improvements. Experiencing great difficulty in finding this money, they were seldom able to participate in schemes of reorganization or to bring their school accommodation up to modern standards.

1. *Educational Reconstruction*, p. 14.

If the dual system was to survive, a way had got to be found to enable the voluntary schools to meet modern demands. It was realized that there could not be a comprehensive system of secondary and primary education, if over a third of the schools were unable to participate.[1] So the 1944 Act solved this problem by constituting two kinds of voluntary schools. All voluntary schools were given an option; they could through their governors or managers elect either to be 'aided' or 'controlled'. If they chose to be 'aided' they were allowed to continue with much the same rights as in the past, but as their part of the bargain they had to meet half the cost of a new building, improvements or external repairs. If, however, they chose to be 'controlled' all responsibility for finance passed to the local authority, but they had to surrender certain rights which they had previously enjoyed. The church concerned ceased to have a majority on the governing body, it gave up most of its rights over the appointment of teachers, and the amount of denominational teaching permitted was curtailed. The Roman Catholic schools all opted for 'aided' status. The position of the Church of England Schools was described as follows by Spencer Leeson, when pleading for funds. 'Only in an aided school', he contended, 'can the full influence of the Church be assured. Out of some 8,300 Church schools, about 3,300 are aided and 4,100 are controlled, the status of the remaining 900 not having yet been settled.'[2]

The government in 1944, as the White Paper indicates, linked these financial concessions with its policy of more public control. Emphasis on public control is an outstanding feature of the 1944 Act in marked contrast to the attitude that prevailed in 1902. Then there was a general desire to limit the role of the State. Such was the dread of state inter-

1. Official returns give the number of secondary and primary schools in the national system in England and Wales in 1963 as 28,974 (County 18,921, C. of E. 7,419, R.C. 2,190, Others 444).
2. *Church of England Newspaper*, 10 June 1955. Article on 'Church Schools – a Challenge'.

ference at that period that the important Bryce Commission of 1895, in accord with the *laissez-faire* doctrines then fashionable, insisted that the unified central department, which it advocated, should have 'little direct executive power'. Its function, it maintained, should be to stimulate, guide, supply information, and hold the balance between conflicting interests. The Board of Education Act of 1899 and the Education Act of 1902 were framed accordingly, and up to 1944 we had a central department authorized only to 'superintend'.

For similar reasons, the Act of 1902 was, except for elementary education, largely permissive in character. Local authorities were *enabled* to do this or that; it was not imposed upon them as a duty – there is a great difference between 'may' and 'must'. This led to wide differences in the standards of provision as between one area and another; and children living in the territory of an authority making good use of the permissive clauses had much better opportunities than those in areas which could with some justice be described as backward. This was true not only of secondary and further education, special schools, aid to students and school health services, but also in some respects of elementary education. For although elementary schools, council or voluntary, had to be available, the Board of Education had not adequate authority, even if it made use as a grant-making department of the power of the purse, to secure a general observance of decent standards of accommodation.

In 1870 the *laissez-faire* philosophy was dominant; in 1902 it still prevailed, though with a question mark; but by 1944 we had abandoned it for a belief in more positive government and the Welfare State. The 1944 Act affords an excellent illustration of our modern political theory translated into legislation. It was indeed the first of our statutes to deal with a great social service with a Welfare State outlook: the statute that dealt with national health came four years later. The very first clause of the 1944 Act gives us a Minister whose duty it is to direct and control local authorities in carrying out national policy.[1] A further clause, 68, redrafted in the course of the debates, shifts power from the circumference to the centre even more pointedly; for it enables the Minister to override local authorities, governors, or managers who, in his opinion, are acting unreasonably. With all the additional powers conferred upon him in the Act to issue orders and make regulations, the Minister has thus become immensely powerful. Sir Ross Barker, a leading exponent of the law of education, described his powers as 'absolute', subject to certain defined obligations and his general responsibility to Parliament.[2]

What, apart from the change in our political theory, were the particular motives that led Parliament to make the centre so strong? Two stand out prominently, and some reference was made to them in the previous chapter: (1) a belief that you cannot approach equality of opportunity unless someone is able to insist that all local authorities and all promoters of voluntary schools observe and maintain certain standards, (2) a recognition of the fact that you cannot hope to distribute fairly available man-power and materials unless the Minister has an effective voice in planning and in the determination of priorities.

Control or Partnership

It is easy from a superficial study of the Act to get a false conception of the nature of the power that the Minister wields. Living in a technological age we are apt to think of 'control' only in the sense given to it in connexion with those many

1. This carefully worded clause will repay study (e.g. consider the significance of 'people' and 'varied') : 'It shall be lawful for His Majesty to appoint a Minister, whose duty it shall be to promote the education of the people of England and Wales and the progressive development of institutions devoted to that purpose, and to secure the effective execution by local authorities, under his control and direction, of the national policy for providing a varied and comprehensive educational service in every area.'

2. *The Education Act*, 1944 (Charles Knight, 1944), p. 8.

inventions that scientific discovery has enabled us to use. We press buttons and manipulate switches, and thereby without effort or talent can achieve immediately results that an earlier generation would have regarded as miraculous. We can also be misled by those advertisements which portray the square-jawed, immaculately dressed 'high executive' sitting at his desk surrounded by innumerable gadgets with which, we are asked to believe, he controls his vast industrial or commercial empire. Control connotes something very different in the sphere of government – and in the administration of industry and commerce, also, in spite of these advertisements – and whoever is entitled to exercise it has to function all the time not in a mechanical setting but in the complex field of human relationships. 'Laws they are not,' said the very wise Hooker, 'which public approbation hath not made them so.'

Under a democratic form of government, such as we now have, Hooker's words are even more true than when he wrote them. The Secretary is accountable to Parliament, and has to justify his decisions, great and small, at question time or in debate. His actions are circumscribed by the system of government outlined in the Act and by the whole law of education. Decisions of major policy are not only subject to Parliament but also to close scrutiny by the Cabinet, and they can have their repercussions in the electorate. Montesquieu once said that the English people were only free at election time; at all other times, he said, the government was their master. That is no longer true, if it ever was: for the government is under constant challenge.

But perhaps the most effective of all restraints upon the misuse of power is custom or tradition. The Victorians believed greatly in checks and balances, the distribution of power. That is important and, as we shall see, in the government of education we have not discarded this notion even though we have given the Minister much the biggest share of power. But it has been well said that while a series of checks and balances is the conventional solution to the problem of power, 'custom and tradition are in such matters far more powerful, and incomparably more effective, than law.'[1] Since the enactment of the 1944 Act we have had several Ministers of Education, and from both of the main political parties; they have usually exercised the powers assigned to them with acceptable moderation, and without any trace of that unpleasant quality that St Augustine called *cupiditas dominandi*. The London County Council, so long our largest local authority and one that during the period had some notable clashes with the Minister, especially over comprehensive schools, aptly described the position of local authorities under the 1944 Act: 'A substantial proportion of the cost of education is met by the Government, and so it is, of course, inevitable that there should be central control, but the relationship between the Ministry of Education and the local authorities has often been described as partnership. If to-day the senior partner has a little more say than formerly and the junior partner somewhat less, the partnership itself still remains and each local education authority has a real measure of freedom and responsibility. The policies of different authorities vary considerably, for example, in the organization of secondary education, and the Ministry has not sought to discourage this diversity.'[2]

This tradition of partnership is the outstanding feature of our educational administration. Although we have now endowed the Secretary with great power, in practice he and his Department of some 3,000 officials function as members of a great fellowship – Department, Local Authorities, Teachers, Voluntary Associations – friends working together with mutual understanding in a great cause. In 1950 the Ministry celebrated a Jubilee; there had been a unified central department for half a century as a consequence of the Board of

1. W. F. Oakeshott, *Education and Power*, Presidential Address to Education Section of British Association, 1950.
2. *The London Education Service* (London County Council, 1954), pp. 92–3. (This publication gives a most readable and authoritative description of the work of a modern local education authority.)

Education Act of 1899. The Minister, that shrewd, lovable, Lancashire man, George Tomlinson, and the Permanent Secretary, Sir John Maud, crystallized the story in a joint introduction, and it was this partnership that they singled out as the crowning achievement. 'It is', they said of the record of the fifty years, 'the story of a progressive partnership between the Central Department, the local education authorities, and the teachers.'[1] The partnership has had its ups and downs, and there are often sharp differences of opinion; but they are mainly differences about means and methods, for there is a remarkable unity of aim and purpose.

The Origins of The Local Education Authority

Our first local education authorities were the school boards, constituted by the Act of 1870 'to fill the gaps' left by voluntary enterprise in the provision of elementary education. Popularly elected, their function was to provide and administer elementary schools, 'Board Schools' as they were called. There are some who think that we would fare better to-day if the local authorities now administering education were concerned only with that great service, and elected or selected for that specific purpose. They prefer, to use the technical jargon, *ad hoc* bodies for the local government of education.

Unfortunately this Victorian example of the school board cannot be safely used as evidence either for or against this opinion. For there were several features of the school board system that are unlikely to recur. Anyone wishing to weigh up the pros and cons of the use of *ad hoc* committees under modern conditions for the local administration of an important social service will get more guidance by closely examining our present method of administering the national health service. Even so, as the school board is our only example of the application of the *ad hoc* principle to the local government of education, it is worth noting some of its characteristics.

1. *Education, 1900–1950*, p. 1.

One serious weakness was that there were far too many school boards – 2,568; and most of the smaller ones were hopelessly unequal to their task and got the institution a bad name. But the larger boards, those in London and the bigger towns, did some valuable work. As the figures indicating the size of the gaps quoted above show, these larger .boards had to build, equip, and staff a great many schools. This formidable task occupied them almost entirely; and in many of our towns the solid structures that they erected are still to be seen, all too durable monuments of the thoroughness and zeal of the men who planned and built them.

School board members were specially interested in the quantitative or statistical aspects of school administration. This was, perhaps, due to the fact that they had urgently to provide so many schools and get so many unwilling children to attend them. Their minutes show that they spent much of their time on class-room measurements – so many children per square yard, staffing ratios, and elaborate attendance returns. Month by month they pored over sheets of figures, and with a Gladstonian zeal for economy closely compared expenditure to date with the estimate for the year. Some of the manuals published for the information of members of education authorities to-day still bear traces of this school board tradition, the passionate belief in the efficacy of detailed attendance returns and other statistical data.

Another feature of school board administration was a liking for centralization and bureaucratic rule. This was no doubt due partly to the fact that the boards were pioneering, and had necessarily to lay down much law in the form of regulations, as there was no tradition of school administration by local authorities. And the very nature of their business and its urgency really demanded considerable drive from the local centre. Moreover the Robert Lowe system of payment of government grant on the basis of results, which then operated, involved consideration of details of the curriculum in ways quite alien to modern practice.

The school board officer was the hub of the administrative

machine in the bigger towns; and the Clerk to the School Board was a considerable personage who by directives, and through 'his' local inspectors and 'his' little army of attendance officers, often exercised a dominating influence in 'his' schools, as he was possessively inclined to speak of them. When the school boards were abolished in 1902 and the County and County Borough Councils became the Local Education Authorities, the bureaucratic tradition of the school boards did not at once disappear in places where it had taken firm root. In many towns the Clerk to the School Board became the Director of Education under the new local education authority, and when that happened secondary and technical education were often administered directly from the Education Office with the same degree of centralization as the school board had applied to the elementary schools under its jurisdiction.

In country areas, on the other hand, where the school boards were weak the County Councils were more free to forge their own administrative pattern. As a consequence, at first county administration tended to be more flexible than it was in many of the county boroughs. Distance in the county areas encouraged this bias towards flexibility and greater decentralization, but there is not much difference to-day in administrative practice as between the County and County Borough authorities. Flexibility has become a normal feature of our educational administration, and the formalism of the school boards has been replaced by a much more human relationship between the education office and the schools.

It is interesting to note that in the U.S.A. the early local administrators, like the school boards in our cities, also evolved a highly centralized system; and some difficulty has been experienced there in breaking away from the rigidity of traditional procedures. 'What is said elsewhere of state mandatory legislation', says a leading American authority on school administration, 'needs to be said with even greater vigour of central regulation and tradition in local school systems. Our common practices must be examined in order that we may discover whether they come from problems which are common, and whether they came from a drive for uniformity 30 or 40 years ago.' And remarking how desirable it is that a school should be closely associated with its own neighbourhood, he notes that under a centralized system of local administration a school tends to be so closely linked with the Education Office as to lose touch with the community it serves.

'A school district of any size', he observes, 'has within it many communities or neighbourhoods. The individual schools should be tied up with the ongoing life in these neighbourhoods. They should be affecting this life for the better. Yet recently the principal of a large Middle Western city school, in speaking of the school and the community, was obviously referring to the entire city, not to her immediate community. Her attention was on the board of education down town, not upon the potential leaders in her immediate community. She was *in* the school community, not *of* it, and the limiting effects of this point of view, could be seen in the school, which in many respects was a splendid one.'[1] One of the worst consequences of a centralized and bureaucratic local administration is that it saps the independence of a school, destroys its sense of being a corporate society, and detaches its loyalty from the neighbourhood that it serves. .

The Local Education Authority: its work and its place in the Partnership

Ever since 1902 the County and County Borough Councils have been responsible for the local administration of education. They are fairly large bodies with a membership of about 100 or more, and unlike the school boards administer several services besides education. And by no means all of their democratically elected members are specially interested in education. So the law requires each Council to appoint

1. Paul R. Mort, *Principles of School Administration* (McGraw-Hill, 1946), p. 226.

an Education Committee and, while arrangements about delegation vary, the Education Committee is to-day in every area the Council's instrument for the administration of education. Normally an Education Committee reports to the Council month by month, though in some areas quarterly; and it then makes recommendations on matters for which it desires, or must obtain, the sanction of the Council.

An Education Committee usually has some thirty or forty members, about two-thirds of whom are, as aldermen or councillors, members of the Council. The law requires that some members with special knowledge or experience of education shall be co-opted, and these make up the other third. The Secretary of State approves the scheme constituting the Education Committee, and his normal practice is to ensure that among the co-opted members are representatives of the Churches and the teachers. There is, also, frequently a University representative. The Education Committee does its work through a number of main sub-committees. Practice varies, but most authorities have sub-committees for Primary and Secondary Schools, Further Education, Special Education, Buildings, Finance, and General Purposes. Because of the volume of their business, some of these main sub-committees set up sectional committees to deal with particular aspects of their work. The sub-committees receive reports from officers of the committee, initiate proposals, decide questions referred to them, and make recommendations on the more important matters for the consideration of the Education Committee.[1]

Every local education authority is required to appoint a Chief Education Officer, and its choice has to be approved by the Secretary of State. Under the direction of the Chief Education Officer there is a professional and clerical staff, usually organized on a sectional basis. Among the principal officers there will generally be a deputy education officer, and assistant

1. For a lucid well-informed account of how our present system of educational administration works, see *Education in England*, by W. P. Alexander (2nd ed. Newnes, 1964).

education officers for primary, secondary, and further education. Much depends on the quality of the Chief Education Officer, his knowledge, experience, humanity, and judgement. As principal adviser of the Education Committee and head of its administrative service he can exercise a far-reaching influence. His relationship with the teaching service is of the utmost importance, and so also is his ability to co-operate effectively with other Chief Officials of the Council. A serious disadvantage of the *ad hoc* method of administering education is that it isolates it from other services, while one of the great assets of our present practice of administering it as a part, albeit a most important one, of the whole service of local government is that it enables the Education Committee and its Chief Officer to influence local developments that affect education, and to ensure that education receives due consideration in connexion with the many facilities that a Council provides. Against these advantages must be offset the dangers inherent in excessive co-ordination on the part of the Council or in meticulous interdepartmentalism, modern tendencies which can make it difficult to administer education with reasonable flexibility as an integral part of a composite system of local government.

While the Education Officer is the only chief officer engaged full-time in the service of the Education Committee, other chief officers and their departments make important contributions to its work. The Clerk of the Council or Town Clerk gives guidance on procedure and legal questions, the Medical Officer usually acts as School Health Officer, the Architect as the Education Committee's architect, and the Treasurer is often the Committee's principal finance officer. Indeed there is no chief officer whose advice is not at some time necessary, and it is always readily available. It is important, however, not to exaggerate the influence of officials. The aim is always democracy, not bureaucracy. For this reason the quality of the Chairman of the Education Committee matters greatly. His guidance of the Committee, his exposition of its policy to the Council, his standing with teachers and others concerned with education in the area, his influence in educational affairs at the national level are all of great significance.

Clearly much hinges, also, on the quality of those who serve on Education Committees, and it is but a truism to say that the future of local government largely depends on the election of men and women of high calibre to its councils. But this is a question that profoundly affects the work and prestige of local authorities generally, and it would be inappropriate to enter into a detailed discussion of it here.

Reference should also be made to a valuable section of the Education Committee's staff – the Inspectors and Organizers, for they maintain direct and daily contact between the Education Committee and the Schools. The local inspectorate fulfils a different function from that of the Ministry's inspectors – Her Majesty's Inspectors, or H.M.Is as they are styled. Its time is largely devoted to informal visits to the schools. 'This', to quote an official description of the London Education Service, 'is perhaps the most important part of their work and enables them to give advice on questions of the curriculum, school organization, and all the problems that arise in schools from day to day'.[1] The Organizers are engaged in promoting various branches of the education service or in advising upon some particular aspect of the curriculum. All authorities have organizers of school meals, while many have organizers of physical education, music, art, crafts, and drama. There are youth organizers, too, who encourage the development of social and recreative activities for young people.

Voluntary enterprise in education is still a characteristic of our national life, undimmed and undiminished by the Ministry's new powers or the increasing scope of the Local Education Authority which now operates in every field of education except the University. In many of these fields local education authorities and voluntary agencies work in close liaison, the authority aiding and encouraging voluntary effort.

1. *The London Education Service*, p. 92.

There is the same kind of co-operation at regional and national levels, and representatives of local authorities are promin nt in such bodies as the National Institute of Adult Education and the National Foundation of Educational Research.

But the closest partnership, as we have noted, is that between the Ministry, the Local Education Authorities, and Teachers. Partnership to be real has, as Dr Johnson said of friendship, to be kept in constant repair. If not in frequent use it rusts and becomes ineffective. This partnership is a very active one, and representatives of the three constituents meet constantly in one capacity or another, officially or un-officially, to discuss problems of many kinds. They meet for specific purposes on advisory committees and negotiating committees; and representatives are often called to the Ministry for consultations on some immediate issue. This would be impractible if the local authorities, of which there are now 146 in England and Wales, had not, like the teachers, responsible associations readily available for consultation by the Minister, and always in a position, if required, to nominate representatives for membership of advisory or negotiating bodies or for informal discussions.

The three major associations of local authorities are the Association of Municipal Corporations, the County Councils Association, and the Association of Education Committees. Because of its special problems and the vast population that it serves the London County Council is regarded for purposes of representation as a separate unit, while Wales, thoug h represented on the other associations, has a Joint Education Committee for the consideration of its special interests. Differences of opinion among the partners are frequent and disagreement is sometimes inevitable, but Sir William Alexander, drawing upon his wide experiences as Secretary of the Association of Education Committees, well describes the nature of the partnership when he observes that 'pro-cedure is essentially by agreement, and that obtains in most matters most of the time.'[1]

1. *Education in England*, p. 27.

Although this partnership is so valuable to education, it would be rash to assume that it is impregnable. In this questioning age a policy-shaping alliance, especially one that from time to time negotiates salaries, is a natural target for the slings and arrows of those disappointed by its conclusions. Much depends on the continuance of good leadership by representatives of local authorities and of the teachers. It would be sad indeed if this partnership, so carefully built up over the years, disintegrated or lost its undoubted prestige; for we should then be left without any effective instrument for the distribution of power, and the government of education would pass more and more into the hands of the Ministry. 'For the best of motives', it has been well said, 'rulers will, like courts, try to add to their jurisdiction. How is this never-ending audacity to be, at any rate, limited? By making sure that effective power is not monopolized. . . . But it would be foolish not to notice that the greed of the State finds justification in the failure of the intermediate bodies to do well what they used to do well, or to find functions in the modern world to replace those which were once their justification.'[1] We can only hope that in the critical years ahead the intermediate bodies – the Local Authorities – will prove equal to this challenge.

They can be assured of a wide measure of freedom so long as the Minister continues to observe with moderation and tolerance the interpretation of direction and control formulated by the Local Government Manpower Committee as follows:

'While the Minister should have a general oversight of the field of education, we think that he has six duties from which the points at which it is necessary for him to exercise control should be derived:

1. He must be satisfied that educational facilities and auxiliary services are provided in sufficient quantity and variety.

1. B. de Jouvenel, *Power* (Batchworth, ed. 1952), Preface by D. W. Brogan, p. 13.

2. He must be satisfied that educational establishments and auxiliary services are well managed, equipped, staffed, and maintained.

3. He must ensure the proper freedom of parents, teachers, and other third parties.

4. He must be satisfied of the qualification of teachers and medical officers to the extent necessary to safeguard their and the children's interests.

5. He must control the fees charged and awards and allowances made to the extent necessary to safeguard the interests of local education and other school authorities, parents, and students.

6. He must control the provision of educational premises.'[1]

1. Report of the Ministry of Education Sub-Committee of the Local Government Manpower Committee (July 1951), p. 6.

CHAPTER SIX

THE TEACHING PROFESSION

The Legacy of 'Two Nations'

'We all teach,' Dr Gilbert Highet reminds us in his delightful book, *The Art of Teaching*; and he devotes many pages to graphic accounts of people, exalted and humble, who though not teachers by occupation, yet by precept and example decisively influenced the lives of others.[1] And needless to say, in his gallery of successful teachers the good parent figures prominently. But let us in this chapter focus our attention on the true professionals, that great company of men and women – in the schools and colleges of our educational system there are over 300,000 of them – who have dedicated their lives to the service of education.

We have called them professionals and headed the chapter accordingly, but it is only recently that, as a nation, we have begun to think seriously of teaching as a profession. For centuries, here and elsewhere, it has lacked that kind of recognition; as Dr Syntax observes:

> The learned callings all agree
> Are physic, law, divinity.

But not teaching: that he writes off as an 'ungrateful trade'. Many reasons have been advanced to account for this ingratitude and to explain why the public which severally in its formative years has come under the influence of teachers, has failed in the past to accord this vocation the honour due to it. Of the various explanations, perhaps the best known is that of Charles Lamb. 'He is awkward, and out of place in the society of his equals,' he says of the schoolmaster. 'He

1. Methuen, 1951

comes like Gulliver from among the little people, and he cannot fit the stature of his understanding to yours. He cannot meet you on the square. . . . He is so used to teaching, that he wants to be teaching *you*.'[1]

The Gulliver explanation is, however, not very convincing, but there are plenty of others.[2] One is that in the bad old days of canings, birchings, sarcasms, impositions, and other customary forms of torture many acquired in their school-days a permanent dislike of their teachers, and this led them to hold a poor opinion of teachers in general. Although schools are no longer like that, centuries of iron rule have, it is suggested, left their mark on the popular attitude to teachers. And it must be admitted that even in this century – the age of the child as it has been called – people sometimes speak of teachers as if they are echoing some unhappy memories of their schooldays. To give one example, in 1928 when in their common rooms teachers were talking about the Dalton Plan and education was becoming very child-centred, the House of Commons was discussing a regulation to which many teachers were opposed. A very distinguished member, Lord Hugh Cecil (member for Oxford University and subsequently Provost of Eton, and later Lord Quickswood) made this remarkable comment: 'I am always,' he said, 'sorry to give up any opportunity of giving discipline to schoolmasters. They are so much inclined by the habit of inflicting discipline on other people, to be extremely self-willed and undisciplined themselves, and I am always glad when they are compelled to submit to a regulation which they find inconvenient.' If one of our more illustrious citizens could in the twentieth century take that vindictive line, founded on a traditional view that had ceased to have any substance, it is reasonable to suppose that others, less en-

1. Essay on *The Old and the New Schoolmaster*.
2. Professor Vernon suggests that 'the low prestige in which the teaching profession is held by most adults probably arises as a compensation for the sense of inferiority when these adults were schoolchildren themselves'. Article on 'The Psychological Traits of Teachers', *Year Book of Education*, 1953 (Evans), p. 51.

lightened, are equally ready to adopt an ungenerous attitude to teachers for much the same reason.

But one of the most impressive features of the last decade has been the growing interest of parents in the processes of education. This fact and the revolution that has taken place in teacher-pupil relationship is bound to have a marked effect upon the public attitude to teachers. Already there are many signs that popular support for education is much stronger than it was before the War. Any government that to-day attempted a policy of drastic economy in education, like the Geddes Axe and the measures that ham-strung the Fisher Act, would have to reckon with a much stronger opposition than any evoked by the economy campaigns of the inter-war period. And with this increasing regard for education there is, as a natural corollary, a growing appreciation of the day-to-day work of teachers within their schools. As far back as 1930 Sir John Adams, after noting the various obstacles to professional advance, felt justified in making this claim: 'We belong to a rising craft: its status has been steadily improving with the nationalizing of education throughout the world, and the increase of the attention given to its scientific side.'[1] Since then there have been great advances; teaching has ceased to be an 'ungrateful trade' and there is a fair prospect of its becoming one of the more esteemed professions of the Welfare State. But in any diagnosis of its prospects due weight must be given to the hampering influence of its worst legacy, the consequences of the age-long division of education into two nations, secondary for the few and elementary for the many. In this country this 'two-nation' concept has been brought to an abrupt end by the 1944 Act. The Elementary School is legally as dead as the dodo, but it will take us some time to lay its ghost. To appreciate its baneful influence a brief excursion into the past is necessary.

Society in the eighteenth and nineteenth centuries drew a marked class distinction between those who taught in

1. *The Teacher's Many Parts* (Univ. of London Press, 1930), p. 36.

grammar schools and teachers who served in schools of the elementary type. Some thought that the Education Act of 1902 would provide an opportunity for narrowing the gulf between grammar and elementary school teachers, for it brought grammar as well as elementary schools within the state system. But it was in fact administered in such a way as to accentuate the distinction between them and between those who taught in them. The grammar schools were governed under separate regulations, while the elementary schools had their own less favourable code. There was a similar demarcation in the inspectorate, H.M.I.s (secondary) and H.M.I.s (elementary) keeping strictly within their allotted frontiers. In the Board of Education's office there were separate branches for secondary and elementary education, and when in 1919 the Burnham Committee was established to settle teacher's salaries on a national basis separate committees were constituted for consideration of the salaries of secondary and elementary school teachers. In many other ways the distinction between secondary (which until 1944 connoted only grammar) and elementary schools, and those who taught in them was intensified. Here we are not concerned with the necessity or merit of these administrative procedures; the sole purpose of this retrospective digression is to establish the point that there is a traditional distinction between the grammar and elementary school teacher, and that it was as marked as ever when the 1944 Act wrought its revolution by abolishing the elementary school and establishing secondary education for all. Our neighbours across the channel drew much the same distinction and there was a derogatory note in their expression, *l'esprit primaire*.

As a postscript to this brief reference to the administration of the 1902 Act, one feature that helped to bridge the gulf should be noted. The pupil teacher system, so characteristic of the training of the elementary teacher, was terminated; and advantage was taken of the new grammar schools, founded under the Act, to recruit admissions to the Training

Colleges from the grammar school sixth forms. Dr I. L. Kandel, with his unrivalled knowledge of world trends in education, notes this reform as the turn of the tide and the beginning of a movement towards a united profession. 'The picture began to change,' he writes, 'first in England and the United States, when future elementary school teachers began to go to secondary schools before they entered institutions for the training of teachers.'[1]

But we have yet many problems to solve before we can look forward confidently to the attainment of a united profession. There are so many unfortunate legacies and of these one of the worst is an inheritance of two divergent traditions about the education of teachers – the public school and older grammar school tradition, which assumed that teachers were born and not made, and the elementary school tradition which assumed that they should be trained but not educated. In the past the grammar schools were content, as the public schools still are, to recruit their staffs from the universities and set them to work without any preparation for their vocation. Their aim was to secure as far as possible cultured gentlemen with a good degree in the subjects they would be expected to teach. Many also for reasons of economy recruited a proportion of non-graduates, usually less cultured and equally unaware of the problems they would have to face.

Of the great nineteenth-century headmasters, Edward Thring was alone in believing that the practice of education, like that of medicine and law, required some preparatory study. 'Somewhat tempered by fear of the gallows,' he wrote a book for the guidance of teachers, which had a large sale both in this country and in the U.S.A. 'How', he asked, 'can those who have never taught a child be authorities on teaching? Is teaching the only subject in which ignorance is knowledge?'[2] In most public schools, in spite of Thring's protest and in spite of modern developments in the education

1. *The New Era in Education* (Harrap, 1955), pp. 323–4.
2. *The Theory and Practice of Teaching* (Cambridge Univ. Press, ed. 1899), p. 17.

of prospective teachers, the old traditional view still prevails. 'Many of the public schools,' said A. de Selincourt, 'and I should think almost all the privately owned preparatory schools, both for boys and girls, are staffed with what might be called amateurs.'[1]

As regards the other tradition, those who, following the lead of Kay Shuttleworth, sought to provide the elementary schools with qualified teachers in the nineteenth century, disregarded culture and developed a system of training designed to promote skill in the practice of teaching. A robust discipline and an ability to secure a limited proficiency in the 3 R's were reckoned the essential qualities of the good teacher. The abler pupils in the elementary schools were the main source of teacher supply; after an apprenticeship to the craft as pupil teachers the best went on to Training Colleges, so-called because they provided a training in what were crudely called 'the tricks of the trade'. The designation has long been unsuitable and the Robbins Committee recommended their renaming as 'Colleges of Education', a title already customary in Scotland.

It would, however, be wholly unjust to the early training colleges to suggest that the men and women they 'trained' were generally narrow in their outlook. But it is important to note the marked contrast between what was deemed necessary in a nineteenth-century grammar school – a university graduate, if possible, but without any other preparation for his vocation – and what was thought to meet best the requirements of an elementary school – a skilled craftsman, college-trained if funds permitted, and if not, one who had learned the techniques in a pupil-teacher apprenticeship.

This two-nation attitude prevailed throughout the nineteenth century, and by no means only in this country. But here, after the Act of 1902 had secured a good provision of new grammar schools within the state system, there were many developments. The Board of Education insisted that entrants to training colleges should normally have com-

1. *The Schoolmaster*, p. 64.

pleted a four-year course in a grammar school. The pupil-teacher system was abandoned. Many new Training Colleges were established. The first colleges were 'voluntary colleges' founded in the nineteenth century mainly by religious organizations, but the 1902 Act enabled local authorities also to provide training colleges under their own auspices and as a result the number of colleges was greatly increased. The normal period of training was until 1960, except in certain specialist Colleges, only two years, and for some time the emphasis in the course continued to be on professional subjects and methods. But, to quote Dr Kandel, 'a change in the direction of more advanced standards came, partly as a consequence of the demand of teachers' associations for a type of preparation more nearly corresponding to that of other professions, and partly because of the changing character of education, at first at the elementary level only. The traditional type of training was no longer adequate when the theory of education began to place stress on the pupil as an individual to be developed intellectually, physically, aesthetically, morally, and emotionally.'[1]

At the same time important developments were taking place in the universities. Towards the close of the nineteenth century they began establishing their own 'training departments' in which graduates, who wished to become teachers, could on completing their degree course acquire some knowledge of the theory and practice of education. Like the training colleges they arrange for their students to have teaching practice in schools, and for their theoretical studies to be closely associated with actual experience in the classroom. When in 1942 Mr Butler set up the McNair Committee to consider problems of recruitment, supply, and training, there were 83 recognized training colleges, 22 university training departments, and 16 art colleges which trained teachers of art. There were also some colleges, not specifically recognized, and among them 6 good colleges of physical education for women.

1. *The New Era in Education*, pp. 323-4.

How to harmonize and unify this diversity with its different traditions was the most difficult of the problems that the McNair Committee had to solve. We shall see how they dealt with it when later in this chapter we examine the present system of teacher education. But one important change of attitude should be noted. Except in the Public and preparatory schools, and a very few of the older grammar schools, the belief is now general that all prospective teachers should be specially prepared for their vocation.

It may well be that a few Public Schools, because of their prestige and the higher remuneration that they offer, can attract persons to their staffs of such outstanding quality that the risk can fairly be taken of letting them teach without any organized study of educational principles or any prior experience of class-room problems. Discussing this point, Aubrey de Selincourt, a writer sympathetic to the grammar tradition, made this interesting comment: 'There are', he remarked, 'Public Schools, as we all know, where the standard of teaching is pretty poor; but few unprejudiced persons would deny that in three or four of them at least, the teaching is incomparably better than anything else the country can offer. The teachers who provide it have not been trained.' But, he continues, 'it would be silly to speak derogatorily of the work done by the departments of education in the Universities and by the Training Colleges. Quite obviously it is both valuable and necessary.' And of the Training Colleges, he wrote: 'Without the instruction they give, even if it does no more than open the students' eyes to the presence of unsuspected difficulties, and suggest to them that a good teacher has a great deal more than his own special subject to learn, our system of national education would indeed be a farce.'[1] Many teachers, perhaps the majority, would make still higher claims for the university training departments and training colleges, and even contend that they are our principal means of raising the standard of education in this country.

1. *The Schoolmaster*, pp. 64–5.

The Freedom of the Teacher

While the long reign of social discrimination has greatly complicated our problem of reconstructing education on a democratic basis, we have on the other hand the inestimable advantage of our heritage of freedom, a priceless possession. No teachers in the world are so free as those in this country, and this we owe largely to those who in the seventeenth century fought so valiantly against attempts to crib, cabin, and confine education by such authoritarian devices as 'the licence to teach', approving, and purging. And we owe not a little to the fact that among the great political thinkers who converted us to a belief in toleration were men, like John Locke and John Stuart Mill, who thought much about education and its place in society.

We have moved far from the days when every recognized teacher was required to teach religion in conformity with the doctrines of one particular faith. Our modern attitude is well illustrated by the care Parliament took to safeguard the rights of teachers, when in the 1944 Act it required that in all primary and secondary schools there should be a daily corporate act of worship and religious teaching. The principle then accepted is described in the White Paper as follows: 'There can be no question of unwilling teachers being compelled to give religious instruction, and, save in so far as teachers may seek employment in aided schools or as reserved teachers, the religious opinions of a candidate for a teaching post will not disqualify him for appointment, and no teacher will be required to give, or be penalized for not giving religious instruction.'[1]

The clause embodying this principle is so significant as a charter safeguarding the rights of teachers in regard to their religious convictions that it is worth examining verbatim, clothed in all its legal finery: 'Subject as hereinafter provided, no person shall be disqualified by reason of his religious

1. *Educational Reconstruction*, p. 12.

opinion, or of his attending or omitting to attend religious worship, from being a teacher in a county school or in any voluntary school, or from being otherwise employed for the purposes of such a school and no teacher in any such school shall be required to give religious instruction or receive any less emolument or be deprived of, or disqualified for, any promotion or other advantage by reason of the fact that he does or does not give religious instruction or by reason of his religious opinions or of his attending or omitting to attend religious worship: Provided that, save in so far as they require that a teacher shall not receive any less emolument or be deprived of, or disqualified for, any promotion or other advantage by reason of the fact that he gives religious instruction or by reason of his religious opinions, or of his attending religious worship, the provisions of this section shall not apply with respect to a teacher in an aided school or with respect to a reserved teacher in any controlled school or special agreement school.'[1]

In this political age, the attitude of the state to the political opinions of teachers has as important a bearing on freedom as its attitude to their religious convictions. Indeed sometimes political opinions colour the attitude to religion, and the issues coincide. Broadly speaking, the world to-day is divided into two political camps, holding views about society so opposed as to appear irreconcilable. 'There is', says one writer, concluding an analysis of the conflicting theories, 'a genuine and irreducible difference between those who attach primary importance to the self-determination of the individual and those who acknowledge the superior reality of the State.'[2] Such a conflict of ideas necessarily involves tensions and controversy wherever the two theories meet.

In countries which acknowledge the supremacy of the state, the teachers' political opinions are determined by its authority. But in countries which, like our own, leave

1. Education Act 1944, cl. 30.
2. T. D. Weldon, *States and Morals* (Murray, 1946), p. 296.

political opinion to be determined by each individual, teachers hold different opinions, and there are generally a few attracted by the political theory and practice of the other camp. We are, however, as tolerant in our attitude to political opinion as we are to religious convictions, but there is this important difference. While the law, as we have just noted, specifically safeguards the right of teachers in respect of religious opinion it makes no reference to politics.

Instead, for our policy about political opinion we rely on custom which, as we suggested in the last chapter, can often be at least as effective as law. Sir Ronald Gould has well described our conventional practice. 'Although there is no specific enactment,' he writes, 'the traditional British attitude of toleration has demanded that there should be no barrier to teaching appointments based on the political beliefs of the teacher nor upon his or her nationality. Although political freedom exists and any attempts to victimize teachers purely for political reasons are resisted, the teachers themselves are emphatic that they should not abuse this position by spreading political propaganda in schools.'[1]

In the U.S.A., where they believe in the self-determination of opinion as fervently as we do, the same tolerance has not always prevailed. 'As a phase of the current wave of reaction against the alleged infiltration of Communism,' to quote a statement by American educationists in a UNESCO publication, 'doubt has been cast by a few vocal people upon the loyalty of some public school teachers. To check on teachers' loyalty or to assure their loyalty, communities and states now sometimes require teachers to take an oath of loyalty to the United States. These oaths vary in nature from those by which the teacher swears that he is not a member of a subversive group, usually defined as one favouring the overthrow of the government by force. The reasoning behind this oath is that those testifying falsely can then be prosecuted for perjury, while those admitting undesirable affiliations can

1. *The Year Book of Education*, 1953, p. 125.

be debarred from employment.'[1] A poll carried out under the auspices of the National Education Association showed that 48 per cent of the teachers polled reported that an oath of some kind had been required of them.

In his comment, quoted above, Sir Ronald Gould rightly stresses the tradition among teachers in this country of taking care not to abuse the trust imposed in them. This sense of responsibility, of 'playing fair', is fundamental to the maintenance of all the freedoms teachers possess, and not only to their political freedom. Indeed the paradox is true that teachers in Britain owe their liberty in large measure to their scrupulous restraint. This applies not only to their high standard of conduct in the realm of politics and other big issues, but also to their good sense in affairs of much less moment. They are normally ready, for example, to show a reasonable respect for the custom or *mores* of the neighbourhood in which they serve. In the U.S.A. there is a tendency in some states for the community or the school board to restrict the teacher's personal life in various ways, e.g. restrictions on smoking or drinking in public, or the wearing of slacks by women teachers.[2] Here such conflicts seldom arise. For teachers usually respect neighbourhood opinion, and show a good-humoured regard for local sentiment. Whatever may be true of the nation as a whole, neighbourhoods generally have confidence in their teachers, and hold them in high regard – a fact impressively established when children were evacuated in World War II.

But to return to big issues of freedom. No freedom that teachers in this country possess is so important as that of determining the curriculum and methods of teaching. Neither the Minister nor the Local Education Authority exercises authority over the curriculum of any school beyond that of agreeing the general educational character of the school and its place in the local educational system. The

1. *The Education of Teachers in England, France, and the U.S.A.* (UNESCO' 1953), p. 319.
2. *The Education of Teachers in England, France and the U.S.A.*, pp. 311–13.

governors, in consultation with the head of the school, are normally responsible for the general direction of the conduct and curriculum of the school, but in practice the curriculum is settled by the head in co-operation with the assistant staff.[1]

When the Ministry of Education compiled a survey of the first fifty years of the central department's administration, the Minister (George Tomlinson) made in an introduction (already referred to) an interesting comment on the absence from the survey of any reference to the curriculum. 'If this Report comes into the hands of readers from overseas, as I hope it will,' he wrote, 'they may be expected to look first for a substantial chapter on educational method and the curriculum of the schools. They will not find it. This does not of course mean that the schools have made no response to the new knowledge about the nature and needs of children or to the changing conceptions of the function of education in a democratic community. The reason is that the Department has traditionally valued the life of institutions more highly than system and has been zealous for the freedom of schools and teachers. In all matters, therefore, affecting the curriculum and methods of teaching it has been content to offer guidance by means of "suggestions" and in the main to rely on Your Majesty's Inspectorate.'[2]

Successive Presidents of the Board of Education, and since 1944 all the Ministers, have stoutly maintained this attitude when pressed to intervene on some aspect of the curriculum. Thus when urged in 1927 to make the teaching of patriotism a compulsory feature of the curriculum as a counterblast to nationalist propaganda in other countries, Lord Eustace Percy, as President, replied: 'If governments, whether local or central, began to prescribe to the teacher a certain method

1. For specimens of articles of government and rules of management of secondary and primary schools, see Alexander and Barraclough, *County and Voluntary Schools* (Councils and Education Press, 1953).

2. *Education 1900–1950*, p. 1. The reference to 'suggestions' is to *Handbook of Suggestions for the consideration of Teachers in Public Elementary Schools* (H.M.S.O., 1937).

of teaching, or even attempt to influence him in such matters, we run the risk of all those evils that we have seen in various forms, both in the Prussia of the past and the Russia of to-day.'[1] Those who want a place to be found in the curriculum for their favourite cause are legion. George Tomlinson, when Minister, once disposed of an importunate enthusiast with the remark 'Minister's now't to do with curriculum', but in 1962 there was an unexpected innovation, the establishment of a 'Curriculum Study Group' by Lord Eccles, then Minister of Education.[2]

It would be misleading to give the impression that the Head is fancy free to do as he likes when settling what shall be taught. While the curriculum is his responsibility he has, in schools where pupils sit for external examinations, to bear in mind the syllabuses that the examining boards prescribe. But all Heads from the nursery school onwards are in our free society subject to challenge about their curriculum from many quarters. They have to carry their staff with them, justify their policy when the school is inspected, have regard to the wishes of parents, and not forget that questions can be asked at Governors' meetings and those of the County or County Borough Council, and even in Parliament. 'Is the Minister aware', asked a Member of Parliament, 'that lessons in make-up are taking place in — school?' And the Minister replied, 'I have seen statements in the Press about these lessons. It is not my practice to interfere with the curriculum of any school.' The Press carried the matter a stage further: 'Could you tell us,' they asked the Head, 'about these make-up lessons at — school?' And he replied: 'There are no lessons in make-up at — school.' 'Then,' asked the Press, 'how did the story get about?' 'Because,' the Head replied, 'I made a speech at a Rotary lunch, in which I said that in my opinion senior girls to-day are prone to overdo make-up, and I saw no reason why, if parents were willing, the girls should not be

1. Quoted in *The New Era in Education*, pp. 131–2.
2. Later a 'Schools Council for the Curriculum and Examinations' was established, with Sir John Maud as its first Chairman.

correctly instructed.'[1] Much ado about nothing, maybe, and a good example of how ready people are to challenge and criticize. But much more important, it shows how easy it is under our democratic system for criticism, however trivial, to be thoroughly ventilated.

The freedom, which teachers in this country possess and so highly value, is not an absolute freedom; from what has been said, it will be clear that they cannot in the exercise of their political liberty, their social conduct, or their choice of curriculum and method do just as they like. This freedom is conditioned by certain unwritten obligations; they have in using their freedoms to accept certain responsibilities and standards, and be ready to justify their actions when challenged, and especially at the bar of public opinion. They have also to pioneer, experiment, and show initiative of a kind not required under a regimented system or under that operating in our elementary schools during the payment-by-results phase. But these obligations do not detract from the value of the freedom; on the contrary they enhance it immensely.

Too often we speak of freedom in education only in a negative sense, as immunity from interference. While that is important, we make a sad mistake if we forget its still more valuable positive attributes – freedom to act, to change, to originate and inspire. The two aspects are, of course, not separate but interdependent: if you interfere, you soon destroy the sense of responsibility. You cannot have it both ways – the right to interfere, and the right to expect initiative and imaginative leadership.

In 1951 a party of teachers visited Russia to study its educational system first hand. Sir Ronald Gould, the General Secretary of the National Union of Teachers, was one of the party; and on his return he spoke on the wireless, drawing an interesting contrast between the Russian way of education and our own. After remarking on the generous staffing there, the cleanliness of the schools, the well-stocked school

1. *News Chronicle*, 18 August 1948.

libraries, and the ample equipment, he told us of the uniform and rigid pattern of the curriculum. What are the advantages he asked, of this rigidity? 'I was given only one answer,' he said, 'that when a child moves from place to place, it is easy to pick up the work in his new school. No doubt that is so, but is it sufficient – or even the main – reason for the enforcement of uniformity?'[1] He then gave us his reasons for preferring the British system, its flexibility and diversity. 'I make no bones about it,' he concluded. 'Give me the English approach.'

The Example of the Universities

Our universities are outstanding examples of our belief in academic freedom. In some other western democracies university teachers have in recent years had to testify to their political loyalty, but there has been no such demand here. Nor has there been any encroachment into university affairs by the state. 'The contrast between the development and control of university education in Great Britain and the State-created, State-paid, State-controlled universities in the great Continental countries, such as France, Germany, Italy, and Spain – is complete and striking.'[2] This immunity from state intervention is the more remarkable because all our modern universities are nineteenth- and twentieth-century foundations, and have therefore grown to their present stature at a time when the state was becoming more active in so many spheres of our national life. Moreover, for many years now the state has been making grants, at an increasing rate, to all our universities; for with rising costs and the need for expansion they have found their

1. The reason given for the enforcement of uniformity is the same as that given in England under the Tudors for insisting upon the use of one Latin Grammar in all grammar schools. Cf., for example, Canon of Canterbury, 1529, 'Of schoolmasters and a Uniform Method of Teaching'. 'Whereas . . . it often happens that a boy who has begun to learn grammar for a year or two under one teacher, is obliged to leave him and go to a new teacher . . . '
2. C. Grant Robertson, *The British Universities* (Benn, 1930), p. 55.

income from endowments and fees altogether inadequate.

The Universities now get about two-thirds of their money from the State, and over 70 per cent of their students are assisted by scholarships. Yet they are completely self-governing, and there is good reason to hope that they will continue free and independent.[1]

How have they managed to maintain this freedom unimpaired? Tradition partly accounts for it. The older universities have their roots deep in the past. Oxford and Cambridge go back to the middle ages, and the four Scottish universities to the fifteenth and sixteenth centuries. They have grown from within. The colleges of Oxford and Cambridge evolved as independent societies, subject to their own statutes and those of the University. They did not escape the close attention of King and Parliament in the seventeenth century, and their teachers like those in the schools caught the full blast of the persecuting zeal of the contending parties. And later they were the subjects of Royal Commissions and parliamentary enactments, but by and large they have enjoyed a remarkable liberty.

But there is much more to it than tradition. The modern universities have not modelled themselves on these famous ancient foundations. They have wisely evolved their own pattern appropriate to their needs and circumstances. The University of London has its own very special history, so have the University of Durham and the federal University of Wales. Indeed all have distinctive characteristics, but an impressive feature of all the modern universities is the manner in which they have succeeded in enlisting the active co-operation and interest of public and other representatives, and have, at the same time, ensured that, much as we have tried to arrange for our schools, all purely academic business is regulated by the teachers in the various faculties of the University: 'Apart from Oxford and Cambridge,' to quote the late Sir Frederick Ogilvie, 'the Universities are governed

1. See the excellent Chapter XVI on 'Academic Freedom' in the Robbins' Report (*Higher Education*, Cmnd 2154, H.M.S.O., 1963).

on a dual system. Purely educational matters are dealt with by an Academic Senate, consisting of Professors, and a proportion of other teaching staff, and presided over by the Vice-Chancellor. Other matters, such as senior appointments, salaries, buildings, finance, are dealt with by a Council or Court consisting partly of Professors, partly of representatives of local interests such as City or County Councils, partly of outside people, and presided over as a rule by a distinguished figure of the neighbourhood, not the Vice-Chancellor. This dual system naturally has its frictions from time to time, but on the whole it works admirably. It ensures that the educational essentials are the responsibility of the academic staff alone. It broadens the landscape, and gives legitimate outside interests some voice in University affairs. It can enlist administrative experts who know their business, and can save Professors for theirs.' And he adds, prophetically, 'It, and not the Oxford and Cambridge system, is certainly the model for the future.'[1]

The practice of academic freedom is, therefore, though always assailable, now more firmly entrenched than ever in our university world. As universities are established in many places, the principle has become more widely known and appreciated.[2] It is not challenged largely because university teachers, like those in the schools, use it wisely. And it should be noted that it comprehends not only freedom to determine courses of study, but also freedom of religious and political opinion. In securing their freedoms on a firm basis the universities have been greatly helped by the fact that in Parliament, on Royal Commissions, and other bodies that have considered their problems there have been distinguished members with personal knowledge of the University way of life, and sympathy with University ideals. In future uni-

1. *British Universities* (Bureau of Current Affairs Pamphlet No. 68, 1948), p. 14.

2. When the Robbins Committee reported in 1963 there were 31 universities in Great Britain. Universities are being expanded substantially and some new ones, including former Colleges of Technology, are being established.

versities should have a further advantage. For with their greatly increased numbers they are every year substantially enlarging the proportion of the electorate familiar with their ideals, and are sending out a growing stream of men and women to occupy influential and responsible positions in our national and civic life.

The government began the practice of aiding universities in 1882, but all the early grants were *ad hoc*, piecemeal subsidies for specific purposes allotted to certain universities. This continued to the end of World War I. Then rising costs and the urgent need for development made government assistance for all universities, and on a more generous scale, essential. It was a critical moment in the history of our universities; a clumsy solution of the problem might have resulted in bureaucratic control and serious encroachments on academic freedom.

Fortunately H. A. L. Fisher was then President of the Board of Education. As he had been a distinguished Oxford tutor for many years and more recently Vice-Chancellor of Sheffield University, he fully appreciated the implications of the problem; and moreover was eminently wise and far-sighted. And there was yet another happy coincidence. To quote Fisher's own words, 'Austen Chamberlain was fortunately Chancellor of the Exchequer. He was himself an alumnus of Cambridge, and the son of the founder of Birmingham University.'[1] Jointly they agreed that the best way of seeking a solution was a Royal Commission: and they persuaded Lord Oxford (H. H. Asquith), the great Liberal statesman and a devoted and distinguished son of Balliol, to be its chairman. 'I felt assured', wrote Fisher, in appreciation of Asquith's readiness to serve as Chairman, 'that its findings, whatever they might be, would be regarded as authoritative and would receive a full measure of parliamentary support.'[2] As a result of the Commission's report, the University Grants

1. *An Unfinished Autobiography* (Oxford University Press, 1940), pp. 115–16.
2. Fisher, *op. cit.*, p. 116.

Committee was established as the channel of government grant and the danger of state control thereby averted. Ever since this Committee, acting under the Treasury and composed mainly of eminent academic people, has distributed the grant – now over £25 million a year – to the satisfaction of both the Treasury and the universities.

The original terms of reference prescribed for the Committee were: To inquire into the financial needs of university education in the United Kingdom and to advise the Government as to the application of any grants that may be made towards meeting them. But as that shrewd American, Abraham Flexner, once observed, a university 'is not outside the general social fabric of a given era. It is an expression of the age.' And as the twentieth century proceeded, we came to believe more and more in the Planned Society. So that universities might plan and their planning be attuned to the national economy, the Treasury widened the scope of the Committee's reference, adding as one of its new functions: To assist, in consultation with the universities and other bodies concerned, the preparation and execution of such plans for the development of universities as may from time to time be required in order to ensure that they are fully adequate to national needs.

In pursuance of its task the Committee pays periodical visits to every university, and a sound planning relationship has developed that has been of great value, especially during the post-war phase of expansion.[1] The demand for university graduates for government services, teaching, industry, and commerce, has grown so rapidly that it has become more and more evident that 'the dependence of the universities on the state is balanced by the dependence of the State on the universities.'[2] It is important, therefore, from the standpoint of national well-being that this fruitful partnership between

1. For a detailed, well documented account of the partnership and its achievement during the years 1946–52, see H. C. Dent, *Growth in English Education* (Routledge and Kegan Paul, 1954), pp. 164–82.

2. *University Development*. Report of University Grants Committee, 1947–52 (H.M.S.O., 1953), p. 76.

the University Grants Committee and the universities should be fully maintained. A device for the expenditure of public funds without the imposition of detailed control inevitably has its critics in spite of its now well-proven merits. The House of Commons Committee of Public Accounts, for example, with customary vigilance recently challenged this unbureaucratic way of apportioning grants. Certain books and accounts of the Universities should, it contended, be open to inspection by the Comptroller and Auditor General and his staff.

Such detailed inspection would, however, almost certainly entail sooner or later bureaucratic intervention in university policy and procedure. The Treasury wisely suggested other ways whereby the University Grants Committee themselves could satisfy the Committee of Public Accounts that universities' methods of contracting, and of recording and controlling expenditure are all they should be.[1] In these uncertain days it is never wise to forecast, but, while there may be further challenges, there is at least good reason to hope that our universities will be able to continue as self-governing communities within the Welfare State and maintain unimpaired the principles and procedures of academic freedom.

Co-operation and Consultation

Although Head Teachers in this country are free to decide the curriculum, it is markedly similar in character and content in schools of the same type. While we have nothing like the uniformity to be found in countries where the curriculum is prescribed, there is, however, an underlying unity. Visitors from overseas, when they notice several schools of the same type with much the same time-table, often express surprise and even doubt whether our teachers are as free in this respect as they are reputed to be.

1. Appendix to Special Report of the Committee of Public Accounts (H.M.S.O., February 1954). See, also, Sixth Report of Committee of Public Accounts, 1955–6 (H.M.S.O. August 1956).

It is not easy to account for this tendency to conform to a national pattern. Before 1944 it could be said of Grammar Schools that their curriculum was conditioned to some extent by the regulations of the Board of Education, which specified certain subjects, and by the requirements of external examining bodies. But the Ministry's regulations that have been in force since 1945 make no reference to the curriculum and the certificate examination has been modified to ensure latitude. The requirements of the universities for open scholarships and admission, and the entrance qualifications for some professions affect the curriculum of older pupils to some extent; but it is broadly true that neither the government nor any external bodies cramp the freedom of the Head Teacher in his choice of the curriculum.

We must therefore look elsewhere for an explanation of the similarities in schools of the same type. Teachers are affected, consciously and unconsciously, by many influences when shaping the curriculum. The views of parents, even when not expressed, carry considerable weight. 'An English School', the Spens Committee observed, 'which departs widely from average practice can do so only with the support of a body of parents of unusual views.'[1] Public opinion, the social climate, the prevailing political philosophy are, also, all factors of importance. 'Even the most independent school', the Spens Committee remark in the passage just referred to, 'is subject to the normalizing influence of social demands, in addition to the silent but powerful national influences from which none is free.'

There are other influences of a more direct character that profoundly affect a teacher's conception of education, and among them the experiences of his own schooldays. Usually the most important are those the universities or training

1. Report of the Consultative Committee on *Secondary Education* (H.M.S.O., 1938), p. 150. For an illustration of the difficulties that arise when parents are confronted with an unusual curriculum, see Holmes, *The Idiot Teacher* (Faber, 1952).

colleges bring to bear on prospective teachers during their formative student years, the knowledge teachers derive from in-service courses, and the stimulus that results from those various contacts with each other through membership of the same common room or of associations and societies. It would be difficult to exaggerate the good done to modern education by societies constituted to promote study of particular aspects of the curriculum – English, History, Classics, Science, Mathematics, Geography, Domestic Subjects, Handicraft, Art, Music, Physical Education, and several others, or from societies formed to promote some particular branch of education like the nursery school, or some important service like the school library or visual aids.

The professional associations, of which there are several, have also done much for the development of education as well as for the advancement of the teacher's status. Except for one or two breakaway associations, they were first constituted to bring together teachers or head teachers of schools of a particular type. They grew up separately, and their history often reflects the 'two nations' fissure:

> Since each group as it rose was determin'd apart
> By conditions of life which none other could share.

This separatism had its merits, as well as demerits: there were obvious advantages in teachers with similar educational problems meeting separately to discuss them. On the other hand, in so far as these divisions had implications of social class or prevented professional unity the pluralism has not always been helpful. Some of the leading associations were founded in Victorian times, when class distinctions were as divisive as

> The unplumbed, salt, estranging sea.

But what that great Headmaster, J. L. Paton, once described as 'the separations and snobberies' that divide education 'against herself' are in our mid-twentieth-century climate disappearing like melting snow; and there are encouraging signs that the profession is moving gradually towards a unity of a kind not incompatible with diversity, but a diversity based on educational considerations only.

Incidentally, it may be worth noting how little is known of the history of the leading associations. Perhaps before long some educational historian will unravel for us the history of the exclusive Headmasters' Conference from the days of Thring onwards, and the no less interesting story of the Headmistresses' Association so firmly established in the same period by Miss Buss and Miss Beale, and on a much broader basis. The origin and growth of the National Union of Teachers is a theme that should tempt anyone in search of an uncharted field of social history. For it is a veritable saga of heroic and persistent warfare against patronage and privilege crowned with ultimate victory when Parliament at last abolished the Elementary School in 1944. 'No great occupation', Dr Asher Tropp notes, 'has shown less interest or pride in its past than the teaching profession, and there exists no satisfactory history of the largest professional association in the country.'[1]

Another important influence is the Inspectorate. Earlier in the chapter reference was made to the Minister's introduction to the survey of the first fifty years of Central administration. After emphasizing that the Ministry did not concern itself directly with the curriculum, he observed that it was content to offer guidance by issuing suggestions, and in the main to rely on the Inspectorate. In a sense these two ways of guiding can be treated as one; for the Ministry's leaflets that offer suggestions about curriculum and method are usually the work of the Inspectorate. When the Minister stressed the word 'suggestions', he did so deliberately: for it is the key to the relationship between Her Majesty's Inspectors and teachers.[2]

The first H.M.I.s were appointed 125 years ago just after

1. In *The Schoolmaster*, 25 December 1953. Article on 'The First Teachers' Association'. 2. See Percy Wilson, *Views and Prospects from Curzon Street* (Blackwell, 1961), pp. 63–78.

a Committee of the Privy Council had been set up to administer the school grants that the state had begun to make to the Voluntary Societies. The Secretary of the Committee, that wise and humane administrator, Kay Shuttleworth, defined what the inspectors were to do and how they were to do it. Their chief duties were (1) to see that public money spent on education was spent for the purposes intended, and in accordance with any conditions prescribed, and (2) to contribute to the improvement of the work they were called upon to inspect, and help to ensure that the public money spent on education was being used to the best possible advantage. In carrying out these duties, they were to rely on persuasion and suggestion. 'The aims of the Inspectorate to-day', the Ministry recently observed, 'differ hardly at all from those envisaged by Kay Shuttleworth.'[1]

Inspectors are appointed by Her Majesty in Council: hence the title H.M.I. They enjoy in consequence some measure of independence; and in an interesting passage, the Ministry has described their relationship to the Minister. 'They do not,' it observes, 'and are not expected to, promulgate in school any particular form of curriculum or any particular methods at the behest of the Minister; they report to the Minister what they find and think, not what they suppose he wishes them to find or think; their reports cannot be altered without their consent (though the Minister can decline to issue them if he wishes to do so). The corollary of this is that from time to time inspectors hold different opinions and express different views in schools. Some measure of diversity is harmless; in the long run, indeed, it is essential to progress. What would be harmful would be any suggestion that an inspector had the right to press his views on a school and require it to carry out its work in his way. Schools do well to remember that an inspector's advice is really advice, and advice that need not be followed.'[2]

When Kay Shuttleworth drew up his famous Minute about

1. *Education in 1949* (H.M.S.O., 1950), p. 96.
2. *Education in 1949*, p. 94.

the duties of inspectors and the manner in which they should be performed, only two inspectors had been appointed. But he had foresight and, as a disciple of Jeremy Bentham, the great administrative reformer who *inter alia* had a profound belief in the value of inspection, he probably realized that in time public education would require many more inspectors. It is just possible, also, that he foresaw that the principle of inspection would eventually become a main feature of other public services, and that the example set by education would, if it was a good one, be valuable as a precedent in other spheres of government. Whether he realized this or not, it has certainly proved to be the case, and for that reason our system of school inspection has attracted the attention of many students of government, not primarily concerned with education. 'The experience of educational inspection', it has been said, 'is so rich in lessons, administrative, financial, and educational, it has been so deliberately fashioned and re-fashioned to changing purposes. . . .'[1] It would however be inappropriate here to dwell at length on the various aspects of inspection as a technique of government, and we must be content to note particularly its bearing upon the work of the teacher in the school.

The size of the modern inspectorate would have staggered Kay Shuttleworth and his contemporaries. There was a big increase after the Act of 1870: at that time there were 98 inspectors and by 1880 the number had grown to 244. The 1944 Act led to another large influx of new inspectors: in 1939 the inspectorate numbered 348, while by 1949 there were 527 in the English inspectorate alone. This post-1944 expansion is partly accounted for by new spheres of work and enlarged services: e.g. school meals, special educational treatment, new nursery schools and classes, community centres, and part-time day release of technical students. Even so, it must be admitted that the increase is formidable, and it is with some relief that one can say that the expansion appears to have been accomplished without detriment to the fine

1. H. Finer, *English Local Government* (Methuen, ed. 1950), p. 362.

tradition established in past years. While the tasks of the inspectorate have multiplied, the epithets used in other days to describe their main functions are still relevant. As 'watch-dogs' they help to ensure that the nation gets value for money, and that parents and children get a square deal. As 'eyes and ears' they keep the Minister and the Ministry informed about developments in education and about local problems as they arise. And as 'missionaries' they move from school to school gathering new knowledge and passing it on to teachers and their own colleagues.

An inspector's contacts with schools are of two main kinds. Periodically schools are inspected with meticulous thorough-ness, and on such occasions the inspector visits as one of a team, carefully chosen to include experts in those branches of knowledge represented in the school's curriculum. But no less important, and often more valuable are the informal visits that inspectors make. Every school is allocated to some one inspector, who keeps in touch with it and, from time to time, arranges if it seems likely to be helpful for specialist or other inspectors to visit and give the teachers concerned the benefit of their expert knowledge.

The friendly approach, initiated by Kay Shuttleworth, had to go into cold storage during the grim period of the payment-by-results grant system. But when that was abandoned and Morant had done his utmost to consign its legacy of bitter-ness into oblivion, the old relationship of suggestion and persuasion was revived. Inspectors came more and more to regard themselves as persons appointed to help, encourage, and stimulate; and paying a tribute to them in 1950 George Tomlinson, one of the shrewdest of Ministers and honest as the day, felt it appropriate to describe them, borrowing Matthew Arnold's famous phrase, as 'men and women, whose privilege it is, to spread abroad "sweetness and light".'[1]

During the present century an important new factor has crept into the relationship between teacher and inspector.

1. *Education in 1950*, p. 1.

The earlier H.M.I.s of the Kay Shuttleworth tradition, while loyal to his injunction to suggest and persuade, were apt to patronize and assume airs of Olympian superiority. Such pomp and circumstance have now disappeared; and, indeed, they had to. For to-day H.M.I. often finds himself inspecting the work of teachers abler and more learned than he is. G.T. Hankin, an H.M.I. who in his day rendered great service in his own branch of study, history, aptly described this new relationship when giving evidence to the Royal Commission on the Civil Service in 1930. 'You are meeting', he told the Commission, when explaining the work of an H.M.I., 'people who are more or less on your own level, both from the point of view of academic qualifications, and of their knowledge of their school. They know their own school; we have a broader knowledge of schools as a whole. You meet the teacher or schoolmaster, and you discuss things with him absolutely frankly, pooling your knowledge. . . . ' And he added, 'I should say in the old days the attitude was rather more paternal. The change is very welcome.'[1]

There is yet another kind of influence that helps to shape educational policy and practice, namely that of various consultative and advisory bodies. Such bodies are now an important feature of our educational system at all levels, local, regional, and national, and in their work the partnership of the Ministry, the Local Authorities, and the Teachers, operates most effectively. On all the leading national advisory councils and committees, there are members of the teaching profession, either nominated as individuals or as representatives of associations.

Of this consultative machinery some existed before 1944. Under the Board of Education Act of 1899 a Consultative Committee was established to advise the President of the Board of Education on questions which he referred to it, and it produced some of the most seminal reports in our educational history, notably the three Hadow and the Spens Reports. After World War I a committee under the chairmanship of

1. Quoted by H. Finer in *English Local Government*, p. 375.

Lord Burnham was constituted to act as a negotiating body to settle the scales of salaries to be paid to teachers. It was composed of representatives of local education authorities and teachers' organizations. As reconstituted after 1944, it had a 'main committee' that dealt with the salaries of teachers in primary and secondary schools, another committee responsible for full-time salaries in further education, and one for teachers in farm institutes. There is also a committee (the Pelham Committee) for negotiating the salaries of the teaching staff in training colleges, and yet another that makes recommendations about the salaries of inspectors and organizers in the service of local education authorities.

The Burnham Committee functioned efficiently for over forty years, and in that period brought about a great improvement in the remuneration of teachers. The two panels (i.e. the local authorities and the teachers) often engaged in fierce argument but goodwill and good sense prevailed. In 1961, however, it became clear that the Minister desired changes in the negotiating procedure, especially an opportunity to 'indicate to the Committee at an early stage . . . his views on the size and nature of a salary settlement'.[1] In the following year Sir Edward Boyle succeeded Lord Eccles as Minister and, after a 'deadlock' in his relations with the Burnham Committee, introduced legislation suspending collective bargaining and empowering the Minister to make Orders determining the salaries of teachers in primary and secondary schools, further-education establishments, and farm institutes. These powers were to continue for two years, and meanwhile there were to be discussions about future negotiating machinery.[2] 'The increasing power of the Minister', declared Mr Chuter Ede, opposing the measure during the second-reading debate, 'is one of the greatest dangers to the future of this country'.

The establishment of the Burnham Committee was one of

1. *Education in 1961* (H.M.S.O., 1962), p. 67.
2. *Remuneration of Teachers Act, 1963.* See also *The Burnham Story* (Councils and Education Press, 1963).

H. A. L. Fisher's major achievements. When he became President of the Board of Education during the First World War he soon realized that the wide variations in the salaries paid to teachers made some such negotiating machinery essential. As an alternative method of securing uniform scales, that of making teachers civil servants was suggested. But Fisher's views on that proposal were clear. 'It offers certain palpable attractions', he wrote, '. . . But [also] . . . such a prospect of danger to educational freedom and to a wholesome variety of experimentation, such a menace to local responsibility and so formidable an accretion of work and power to the Board at Whitehall that I dismissed it from my mind.'[1]

Another of Fisher's reforms was the creation of the Secondary Schools Examination Council to co-ordinate the work of approved university examining bodies.[2] With the passing of the Education Act of 1944 the consultative machinery was strengthened. The Consultative Committee was replaced by Central Advisory Councils for England and Wales respectively, and they were empowered to advise not only on matters referred to them but also upon 'such matters connected with educational theory and practice as they think fit.' Scotland has a similar council. The Burnham Committee was given statutory status and the Minister vested with authority to see that salaries paid by local authorities to teachers accorded with scales agreed by this negotiating body and accepted by him. He was empowered to approve or reject the Burnham Committee's proposals, but he was not authorized to alter them. But, as explained on the previous page, Burnham is now unhappily in eclipse.

Of the new consultative bodies set up since 1944 the most important are two National Advisory Councils, one for Education for Industry and Commerce, and the other for the Training and Supply of Teachers. The first will be considered in Chapter Eight, and the second in the next and final

1. *Unfinished Autobiography*, pp. 96–7.
2. Its scope and membership has been recently widened. See Note 2, p. 163.

section of this chapter. But here it is appropriate to note that on both there is a strong representation of teachers. There are, too, a few independent bodies, some aided by the Ministry, which include on their executive councils representatives of the Ministry, local education authorities, and teachers. Among these are the National Foundation for Educational Research, the Educational Council for Visual Aids, the Central Bureau for Educational Visits and Exchanges, the National Institute for Adult Education, and the Institute of Christian Education.

The Education of Teachers

It is unnecessary to labour the point that the 1944 Act will be of little value unless there is always available a good supply of teachers of the right calibre and with the varied qualifications required to staff adequately many different schools and institutions. Fully recognizing this, Mr Butler in 1942 set up the McNair Committee to study this problem and advise. It produced a report of great constructive value, and as a result changes have taken place which are transforming our system of preparing teachers for their vocation.[1]

For what has been said earlier in this chapter about the 'two nation' cleavage in the development of our system of educating prospective teachers, it will be appreciated that it was essential to find some way of breaking down historic barriers and bringing the universities and training colleges into close association. There was a difference of opinion in the McNair Committee about the best way of accomplishing this, and alternative schemes were proposed. But in all but one region a similar pattern of integration has been adopted, and we have got therefore very near to a universal system, without any pressure from the centre.

Under this system the University (or University College) is the focus of teacher education in its region, and it establishes an Institute of Education in which the university

[1]. The McNair Committee's Report was published in 1944 under the title *Teachers and Youth Leaders*.

education department and the training colleges co-operate. The Institute is governed by a Council on which the university, the training colleges, and the local education authorities are represented, and in some instances there are also representatives of teacher associations. This Council is the supreme authority for teacher education in the region, subject only to the statutes of the University and the regulations of the Minister. But – and here the university's care for academic freedom will be noted – in all business not administrative the Council is advised by an Academic Board which itself sets up panels to report to it on various aspects of teacher education. 'Broadly speaking,' Mr E. F. Marshall writes, with intimate knowledge of the working of the largest Institute, 'in the various committees and panels and boards of studies the teaching staffs of universities, training colleges, specialist colleges, and university training departments are meeting and discussing problems in a way which would have been impossible ten years ago.'[1]

The institutes are now through the difficult pioneer stage and it may well be that the time is ripe for a careful stocktaking, that will afford some guidance for the next stage in their development. There are many crucial questions which can be answered only after a close study of how in their different ways and confronted with their different problems the Institutes are discharging the main tasks assigned to them. What influence are they having on the courses of study in the university education departments and training colleges? Are they proving effective as a planning authority for teacher education in their regions? Are they providing good regional centres for in-service courses and discussion groups, and for further study under expert guidance? Are they proving equal to the highly responsible and invidious duty of deciding which students should be recommended at the end of their course for qualified status? Are they justify-

1. *Year Book of Education*, 1953, p. 138. Mr Marshall, now Principal of Shoreditch Training College, was previously Secretary of the University of London Institute of Education.

ing the hope that by their leadership we shall before too long secure a national system of teacher education that is both unified and flexible? And most important of all, what can be said of their standards and values?

While we have as yet no authoritative survey, we have the advantage of a careful study of the work of the institutes by Mr C. A. Richardson, who was Chief Inspector for the Training of Teachers during the period when the institutes were getting into their stride. Shortly after his retirement from this position, he was persuaded to write an up-to-date account of teacher education in England for a UNESCO publication. He was able to bring to this task the unique knowledge of a skilled observer who had been in continuous touch with all the institutes. While cautious in his judgements he is clearly convinced that the institutes are proving effective instruments of reform, and are capable of bringing about 'changes more profound than any in the history of training. 'There seems little doubt', he concludes, 'that, in all fundamentals, the way in which the system of training is now developing is that best calculated to serve the purposes for which it is designed.'

Having noted the confident tone of Mr Richardson's diagnosis, it is proper to add, while not sharing his anxiety, that in his opinion 'there is one potential source of danger', namely the attitude of the universities. In the past, as he observes, they have sometimes been lukewarm and even sceptical about teacher education; and 'the university departments of education had to struggle for a firm foothold and then fight hard to establish themselves on an equal footing in esteem with other university departments.' Now that the universities have accepted a dominant role in teacher education as the focus of the whole system, it would indeed be fatal if they did not back the new institute wholeheartedly or if they made them 'conform too rigidly to the pattern of university routine, tradition, and convention.' It is a relief, therefore, to find that, having sounded his note of warning, Mr Richardson is able to conclude with the comment:

'Although it is perhaps too early yet to judge the final out-come, all the signs are that, in general, the universities will exert their influence wisely, considerately, and with high regard to the prime importance of the contributions coming from the other parties to the common venture. The omens are good.'[1]

The McNair Committee also wanted a bridge built at the national as well as the regional level – a central council. Although their proposals were not strictly followed, the principle of a central council was adopted; and in 1949 a National Advisory Council was established, composed of representatives of all the interests concerned with the educa-tion of teachers. It has a two-fold duty: to keep under con-tinuous review (1) the education of teachers and the stand-ards of qualification, and (2) their recruitment, supply, and distribution. The tasks assigned to them are difficult enough at any time, but especially so under present conditions. For many of their problems, some of great urgency, are a con-sequence of the circumstances of to-day. Our educational system, in process of reconstruction and expansion, requires not only many more teachers but also a greater diversity of knowledge and experience. Care has to be taken to ensure as far as possible that the differing needs of nursery, infant, junior, and secondary schools are met; and that staff is available for such specialisms as housecraft, art, music, handicraft, physical education, the teaching of handicapped children, and the teaching of technical subjects. Full em-ployment and the competing claims of other careers have added greatly to the complexity of the Council's task; but while there have been particular shortages, notably for the teaching of mathematics and science, the general level of recruitment has been well sustained.

The abnormal birth-rate during and just after the War has been another complicating factor, and in their first Report the Council remarked upon some of its implications. 'As the children pass up the schools,' they note, 'so teachers must be

1. *The Education of Teachers in England, France and the U.S.A.*, p. 123.

found for an exceptionally large number of infants in 1953 and 1954, then for an exceptionally large number of juniors in 1956 and 1957. The pressure in the secondary schools will be in 1960 and the following years.'[1]

One other major reform recommended by the McNair Committee was not implemented until 1960, namely that in all Training Colleges the duration of the course should be three years. The colleges of domestic science and the women's colleges of physical education had already established three-year courses, and it is a characteristic also of the Froebel Colleges, who have done so much for the education of young children. It is also the usual period of training in Scotland and Northern Ireland. But prior to 1960 the normal length of the course in training colleges in England and Wales was two years. It had long been recognized that this was inadequate as a preparation for teaching, but it was impossible to extend the course so long as there was the acute shortage of teachers in the primary schools caused by the abnormally large influx of children due to the high war-time birth-rate. With a course of only two years' duration students had to rush through their curriculum without reasonable opportunities for study and reflection; and they too often had to begin their career in the schools while still immature and with much ill-digested knowledge. When condemning this hasty introduction to a life-long vocation, the McNair Committee remarked, 'many students in training colleges do not mature by living: they survive by hurrying.'[2] It was a preparation ludicrously short in comparison with that for other professions, and it was unfair both to the students and their tutors. It was, also, an anachronism, a legacy from the days when a narrow, restricted training was considered sufficient for those destined to teach in elementary schools. The scope and content of the two-year course had changed beyond recognition, but its brevity had survived as a relic of old, unhappy, far-off discrimination.

1. *Training and Supply of Teachers* (H.M.S.O., 1951), p. 3.
2. *Teachers and Youth Leaders*, p. 65.

When 'the bulge' of additional children passed beyond the primary stage, it became practicable to introduce a three-year course; and it was a great day for education in this country when this reform, so long deferred, became after much preparation in the colleges a living reality. About the same time a big building programme, adding about two-thirds to existing training college accommodation, was put in hand. Not only were new colleges built and existing ones enlarged, but there was also a welcome policy of modernizing the character of the accommodation. Architects were asked 'to enlarge and improve existing colleges and to build new ones, in such a way as to create an entirely new environment.'[1] With the addition of a third year the temptation to add subjects to the curriculum was strong, but so, fortunately, was the resolve to resist it. When pressing for a three-year course the McNair Committee made very clear its opinion that the purpose of the additional year would be frustrated if it was used mainly 'as an excuse for a general increase in the number of subjects'. Happily the view that has prevailed in the colleges had been that much of the extra time should be used to provide opportunities for reflection, private study, discussion, and cultural interests.

Impressed by the progress made by the Training Colleges since the publication of the McNair Report and by the constructive achievements of the Institutes of Education, the Robbins Committee made a number of recommendations designed to raise the status of teacher education. We have already noted one of their suggestions, namely that the training colleges should be called Colleges of Education: but there were other more important proposals made with the intention of associating them much more closely with the universities and of providing their students with opportunities for graduation. We can certainly look forward with some confidence to teacher education assuming a key position in the pattern of higher education now emerging.

1. *Education in 1959* (H.M.S.O., 1960), p. 80.

CHAPTER SEVEN

SOME IMPORTANT INFLUENCES

'A Free Country'

Eighty years ago John Stuart Mill was able in his *Autobiography* to claim that nine-tenths of the affairs dealt with by governments in other countries were here handled by 'agencies independent of it'. Since then the area of the state has been greatly enlarged, but the old British tradition of voluntary service and independent enterprise has survived. Of no aspect of our national life is this more true than of education. Some local education authorities in our larger towns issue annually for the information of their citizens a booklet giving particulars of the various societies in their area that promote or provide educational and cultural opportunities, together with their programmes for the session or year. Such publications sometimes run to many pages, so numerous are the societies and so vigorous the group life and so many the interests that they cherish and serve.[1]

It is sometimes said that we owe this group habit to those valiant independents of the seventeenth century, who refused to accept the conforming way of life that the two other parties in the Civil War preferred. Our method of running our societies and meetings certainly often reflects the spirit of those first dissenters and recalls the democratic way in which their little congregations conducted their services and their discussions of great issues. 'Their genuine experienced democracy', A. D. Lindsay reminded us, 'was not political, but the democracy of the voluntary society – a society which did not use force in the putting into practice of its decisions,

1. A good example is *Leisure and Learning*, an annual publication of the Manchester Local Education Authority.

but was a fellowship of discussion. They assumed that each member contributed to the discussion what he had to say, and that then men came to some agreement, to what the Quakers were to call the sense of the meeting.'[1]

When the great French historian Élie Halévy wrote his *History of the English People*, nothing impressed him so strongly as the scope and intensity of this group life, and the influence exerted by many institutions, thriving unfettered and autonomous in an atmosphere of complete freedom. 'From whatever point of view we study the institutions of Britain,' he wrote in a concluding chapter, 'we are brought back to the same formula. England is a free country . . . this means at bottom that England is a country of voluntary obedience, of an organization freely initiated and freely accepted.'[2] The educational and cultural value of this group life is one of the strongest arguments for a generous provision of community centres and village halls.

The Influence of the Churches

The decline in churchgoing leads many, and not least zealous church folk, to say that the influence of the churches in our society is much less than it was in Victorian and Edwardian days. We are concerned here only with their influence on and in education, and experience suggests that their contribution to education – the Bible class, the Sunday School, youth service – varies much from one locality to another. And it is a reasonable guess that it has always done so.

In one respect there has certainly been a marked advance. Fifty years ago sectarian bitterness about religious education was still intense, and until the nineteen thirties any reference to religious education in Parliament, at a conference, or in a committee was almost certain to provoke a storm or, worse still, a dismal exchange of unprofitable and unpleasant argu-

1. *The Modern Democratic State* (Oxford Univ. Press, 1943), Vol. I, p. 117.
2. Pelican Edition, 1938, Vol. III, pp. 219–20.

ment. As a result religion became subject to a kind of taboo in educational circles; officials, teachers, members of education committees observed a discreet silence so as not to provide controversialists with a pretext for engaging in wordy warfare. Many teachers took great pains over 'the religious lesson' as it was called; but as a rule they studied their material and did their thinking unaided and in isolation. For so long as the taboo prevailed, neither the Board of Education nor Local Education Authorities thought of arranging in-service courses and teachers normally relied for guidance on expositions of the Scriptures that were meagre and out-of-date.

In an appendix to his Bampton Lectures Dr Spencer Leeson assembled some interesting illustrations of what he described as this 'general reluctance to mention religion.'[1] He cites, for example, Sir Robert Morant's inspiring preface to the Code of 1904, with its emphasis on character-training; 'in this,' Dr Leeson comments, 'the word religion does not occur, nor is there any reference to belief of any kind,' And later, he notes how in 1926 the Hadow Report on *The Education of the Adolescent* is almost as discreet, making only a vague reference to the place of 'religious knowledge' in the modern school. By making such reticence inevitable the earnest gentlemen who quarrelled about religious education did a great disservice to the cause that they espoused; they certainly provide some justification for Bishop Creighton's acid comment that there are none who do so much damage as those who go about doing what they believe to be good.[2]

In 1933 Lord Halifax, himself a devout Churchman, was President of the Board of Education, and he took a step which marks the beginning of the end of this long reign of 'general reluctance to mention religion'. He summoned a repre-

1. *Christian Education* (Longmans, 1946), Appendix III. Spencer Leeson's death in January 1956 was a grievous loss to the cause of religious education. By his gifts of leadership and his unique experience, he made a great contribution to its development under the 1944 Education Act.

2. *Life and Letters of Mandell Creighton*, Vol. II, p. 503.

sentative conference to meet at the Board of Education to consider what could be done to help teachers to equip themselves for the teaching of religion. Two years later, the Institute of Christian Education was founded, and still further evidence of the changed attitude came when in 1938 the Spens Committee, discussing the curriculum of secondary schools, devoted a whole chapter to 'Scripture'.[1]

The tide had turned. The teaching of religion had at long last been rescued from the slough of controversy, and it was becoming possible to discuss openly and with goodwill the educational issues. William Temple outlined the nature of the task. 'The need for improvement', he said, 'is chiefly on two sides. There is first the clarifying of the aim with which we set out upon the enterprise of religious instruction and religious education. There can be no doubt that many of those engaged in it have no clear aim at all before them. The second great purpose is to take care that what is being presented is the most enlightened interpretation of our tradition in accordance with modern scholarship and living contemporary thought. Here, once more, we notice that many of those engaged in teaching have not had the opportunity of keeping themselves in touch with the best work done in the field, and that consequently, through no fault of their own, teaching in this subject has been less effectual than in most others.'[2]

Religious Education To-day

During the war years, much progress along these lines was impossible. But, as Thucydides remarked, war is a stern schoolmaster, and the crises and challenges of that grim period brought the churches more closely together than ever before. Consequently, when the Education Act of 1944 was being prepared, they were able for the first time in our educa-

1. Report of the Consultative Committee on *Secondary Education*, Chapter V.
2. *Religion in Education*, October 1936, Vol. III, p. 182.

tional history to exercise a combined influence and make joint recommendations. This co-operation bore fruit, as the clauses about religious education in the Act testify; subject to the conscience clause, they ensure (1) daily worship, and (2) religious teaching in every school within the national system. While these provisions do little more than give a statutory benediction to what had been normal practice, they have proved a great stimulus to the development of religious education and kindled a public interest in this aspect of school life. And improvement in the quality of religious teaching has been greatly assisted by an important change in the law embodied in the Act, namely the repeal of what was known as 'the time-table clause'.

This clause was included in the Act of 1870 in the belief that it would facilitate the withdrawal of children from religious teaching when parents wished to take advantage of the conscience provision. It stipulated that religious teaching must only be given at the beginning or end of the school session. This made it imperative that all religious teaching throughout the school should be given at the same hour, thus making it impossible for Head Teachers to arrange for it to be given only by those specially qualified to teach it. Now that it can be taught at any time, it can like any other subject be assigned to teachers who make it their chief interest and can, in William Temple's phrase, present it 'in accordance with modern scholarship and living contemporary thought.'

The other important provisions in the Act about religious education concern the syllabus. The voluntary aided schools – rather less than half the Church of England schools, all Roman Catholic schools, and the thirteen Jewish schools – use syllabuses of their denominations.[1] The Act requires that all the County Schools shall use what it terms 'an Agreed Syllabus', and this same kind of syllabus is also to be largely

1. For a masterly survey of the aims and problems of voluntary and particularly aided schools, see article by A. C. F. Beales on 'The Future of Voluntary Schools' in *Looking Forward in Education*, pp. 81–107.

followed in the voluntary controlled schools. This means in effect that religious education in the great majority of the primary and secondary schools of England and Wales – nearly 19,000 out of about 29,000 – will be profoundly influenced by 'agreed syllabuses'. Another significant innovation in the Act is that religious teaching can now, like any other branch of study, be inspected by H.M.I.

'Agreed Syllabuses' had been used in Council Schools in many areas for some years before the Act; the West Riding of Yorkshire (1923) and Cambridgeshire (1924) had been pioneers in this development, and had demonstrated how valuable such syllabuses can be as a guide to teachers when planning their actual schemes of work. Some authorities adopted one or other of these syllabuses, while several arranged for syllabuses to be similarly prepared for use in their areas. By 1944 some of these syllabuses had become well known and were widely used, especially the Cambridgeshire syllabus. They had proved helpful not only as a basis for schemes of work but also because they frequently included valuable suggestions about the form and content of the daily service.

The Act lays down the procedure for the preparation of these syllabuses, and this follows generally the basis that had proved successful in Cambridgeshire and elsewhere. Its aim is to bring scholarly churchmen of the Anglican and Free Churches into conference with practising teachers for the purpose of affording the best possible guidance in the teaching of scripture throughout the school age range. Fifty years ago such co-operation would have been impossible; and in comparing the influence of the Churches in education then and now it is necessary to bear this in mind. It may well be that, although church-going has much declined, the Churches because of the absence of sectarian bitterness are able to exercise a more effective and more wholesome influence. Many will find it difficult to understand the importance attached to these agreed syllabuses as a mainspring of this revival in religious education, but the story of religious education has many incomprehensibles. No one of our day knew the story of its intricacies so well as did Spencer Leeson, nor was anyone better equipped to measure the value of the Agreed Syllabus as an instrument of reform. 'This', runs his verdict, 'is a new and important phenomenon, and it will have a significant place in the history of English Christianity.'[1]

Secularists will question the action of the Coalition Government in giving such a strong backing to religious education in 1944. The debates that led to the passing of the Act show unmistakably that Parliament then believed that in encouraging religious education it was reflecting the prevailing climate of opinion. And when replying for the Government at the close of the second reading debate, Mr Chuter Ede carried the House with him when he claimed that although never in our history were there so few adherents to particular denominations, yet there were a great many people who regarded themselves as Christians and wanted something more for their children than the secularized education provided in many other countries.

The Place of the Parent in Our Educational System

In an earlier chapter, we listed the parent as one of the claimants to control in education, but we have not yet examined his claims. Should he be allowed to bring up his children as he likes? That is the main issue as regards his claim, and it is one that was much debated in the Victorian age.

In the years before 1870 parents could do pretty well as they liked about their children. Under the duress of poverty thousands allowed them to be exploited as child labour, and it was calculated in 1870 that only two-fifths of the children between the ages of six and ten were attending school, and only one-third of those between ten and twelve. Shortage

1. *Christian Education*, p. 153. For a survey of what is being accomplished and the problems that arise, see *Religious Education in Schools* (published for Institute of Christian Education by S.P.C.K., 1954). See also the excellent Chapter 7 on 'Spiritual and Moral Development' in the Newsom Report.

of school accommodation partly accounts for this, and economic conditions were also an important factor, making life extremely difficult for many parents. Even so, there was a shocking background of parental indifference and neglect, and considerable brutality.

Most of us, to-day, would say that confronted with a situation of this kind Parliament ought without hesitation to have made education compulsory in the Elementary Education Act of 1870. But with their strong belief in individual liberty members were reluctant to take what seemed to them such a drastic step. So 'compulsory education' figured in the protracted debates of 1870 as almost as controversial an issue as 'the religious question'. As often happens, the question of principle was sometimes obscured by practical considerations, especially the argument that it was no good introducing compulsion until 'the gaps' in school accommodation had been filled.

But it is the question of principle that makes the debate interesting, and the assumption by so many members that to compel a parent to send his children to school was an unwarrantable interference with the liberty of the subject. As one member put it: 'the principle of compulsion is foreign to our tastes, habits, and sentiments.' While another said: 'For what was compulsion? Making a man do what he disliked: something that England would never tolerate.'

The net result of this long debate was, as you might expect, a compromise: those school boards which wished to introduce a compulsory system were allowed to do so in their areas. But the debate continued in the Press, and in those places where public opinion is formed. It centred around three focal points: (1) the social evil of neglected children; (2) precedents; (3) the limitations of *laissez-faire* as a social creed. Social reformers by their writings and statistics saw to it that the public conscience was aroused about child neglect. And as to precedents, the piecemeal factory legislation of the period provided examples of compulsion applied in workshops with the intention of ensuring that child employees received a bare minimum of part-time schooling. Such precedents carried weight, for our legislators usually find an innovation more acceptable if it can be shown that it is not as new as it seems.

No less effective was the new trend in political thought. Some of the leading political thinkers had helped greatly to swing opinion towards compulsion by enunciating principles to justify departures from the strict orthodoxy of *laissez-faire*. Of these the most influential was John Stuart Mill who in his later years had come more and more to realize that to do justice positive action by the state was sometimes essential. This was particularly true, he held, when an individual was unable to protect his own interests; and who, he asked, was more defenceless than a child?

So while his strong individualism made him to the last a staunch opponent of state education – 'a mere contrivance', he called it, 'for moulding persons to be exactly like one another,' he nevertheless maintained that it was wholly wrong to leave it to the parent to decide whether his children should be educated or not. 'Is it not', he wrote, 'almost a self-evident axiom that the State should require and compel the education up to a certain standard of every human being who is born its citizen.'[1] It is important to note – for it has left its impress on our law of education – the distinction that Mill draws between compelling parents to send their children to school and compelling them to ensure that their children received education. How they were educated up to the required standard was in his view a matter for the parent to decide, and if parents preferred some other way than that of sending them to school they should be free to make whatever arrangements they wished.

Of the other Victorian prophets who proclaimed their views on compulsory education, Matthew Arnold is perhaps the most interesting not only because of his eminence as a man of letters but more especially because as an H.M.I. who had studied continental systems of education, he wrote with

1. *On Liberty* (Thinker's Library edition, Watts), p. 130.

practical knowledge and experience. He contended that if compulsory education was to be effective, three conditions must be fulfilled: (1) the law of compulsory education should be applicable to children in all grades of society, (2) the education provided should be of a kind to evoke the appreciation of parents, and (3) there should be a reasonable standard of living so that the attitude of parents would not be dictated by economic necessity.[1]

One important question that greatly exercised the minds of Victorian legislators was whether, if education was compulsory, it should *ipso facto* be free. Mr Butler had to resolve much the same issue when in 1944 he introduced secondary education for all. Charles Kingsley contended that it should be free, arguing from his knowledge of social conditions that unless it was parents would find it difficult to pay fees, however small, and if compelled to do so they would be more than ever hostile to a system of compulsory education. Matthew Arnold, on the other hand, thought that compulsion and fee-paying could co-exist, observing that 'in Prussia, where schooling is compulsory, and really compulsory, there is no primary school which does not levy a school fee, though a low one.'[2]

Having accepted in a limited way the principle of compulsion in 1870, the Victorian Parliament pursued a policy of gradualism, but it operated with more speed than such policies usually do. In 1880 they passed a law making elementary education generally compulsory, and in 1891 another Act abolished fees in all but a few elementary schools. The voluntary schools, which for long regarded 'children's pence' as a necessary and traditional source of income, were compensated by an extra government grant (the Act of 1918 made all elementary education free, abolishing the few exceptions). By the end of the nineteenth century, therefore, elementary education in this country had become com-

1. See W. F. Connell, *Educational Thought and Influence of Matthew Arnold* (Routledge and Kegan Paul, 1950), pp. 124–6.
2. *Educational Thought and Influence of Matthew Arnold*, p. 129.

pulsory, and with a few exceptions free. The foundations of our law of school attendance had been securely laid.

If we now examine the parent's place in our educational system to-day, we shall be able to note the structure built on this Victorian foundation. The 1944 Act, except in one instance, always refers to 'the Parent' in the singular, and it is usual to regard the father as responsible under the law for the education of his children.[1] But in these days when fathers are often absent on service or at work away from home and when there are a number of broken homes, it is not always practicable to adhere to the usual interpretation. So the 1944 Act defines 'the parent' as including 'a guardian and every person who has actual custody of the child.'

The parent is still 'compelled', as he has been since 1880, but there are two fundamental changes. Of these, one is the change in what the law requires of the parent. Until 1944 the stress was on literacy: every parent was required 'to cause his child to receive efficient elementary instruction in reading, writing, and arithmetic.' To-day the obligation imposed on the parent is much stiffer: to cause his child 'to receive efficient full-time education suitable to his age, ability, and aptitude, either by regular attendance at school or otherwise.' The other change, no less revolutionary, is one of attitude or relationship. In the years after 1880 many parents were definitely hostile to education, and regarded the 'School Board man', as the attendance officer was commonly called, as an enemy. Indeed in some localities these officers had to operate in pairs because of the rough handling that awaited them if unaccompanied. The conditions which Matthew Arnold specified as a prerequisite of a compulsory system had not been fulfilled, and its administration was full of difficulties.

To-day the practice of regular attendance is generally accepted, and parents usually appreciate the educational

1. The exception is in regard to boarding school education, where the Act evidently intends that both parents should have an opportunity of saying that they prefer a boarding school education for their child.

opportunities available for their children. 'Gradually the school attendance officer has outgrown completely the hostility that he encountered as "the School Board man", and although he still has to prosecute, the number of obstinate and irresponsible parents is now relatively small; the experience of school attendance committees has shown that the absences due to parental failure are not more than about ten per cent. There are however other causes of absence, social and domestic, which call for sympathy and help and not for severity. Further, it has become more and more appreciated that in the social background of education, there is good work to be done if children are to profit by their schooling; and there has been a tendency to assign more and more of these humane services to the school attendance department.'[1] So the formidable School Board man of the last century has evolved to become the friendly, helpful School Welfare Officer of to-day.

The modern parent has some further responsibilities under the law besides that of seeing that his children receive an appropriate education. He must allow them, when in school, to undergo medical inspection. And so that there may be early ascertainment of disabilities, he can, if he has a child of pre-school age thought to be suffering from some defect, be required when the child has reached the age of two to submit him for medical examination. And if the local authority decides that his child needs special educational treatment at a Special School he must agree to his attendance there between the ages of five and sixteen.

But parents also have valuable rights and safeguards under the law. Of these an important one is the right to appeal to the Minister who, as we noted in an earlier chapter, has power to override any decision by a local authority that he deems unreasonable. And the Minister himself can be appealed against, for under our parliamentary system an aggrieved parent can have his complaint ventilated in the

1. W. O. Lester Smith, *Compulsory Education in England* (UNESCO, 1951), p. 30.

House of Commons by a member of parliament. The conscience clause enables a parent to secure that his children do not receive religious teaching or attend worship if he does not wish it. The 1944 Act also provides that 'so far as is compatible with the provision of efficient instruction and training and the avoidance of unreasonable public expenditure, pupils are to be educated in accordance with the wishes of their parents.'[1] It is proving a difficult clause to administer, especially as regards the selection of a child's secondary school, and although local authorities normally consider sympathetically all that a parent has to say, the administration of the clause has been a source of contention and even litigation.[2] Parents also have the right to ask that their child shall receive a boarding school education, and this is arranged if the local authority agrees that it is desirable.

These legalities can, however, easily occupy too much of our attention, conveying a false impression of the place parents occupy in our modern educational system. For to-day the emphasis is not on parental rights and obligations, but on co-operation and goodwill. As evidence of this we need only remind ourselves of the remarkable growth of parent-teacher and similar associations. There are now said to be at least 2,000 parent-teacher associations, and there can be few schools without some definite organization for establishing a close and friendly relationship with parents. This movement is a good omen for the future of education in this country. For, as has been rightly said, such societies 'stimulate the idea that the schools belong to the people, and that their improvement lies in the people's hands.'[3]

1. Clause 76. See also Clause 37 (2) and (3).
2. For a criticism, see article by A. C. F. Beales on 'The Future of Voluntary Schools' in *Looking Forward in Education*, p. 100.
3. *Social Group Work in Great Britain*, edited by P. Kuenstler (Faber, 1954). Article by Mary Morris on 'Adult Groups', p. 125.

Independent Schools

As we have just noted, the law leaves parents free to decide in what way their children shall receive an appropriate education. A minority – less than ten per cent – choose to send them to schools outside the national system; and in this category there are some of the best in the country and at the other extreme a few – the Dotheboys Halls of to-day – that, in the words of a Departmental Committee's Report, 'are harmful to the mental and physical welfare of their pupils.' To protect children from the injustice of being sent to the bad type of private school, the 1944 Act provided for the establishment of a register of independent schools; and schools will not be accepted for registration if the premises are unsuitable, the accommodation inadequate, the teaching inefficient or the proprietor not a fit person to be in charge of a school. These provisions of the Act came into operation in 1957 and any-one now conducting an unregistered school is liable to certain prescribed penalties. Proprietors of schools refused registration may appeal to an Independent Schools Tribunal.

The provision of the 1944 Act for the establishment of a Register of Independent Schools is, however, not only important as a preventive of bad schools. It is also significant as a reaffirmation by Parliament of our traditional doctrine that parents should be free to send their children to schools outside the national system, if they so wish. Even strong believers in a controlling state have shown no desire to depart from this doctrine. 'I do not favour private education,' declared Aneurin Bevan, 'but I would not prohibit it, pro-vided the welfare of children is safeguarded by State inspec-tion. In a class society I am afraid it is impossible wholly to prevent class education. Different levels of income will always find expression in different standards of expenditure. The permanent solution is greater equality in the distribu-tion of wealth.'[1] But he added that he was opposed to any

1. *Tribune*, 7 January 1955.

state financing, either directly or indirectly, of schools outside the national system.

The Public Schools

During the Second World War there was much said and written about the future of the Public Schools, and for two main reasons. Those who valued the Public Schools feared that economic conditions after the war would make it impossible for many of them to continue without some support from government or local funds. On the other hand, their critics contended that, as their pupils were mainly drawn from the upper middle class, they would be out of place in a society becoming increasingly egalitarian. But, said Mr Rex Warner, in a book written during the controversy, 'on one point all agree, that the Public Schools are, for good or evil, important; and indeed the fact is self-evident, as may be shown by an investigation into the antecedents of any Cabinet or any powerful group of interests, whether economic, political, ecclesiastical, military, or educational.'[1]

In the hope of bridging the gulf between the Public Schools and the national system, Mr Butler in 1942 set up a committee under the chairmanship of Lord Fleming which two years later presented the document now known as the Fleming Report. Its terms of reference were: 'To consider means whereby the association between the Public Schools (by which term is meant schools which are in membership of the Governing Bodies' Association or Headmasters' Conference) and the general educational system of the country could be developed and extended: also to consider how far any measures recommended in the case of boys' Public Schools could be applied to comparable schools for girls.' This, as the Fleming Committee observed, gives an entirely new definition of a Public School. 'Most people,' they said, 'when they speak of a Public School mean a Boarding

1. *English Public Schools* (Collins, 1945), p. 7.

School, and are probably thinking only of a small number of expensive independent Boarding Schools. The Public Schools, according to our terms of reference, consist of 89 independent schools and 99 schools which are aided either by grants from the Board of Education or by the Local Education Authorities. Thus more than half the Public Schools with which we are concerned already receive aid in some form or other from public funds, and about half are entirely or mainly Day Schools. At some of the latter, the education given is no more expensive than that given at many Aided or Maintained Schools outside our terms of reference, and is not appreciably different in quality or kind.'[1]

So the Committee wisely divided their task into two distinct parts: (1) the Boarding Schools, and (2) the schools already receiving grants from public funds. The first was the difficult problem – how to associate in the national system these very independent boarding schools. Although their ideals are largely shared by most schools in this country, and their curriculum is that of the grammar school, they have some distinctive characteristics. They attach great importance to the prefect system both as a method of school government and as a training in leadership. They usually arrange for their pupils to live in separate houses where under the influence of a house-master they can learn by experience the arts of living together as members of a small community. They set great store upon prowess in team games, and almost venerate their playing fields. But they value especially the school chapel, its worship being an integral part of their community life and their education. All but twelve of the independent boarding schools are closely linked with a religious denomination. Three other characteristics should be noted. All these schools have independent governing bodies, on which public authorities are seldom represented: and they are in effect self-governing corporations. And

1. *Report of the Committee on Public Schools and the General Educational System*, p. 2.

although unlike the proprietary private schools they are non-profit-making, yet they are obliged to charge high fees largely because of the generous staffing and the absence of government grant. And partly for this reason, with certain rare exceptions, like Christ's Hospital, they draw their pupils from a limited class.

The Fleming Committee came to the conclusion that the best way of associating these schools with the national system would be by the provision of bursaries for qualified pupils. They suggested that some should be awarded by the Ministry and others by local authorities. It was hoped that this would result in those schools that decided to participate recruiting at first about 25 per cent of their pupils from the primary schools, and that eventually these boarding schools would 'be equally accessible to all pupils.'[1] The Report is an admirable document that will repay study by anyone interested in the history and the future of the Public Schools, or in the *pros* and *cons* of a boarding school education. But a more detailed account here of its proposals for associating these boarding schools with the national system would be of little practical value; for the proposals have, as many at the time surmised they would, proved singularly ineffective.

It is, therefore, more profitable to consider why this projected scheme of bursaries failed. Many factors have no doubt contributed to the stalemate situation that now prevails. But the fact that the Ministry itself did not implement its own special part in the scheme was not particularly encouraging. Instead the Minister stimulated local authorities to enter into arrangements with these independent boarding schools, and several did so. But the total number of admissions under local authority auspices has never been large – ten years after the Fleming Committee was appointed it was estimated that only about 2,000 pupils in these schools were being assisted by local authorities.[2]

1. *Report of the Committee on Public Schools and the General Educational System*, p. 66.
2. See Article by H. Raymond King in *Year Book of Education*, 1952.

An important factor has undoubtedly been the high cost of education in good boarding schools. For a few pupils the provision of such schooling can be well justified – e.g. for children of parents who because of their employment have to reside out of the country or have no settled home life. Health, home circumstances, instability, and neglect were advanced by some as good grounds for selection for a boarding school education, but other more appropriate residential schooling is available for many children in these categories and unless such children showed good promise of ability they were unlikely to commend themselves to the authorities of the independent boarding schools. Further, it is vital to the success of a scheme of this character that the assisted children should be able by their merits to establish for themselves a reputation in no sense inferior to that of their fellow pupils.

But merit did not prove an acceptable determinant either. For there was a strong feeling that it would be an unjustifiable slight upon the good secondary day schools in the child's locality to 'cream off' the ablest children and encourage their parents to agree to send them to Public Schools. Selection by merit was further complicated by the fact that the normal age of admission to public schools is thirteen and the normal age of transfer to secondary education under the national system eleven to twelve. The Fleming Committee made various suggestions for overcoming this difficulty, and it is possible that if there had been a strong demand from parents for a public school education for their children this difficulty would not have proved, as it did, an obstacle to the success of the Fleming Scheme.

But experience has shown that parents are not nearly so keen on a boarding school education for their children as some of the witnesses heard by the Fleming Committee said they would be. 'In most areas', says a writer after a careful study of local reactions to the Fleming Scheme, 'there has been a lack of applications for subsidized places. It would seem that apart from those families where it is traditional to use the independent schools, there is no effective demand for a public school education. This relative indifference contrasts strikingly with the strength of demand for places in secondary grammar schools.[1] It should also be noted that a few local authorities have established their own boarding schools, while others are able to arrange for children, whose home circumstances or distance from school make it desirable, to be accommodated in hostels associated with grammar schools in their area.

For these and other reasons the problem of building a bridge between the Public Schools and the national system has proved intractable; and in any diagnosis of the problem, it should not be forgotten that there is a substantial body of opinion that does not want this kind of bridge to be built.[2] So the future of the public schools remains one of the major unresolved issues of our time. If the incidence of taxation should deprive them of the steady support of the social classes that they normally serve, it will become an issue that can no longer be shelved. In that event some form of association with the national system will doubtless be discussed with more sense of urgency. 'If it cannot be achieved,' Sir Ernest Barker once observed, 'the future of the boarding public school is dark and dubious.'[3] Meanwhile, as the Fleming Committee remarks, 'the trend of social development is leaving the Public Schools out of alignment with the world in which they exist.'[4]

The other problem that the Fleming Committee had to consider was relatively simple; for the schools concerned were already in receipt of government grants, were mainly day schools, and had a fairly close relationship with the local authorities of the areas in which their pupils lived. The most debatable question the Fleming Committee had to decide about them was whether they should continue to charge fees

1. Olive Banks, *Parity and Prestige in English Secondary Education*, p.237.

2. See, for example, the Labour Party's pamphlet, *Challenge to Britain*, 1953, p. 24.

3. *Britain and the British People*, p. 100.

4. Report of the Committee on the *Public Schools and the General Educational System*, p. 30.

when all secondary education within the national system became free. As usual, there was a compromise. Regulations issued by the Ministry of Education in 1945, based largely on the Fleming Committee's advice, allow these Direct Grant Schools, as they are officially called, to charge approved fees for half the places in the school. But the fees have to be graded in accordance with an approved income scale. The other half of the admissions are free places or places reserved for local authority entrants.

There were 232 direct grant grammar schools at the time of the Fleming Report, but the total was subsequently reduced to 164. It has, however, since been increased to 179. Among these direct grant schools are some of our most famous day schools such as Manchester Grammar School and the North London Collegiate School for girls, founded over a century ago by Frances Mary Buss. One can sense their quality and gain some idea of the intellectual stimulus such schools afford from these words of the late Sir Ernest Barker, one of the major prophets of our time, about his days as a pupil at the former school. 'What a mother it was!' he wrote. 'It gave me a great drill and a stirring stimulus. Some men may find . . . that their college days have meant more to them, and left them with more of the permanent friendships of life than their days at school. I can hardly say that it was so with me. My school meant at least as much to me as my college. It taught me to work, to read, and to think. It gave me great friendships. It filled me entirely and utterly for nearly the space of seven years. Outside the cottage I had nothing but school, but having school I had everything.'[1]

1. *Father of the Man* (National Council of Social Service, 1948), p. 65.

CHAPTER EIGHT

EDUCATION AND INDUSTRY

Education as a Preparation for Life

Most of us in some way or another think of education as a preparation for life. 'Life – that's the trade I would teach him,' said Rousseau when planning the education of little Émile. And Herbert Spencer describes the main purpose of education as 'preparation for living'. This at least is certain, that no one can get far in his thoughts about education without considering what man needs to make the best of life. Such reflections can take us into countries of the mind familiar only to those learned in the disciplines of philosophy. But our own experience tells us that however the world changes, much that we need to learn to acquit ourselves well in life's campaign is unchangeable. Although education is sensitive to social change, and differs much from one country to another, it is no less true that many of the lessons it should teach are unaffected by time or place. There are certain immutable rules, fundamental to character, that all must learn and observe to be decent members of society. They are, as Sophocles reminds us in the *Antigone*,

> Unwritten laws, eternal in the heavens,
> Not of to-day or yesterday.

On the other hand, it is no less important for education, as a preparation for living, to provide the knowledge and training necessary for life in a particular country at a particular time. It is the duty of home and school to do their best to equip children with the essentials for leading a useful and satisfying life in the context of contemporary society. These two aspects of education, the changeless and the changeable, are interdependent, for it is important that the eternal laws, such as those concerning good and evil, should be related to actual problems and immediate challenges. Teaching of any kind that ignores actual conditions and present need can be irrelevant and time-wasting. Years ago we used to hear tales of children in the heart of Africa learning by rote the dates of the Kings and Queens of England or the names of the ports, capes and bays on the coast-line of this little island. But we need not go so far afield for examples of irrelevance; there can be few of us who teach, or have taught, innocent of the offence.

Teaching cannot always be up to date. There is an inevitable time-lag between the discovery of new knowledge and new skills and the teaching of them; 'the academies', said Bagehot, 'are asylums of the ideas and the tastes of the last age.'[1] New knowledge takes time to percolate: and we must not expect to find the latest discovery or the newest techniques in schools or in the text-books that they use:

> Non, non, ce n'est point comme à l'Académie,
> Ce n'est point comme à l'Académie.

In these days of rapid change it is more than ever possible for the curriculum and its exposition to be out-moded; and we can also, so swiftly does the kaleidoscope move, find ourselves, as we grow older, hopelessly out of step with our pupils. 'Because of the fantastic rate of change of the world in which we live,' says Miss Margaret Mead, giving an anthropologist's view of the nature of the problems that confront teachers to-day, 'children of five have already incorporated into their everyday thinking ideas that most of their elders will never fully assimilate. Within the life-time of the ten-year-olds the world has entered a new age, and already, before they enter the sixth grade the atomic age has been followed by the age of the hydrogen bomb. . . . Teachers who never heard a radio until they were grown up have to cope with children who never knew a world without television. . . . The children whom we bear, and rear, and teach are not only

1. *Physics and Politics* (Kegan Paul, 7th ed., 1885), p. 60.

unknown to us and unlike any children that have been in the world before, but also their degree of unlikeness itself alters from year to year.'[1] Such reflections lead her to the conclusion that special responsibilities that fall upon 'the new, emerging teacher' are those of (1) keeping as far as possible abreast with new knowledge and social change, and (2) discovering how best to prepare pupils for 'a world which does not yet exist'.

To the unavoidable difficulties that beset us when trying to make education a preparation for life, we are inclined to add others of our own making. We sometimes allow prejudice to stand in the way of reforms essential to bring education into line with the needs of the day. Consider, for example, our long refusal to admit science into the grammar school curriculum. Bacon's *New Atlantis*, published at the end of James I's reign, marks the beginning of a campaign to interest the nation in the study of the sciences and in scientific research, but the movement so well begun in the early years of the seventeenth century meandered hither and thither before it forced its way into the grammar school curriculum. The hostility and apathy that it encountered in academic circles now seem incredible. 'Rather than have Physical Science the principal thing in my son's mind,' wrote Dr Arnold, 'I would gladly have him think that the Sun went round the Earth, and that the Stars were merely spangles set in a bright blue firmament.' It was only after an arduous, uphill struggle in the second half of the nineteenth century, with T. H. Huxley throwing the whole weight of his forcible advocacy into the fray, that science crept into the curriculum, and it did not acquire much prestige as a subject of study until well into the present century. There are still quite a few people living who had a grammar school education in schools which made no provision for the teaching of any science.[2]

1. *The School in American Culture* (Harvard Univ. Press, 1951), pp. 33-4.
2. For a good account of the struggle to secure the introduction of science into the grammar school curriculum, see Archer, *Secondary Education in the XIX Century* (Oxford Univ. Press, 1921).

There has been a similar resistance to the provision of technical education at the secondary stage. It encountered until recently a two-fold opposition: (a) some were inclined to look down on it as socially inferior, and as certainly no part of a liberal education, and (b) others crabbed it as 'vocational', a capitalist device for exploiting children for the benefit of employers. Such attitudes are a hangover from a conception of society that originated in Ancient Greece, but has long since been discarded; they are, as John Dewey observed, relics of 'a political theory of a permanent division of human beings into those capable of a life of reason . . . and those capable only of desire and work.'[1]

There were two notable attempts towards the close of the nineteenth century to end this distinction between liberal and technical secondary education. The enlightened men who framed the Welsh Intermediate Education Act of 1889 took the unusual course of outlining in that Act the studies that the schools established under it would be expected to pursue. In that way they hoped to secure for Wales a system of secondary education unhampered by traditional assumptions about the curriculum. So in addition to the grammar school studies then usual, they specified 'natural and applied sciences', and included also subjects 'applicable to the purpose of agriculture, industries, trade, or commercial life and practice.' But these good intentions were largely frustrated, the academic tradition persisting and prevailing although 'there was in fact a great need, especially in rural areas, for schools which would undertake both "intermediate" and "technical" education.'[2]

Six years later the influential Bryce Commission made a vigorous plea for a new conception of secondary education, and sought by its arguments to show how stupid it was to exclude technical education at the secondary stage. 'Second-

1. John Dewey, *Democracy and Education*, p. 305. Quoted in Spens Report, Chapter V, p. 414.
2. *Report of the Consultative Committee on Secondary Education* (Spens Report), p. 343.

ary instruction is technical,' it contended, 'i.e. it teaches the boy so to apply the principles he is learning, and so to learn the principles that he is applying or so to use the instruments he is made to know, as to perform or produce something, interpret a literature or a science, make a picture or a book, practise a plastic or a manual art, convince a jury or persuade a senate, translate or annotate an author, dye wool, weave cloth, design or construct a machine, navigate a ship, or command an army.' And, it continued, 'Secondary education, therefore, as inclusive of technical, may be described as education conducted in view of the special life that has to be lived with the express purpose of forming a person fit to live it'.[1]

This wider conception of secondary education, however, proved unacceptable at that time. The secondary schools, founded under the 1902 Act, conformed to the grammar school tradition, though with an ever widening curriculum; and it was left to the Junior Technical and Central Schools to demonstrate the educative value of technical studies at the secondary stage. But the Spens Report (1938) with its strong emphasis on technical studies has brought us back sharply to the Bryce doctrine. And the 1944 Act by giving us secondary education for all has provided the opportunity, and indeed the necessity, for a new approach to the secondary curriculum. The old prejudices – the false antithesis of liberal and technical education and the groundless suspicions about vocational studies – have lost their icy grip; and we can look forward with more hope to the creation of an educational system that will provide a much better preparation for life and one more appropriate to this century of change and challenge.[2]

1. *Report of Royal Commission on Secondary Education* (1895), p. 136. Quoted in Spens Report, pp. 59–60.
2. For a good account of changing attitudes to the curriculum see H. C. Dent, *Change in English Education* (Univ. of London Press, 1952), Chapter IV.

Some Aspects of an Industrialized Society

It is a truism, though one sometimes not fully appreciated, that if education is to be a preparation for living it must be closely related to the kind of society in which the majority of the pupils are expected to live their lives. Ours is a highly industrialized society, and this affects our problems in education in two quite different ways. On the one hand, it conditions the home background of the majority of our children, and in their education we not only have to have regard to this background but also to the fact that the majority of them, when they grow up, will live their lives in a similar environment even though after the manner of this mobile age they move about from one district to another. On the other hand, it makes it necessary to provide an education designed to fit boys and girls when they grow up to help the country to maintain that eminence in industry and commerce on which our livelihood depends.

Although there are large tracts of our countryside that make it easy to forget it, ours is a very crowded island. Three hundred years ago the population of England and Wales was not more than about $6\frac{1}{2}$ millions; a century ago it had nearly reached 18 millions; but now, largely as a result of the longer span of life, the figure has mounted to 44 millions. The total for the United Kingdom is 50 millions. England itself has about 760 people to the square mile, as against some 190 in France, and rather more than 40 in the U.S.A. Less than 20 per cent of us live in areas that can fairly be classed as rural, and about two-fifths of the inhabitants of the United Kingdom are packed into the populous regions in and around London, Manchester, Birmingham, and Glasgow or in Merseyside, the West Riding of Yorkshire, and Tyneside.

The educational needs of areas of a very urban character are, therefore, for us a major problem. It is difficult to generalize about such areas or the problems that they create: for there are wide differences. For example, a teacher's task in a suburban school is by no means the same as in a school surrounded by slum dwellings that still await clearance. Dockside, central areas, housing estates, new towns all present their special problems, nor are they static problems. For districts change their character, and how and why they do so can be a fascinating human story when told by someone with a gift for writing with imaginative insight about man and his environment. Sometimes such studies take the form of childhood recollections, and they then often shed a still brighter light on educational problems. With the skill of a master H. G. Wells gives us in *The New Macchiavelli* his childhood memories of a developing suburb during the heyday of the speculative builder, and recently Richard Church with the penetrating vision and word mastery of a poet has in *Over the Bridge* told us how he and his brother in childhood reacted to social change and satisfied their desire for adventure in an area of London south of the river. James Kenward too has written sensitively about *The Suburban Child* of a generation ago, and had the good fortune to get Edward Ardizzone to illustrate his story. 'Parks are unjungular,' his childhood memories remind him, 'they have so obviously been explored.'

While our urbanized areas differ so much and undergo so many changes, it is broadly true that all who grow up in them share the advantages and disadvantages of life in a mass society. This, to make an obvious point, is very different from the quiet, unhurried life of a rural environment, and different also from the life our forebears lived before the industrial revolution. That life was often one of grim poverty and much social injustice, 'but,' to quote G. M. Trevelyan, 'migration to the factories had meant loss as well as gain. The beauty of field and hedge, the immemorial customs of rural life – the village green and its games, the harvest home, the tithe feast, the May Day rites, the field sports – had supplied a humane background and an age-long tradition to temper poverty. They were not reproduced in mine or factory, or in the rows of mass-produced brick-dwellings erected to house the hands.'[1] The traditional social relationships based on neighbourhood

1. *English Social History*, pp. 475–6.

were destroyed, and no attempt was made except by a very few enlightened employers to provide in the new urban setting any opportunities for decent living. It is a sad fact that when men discover some new source of wealth – coal, diamonds, oil, or what you will – they set about exploiting it with little regard for human well-being.

Much has been done to repair the damage to our own society caused by the industrial revolution, but there are some who hold that it dealt a blow from which our culture shows little sign of recovery. After remarking that it destroyed 'the popular culture that had enriched Shakespeare's England', Professor M. V. C. Jeffreys contends: 'In default of a true popular culture, the mass of the people – so long denied opportunity for profitable recreation – have readily accepted a sham culture of which the cinema is the most powerful single vehicle. Since we have neither a unified view of life in which our knowledge and ideas all find their place, nor a live cultural tradition in which all sections of the community share, it follows that we have no adequate cultural interpretation of our contemporary world. Our culture is too incoherent and fragmentary to give us spiritual or even intellectual mastery of our situation.'[1]

Our Welfare State has not so far given much attention to the cultural and social needs of its citizens: the emphasis has been on material necessities, on the standard of living rather than on the quality of life. The metropolises of our great conurbations certainly offer valuable cultural and educational opportunities, but the scope of the leisure-life in the areas clustered around them varies greatly as does that of the neighbourhoods that compose them. For growing up in a mass society, it is the educative quality of the neighbourhood that matters most and if it lacks a sense of community an urbanized neighbourhood can be depressingly impersonal and soul destroying:

> What life have you, if you have not life together
> There is no life that is not in community.

1. *Glaucon*, p. 48.

Much consideration is now being given to the conditions under which people work: to problems of management, works' councils, industrial fatigue, questions of lighting, humidity and noise, and so forth. And recently the industrial psychologist, recognizing the wisdom of Aristotle's famous saying that 'man is a social animal', has turned his attention to social life within the factory and shown by experiment that it has an important bearing on the worker's well-being and on morale.[1] But as yet we have done comparatively little to improve the social and recreative life in places where these same workers live. As a result mass entertainment is the characteristic recreation of the mass society. It is no criticism of this form of entertainment to suggest that it is no substitute for an interesting, active neighbourhood life in which the individual counts and can in a congenial group succeed in his natural quest for significance.

In many neighbourhoods much has been accomplished by voluntary effort with little official encouragement. In some places the adult education movement is well established and greatly appreciated: there are now more than 800 community centres, and there are innumerable clubs under the auspices of the various organizations within the youth service. There are areas, too, where the Arts Council has met with remarkable success, stimulating an interest in art, music, and drama. And we have in the 1944 Act a clause that makes it the duty of Local Education Authorities to secure the provision of adequate facilities for 'the leisure-time occupation' of the people.[2] But it has never been administered with enthusiasm, and has always been at the tail end of the priority queue. As a result, in spite of much praiseworthy voluntary enterprise, the educational, social, and recreative needs of our industrialized society, so long ignored, are still not being met with any degree of adequacy.

1. See Elton Mayo, *The Social Problems of an Industrial Civilization* (Routledge and Kegan Paul, 1949), and J. A. C. Brown, *The Social Psychology of Industry* (Penguin Books, 1954).
2. Clause 41 (b).

Education for Citizenship in an Industrial Society

At the beginning of the last section it was suggested that a highly industrialized society sets the educator two distinct problems: (1) that of providing an education helpful to those living in populous areas, and (2) that of providing an education helpful to our industry and commerce. Let us now briefly examine this second problem. It raises in an interesting form the issue we considered in Chapter Two, namely whether you should in education put the stress on individual development or on the claims of society. In this country, as we then noted, we try to maintain a reasonable balance, and sometimes describe our aim in a phrase used by the Hadow Committee in their report on *The Education of the Adolescent* – 'social individuality'.

No one in our time has urged the claims of the individual more effectively than Lord Russell, and his opinion, therefore, on this issue is of particular interest. 'Considered *sub specie aeternitatis*,' he observes, 'the education of the individual is to my mind a finer thing than the education of the citizen, but considered politically, in relation to the needs of the time, the education of the citizen must, I fear, take the first place.'[1] In practice the two aims are often not incompatible, for children and young people are more interested, and therefore develop more naturally, when their studies are related to the actualities of life. In World War II many a boy, who had taken little interest in mathematics hitherto, worked at it with zest when, as a member of the Air Training Corps, he discovered its bearing on mechanics and the problems of flight. The war-time government training schemes for the rapid development of technical skills provided many illustrations of similar development of latent capacity.

One of the chief attributes of good citizenship is a desire to serve the community, and one of the most important services that a citizen can perform is that of helping in an industrial or

1. *Education and the Social Order* (Allen & Unwin), pp. 27–8.

commercial occupation to maintain the standard of living. Over 600,000 boys and girls in Great Britain enter employment every year, and on their aptitude and attitude to work the material well-being of our Welfare State largely depends. Effective citizenship also requires some understanding of contemporary affairs, and as we live in a scientific and technological age this involves a familiarity with the achievements of science and technology.

For such reasons there would seem to be a strong case for emphasis on scientific and technical studies in our curriculum. 'If industrialism and democracy are the outstanding and significant forces in the modern world,' says Sir Walter Moberley, 'no philosophy of life or of education, which gives to them only a secondary place and a subsidiary function, can hope to convince.'[1] This applies not only to the university stage but no less to the whole range of education. It should, for example, not be forgotten that interests and attitudes are formed early in life, and it is important, therefore, to remember the significance of the junior school as the place where the prospective citizen often acquires from his teachers view-points that remain through life.

It is in the formative years of childhood that the foundations of citizenship are laid, and the well-being of our community life is much affected by the interpretation of service communicated at this stage. In her excellent book on *Activity in the Primary School* Miss M. V. Daniel assigns three 'functions' to education at this stage: (1) the development of mind and body, (2) the needs of the community, and (3) the preparation for everyday life. Discussing this third function, she observes: 'Vocational training in the limited sense certainly has no place in Junior School work; but in our modern society the ability to read, write, and perform the elementary processes in Arithmetic are essential for every occupation and for the simplest requirements of our community life. The Primary School is failing to fulfil its purpose, therefore, as long as it fails to teach the fundamental subjects upon which

1. *The Crisis in the University* (S.C.M. Press, 1949), p. 98.

earning a livelihood and taking part in the life of the community depend.'[1]

As to the secondary stage we have already in the first section of this chapter noted our traditional reluctance to admit technical studies into the curriculum. When the 1944 Act, by establishing secondary education for all, provided a new opportunity for doing so, many hoped that it would lead to the establishment of a large number of secondary technical schools, affording a good general education and, towards the end of the course, providing teaching related to major industries in the locality. Such hopes have, however, not been realized, and we have now only 204 schools of this type as against 3,906 secondary modern schools. 'There are too few of these schools,' Mr R. A. Butler observed, when commenting upon developments under the Act, 'and too many of those we have are poked away in corners of technical colleges and are failing to receive proper recognition and support.'[2]

Of the value of these secondary technical schools no one closely acquainted with them has any doubt. As a preparation for good citizenship in a modern industrial society, they could hardly be improved upon. Liberal studies are not neglected. Describing the life of a large Girls' Technical School in an area of new houses, the Headmistress writes: 'The school possesses a good library, and high in importance for the making of a good life I would place the teaching of English. . . . The English staff work to see that its thousands of books are well used. Every girl has her book list and is keen to read the volumes on it. Serious reading is giving the school literacy and culture. The influence of the library is incalculable.' And, again: 'The girls are very sophisticated but when the changing values and temptations of the outside world have to be faced, they may find this sophistication, allied

1. Blackwell, 1947, pp. 46, 47.
2. Lecture on 'The 1944 Act seen against the Pattern of the Times' in *Jubilee Lectures* (Evans, for Univ. of London Institute of Education, 1952), p. 53.

with the Christian principles and training we hope the school has given them, help provide a philosophy, with which they may face the world, and also help them to continue to appreciate things of lasting value when they have left school.'[1] With this background of a good general education, these schools also provide sound technical teaching designed to fit their pupils for their vocation, and ensure a good foundation for the abler ones who intend to proceed to Technical Colleges. For example, in the award of Higher National Certificates in mechanical engineering in 1952–3, 32 per cent of the successful candidates were products of the secondary technical school.[2]

While the prides and prejudices referred to in the first section of this chapter still act as a brake on the promotion of secondary technical schools, there are other promising developments at the secondary stage that should be noted. The new comprehensive schools have their technical sides, and more secondary schools are developing on multi- or bi-lateral lines with often a strong technical side. Such combinations may be expected to become more common; for they are well-suited to the educational needs of certain areas, and not least to those of rural communities. Agriculture is one of our great industries: in spite of many urban encroachments upon good fertile land, we produce enough food to feed nearly half of our teeming population, and having regard to the gravity of the world food situation it is our duty to produce still more. The reconstruction of education in the countryside is, therefore, important; and it is, also, one of the most fascinating problems of our time. 'Many people', it has been well said, 'have a somewhat emotional belief that the countryside represents the unchanging face of England. In fact, however, the country is changing and has changed far more than the towns in the last seventy years.'[3] And in this

1. *The School as a Christian Community*, pp. 101–2.

2. See P. F. R. Venables, *Technical Education* (Bell, 1955), p. 224.

3. Adam Curle, Article on 'Education and the Future in Rural Areas' in *Looking Forward in Education*, p. 156.

moving picture, advances in agricultural science and engineering are dynamic influences, making new demands on the curriculum not only in farm institutes but also in rural secondary schools of every type.

The Wide Range of Technical Education

We use the term 'technical education' very loosely in this country to cover a wide range of institutions, courses, and classes in a multiplicity of subjects. Its use at the secondary stage has already been noted, but for the remainder of this chapter it is proposed to consider only the provision made for students who have left the secondary school. Officially the term is interpreted to include education in technical, commercial, and art subjects for all students over compulsory school age; the number of students is increasing at all levels, and the approximate figures for England and Wales are now: Full-time 156,000, Sandwich Courses 19,000, Part-time Day 608,000, Evening (technical) 778,000, Evening Institutes 1,075,000.[1] The immense range of the subjects studied and of the courses and classes attended defies desscription, but some idea of their amazing diversity can be obtained by examining the relevant statistics included by the Ministry of Education in its annual publications or by looking at one of those attractive prospectuses issued as a guide for potential students by some Local Authority responsible for an area at the centre of one of the vast conurbations.[2]

Confusion sometimes arises from the contemporary fashion of speaking of 'technological education' as well as 'technical education'. Those who use these terms deliberately intend a distinction. By 'technological education' they mean education appropriate for students preparing for one of the professions requiring technical knowledge, e.g. a branch of

1. *Education in 1963* (H.M.S.O., 1964), pp. 34 and 56.
2. E.g. the London County Council's annual publication *Floodlight* or the Manchester Local Authority's *Opportunity*.

engineering, or for management in industry or commerce. And they restrict the more familiar term 'technical education' for use as a description of courses intended for craftsmen or technicians or for students seeking to qualify as such. It would, however, be difficult, if not impossible, to classify the various technical institutions on this basis; for colleges providing 'technological education' normally provide 'technical education' also.[1]

Ever since the seventeenth century technical education has had powerful advocates. The Royal Society, founded in 1662 by a group of influential men with a wide variety of scientific interests, had the promotion of technical studies as one of its main objectives. 'The practical or utilitarian motive was clearly present from the first,' Sir George Clark tells us, 'both in the narrower form of a desire to improve technology and in the wider form of a desire to promote national prosperity.'[2] And through the years technical education has always attracted the devoted support of all sorts of eminent persons – the Prince Consort, George Birkbeck, T. H. Huxley, Quintin Hogg, to mention but a few who from different motives rendered outstanding service. And the history of many of our Boroughs bears witness to the zeal with which enlightened local leaders promoted technical education.

It can also be claimed for technical education that it makes a wide appeal: for it benefits not only those who attend its courses and classes but also the firms which employ them. And, indeed, it benefits us all: for our standard of living is dependent on the efficiency and skill of all engaged in industry and commerce. But even so, advances in technical education have always been fitful and uneven; and although

1. For a masterly and encyclopaedic survey of the whole range of technical education, its aims and organization, see P. F. R. Venables, *Technical Education*. It includes chapters by specialist authors, dealing respectively with Engineering, Building, Art, Women in Further Education, and Commerce.

2. *Science and Social Welfare in the Age of Newton* (Oxford Univ. Press, 2nd edition, 1949), pp. 12–13.

we have many technical colleges and institutions of which we can be justly proud, the general provision has never kept pace with our industrial and commercial needs or been worthy of our position as a great industrial nation.

This record of slow and uneven development is no doubt due to a variety of social and economic factors. One, surely was the comparative ease with which our industry and commerce prospered: there was a long period when complacency about our technical prowess and commercial abilities appeared to be justified: it seemed not improper then to claim that

> Time and the ocean and some favouring star
> In high cabal have made us what we are.

One of the great events in our industrial history is the Great Exhibition of 1851, prototype of our Festival of Britain a century later. At that time the Prince Consort, and those who with him were instrumental in promoting the Exhibition, believed that it would prove a great stimulus to technical education. Lord Playfair, one of the leading protagonists of technical education at that period, seized the opportunity to stump the country on behalf of the cause he had so much at heart. He subsequently recorded in his diary his impressions of his campaign. 'Having great faith in the education of public opinion,' he wrote, 'I began a crusade in favour of Technical Education. It was weary and dreary work. My voice sounded to myself as the voice of one preaching in the wilderness.' Twenty-five years later Sir Philip Magnus, another staunch advocate of technical education, commenting on these depressing words, remarked: 'The experience of others has not been very different.'[1] Indeed all who labour for the advancement of technical education must often find it heavy going.[2]

1. Lecture on 'Industrial Education' in *Education in the Nineteenth Century*, edited by R. D. Roberts (Cambridge Univ. Press, 1901), p. 159.
2. For an outline of the history of technical education since 1851 see M. Argles, *South Kensington to Robbins* (Longmans, 1964).

The Percy Report and its Consequences

World War II led to a change of outlook: economic survival and defence against possible aggression made an increasing supply of technologists and technicians an imperative necessity. In 1944 a Departmental Committee was appointed, with Lord Percy as its chairman, to consider the needs of higher technological education in England and Wales, and the respective contributions that universities and technical colleges might be expected to make.[1] It reported in the following year, and although its report covers no more than some thirty pages it is a constructive document of much importance.

Among its main recommendations were: (1) The selection of a strictly limited number of Technical Colleges in which there should be developed courses of a standard comparable with that of a university degree course. The colleges should, as far as possible, be self-governing. (2) The award by these colleges (which the report describes as Colleges of Technology) of a qualification corresponding in standard 'with the University first degree' and conforming to a national standard. (There was a difference of opinion about the title to be assigned to this qualification. The Chairman contributes a most interesting note on this point, which explains why in his opinion the award could not have the title of a degree. 'In all civilized countries,' he observes, 'the power to confer degrees is the distinguishing mark of a University.'[2]) (3) A few National Schools of Technology for the needs of small but important industries should be established within existing colleges. (4) 'Sandwich Courses' should be developed. These are courses in which the student spends part of his College course in full-time study in college, and part in industry. (5) The development of research in connexion with

1. *Higher Technological Education* (H.M.S.O., 1945). For complete terms of reference, see p. 3.
2. P. 25.

advanced technological studies. (6) Regional Advisory Councils and Academic Boards should be established throughout England and Wales.

How relevant these recommendations were to the contemporary situation may be gauged from the fact that they have all figured prominently in post-war policy and discussion concerning technological education. Items 3 to 5 above proved comparatively non-controversial, and there were some interesting developments along the lines proposed. A few national colleges for small but important industries have been established. The development of 'sandwich courses' has been accelerated as a result of current policy.[1] Research has been encouraged, but more is needed.[2] Ten Regional Advisory Councils and Academic Boards were set up in 1946, and as an apex of this elaborate regional structure a National Advisory Council of seventy-two members was constituted. The latter has been charitably described as 'a somewhat cumbrous body'.[3] As to the regional councils and boards, it is questionable whether they are worth the time and effort they consume.[4]

Real progress along the lines of the important recommendations summarized in items (1) and (2) was held up by a prolonged and somewhat discreditable controversy. It had various side-lines but the central issue of the dispute was whether the nation should look to the universities or the major technical colleges for the increasing number of technologists so sorely needed. In this conflict the universities received some influential support at a high level, and the first major decision of the Government was a subsidy to enable the Imperial College of Science and Technology, a constituent college of London University, to double its intake of students. Controversy in any sphere of education usually

1. See White Paper: *Technical Education* (Cmd 9703, H.M.S.O., 1956).
2. Ministry of Education, Circular 94.
3. H. C. Dent, *Growth in English Education*, p. 137.
4. For a critical examination of the system of regional councils, see P. F. R. Venables, *Technical Education*, pp. 135–41.

has a paralysing influence on policy, and this rather stupid battle had just that effect. Too much attention was given to the 'university or technical college' issue, and far too little to the urgent need for an expansion and reconstruction of technical education as a whole. While students were coming forward in ever-increasing numbers, the provision for them in existing institutions was proving more and more inadequate. The number of full-time university students of science (excluding medicine) and technology rose from 12,949 in 1938–9 to 29,013 in 1955–6, an increase of 124 per cent. These students represented 34.5 per cent of the university population as against 26 per cent in 1938–9. In technical institutions the increase in this period was: full-time, 25,000 to 74,000; part-time day, 92,000 to 427,000; evening, 1,268,000 to 1,781,000.[1]

Now, largely as a result of the Robbins Report, the pattern of higher education in Britain is changing rapidly. It envisages about 60 institutions of university status by 1980, including six more new universities, the colleges of advanced technology (already accorded university status), five S.I.S.T.E.R.s (special institutions of scientific and technological education and research).

The New Prospect for Technical Education

What had been particularly lacking during those years of expanding student-population was a strong lead at the centre and a dynamic national policy. There was too much argument: and too little action. But once it was appreciated how rapidly technological and technical education were expanding in the U.S.S.R. and the U.S.A. the hollowness and futility of the 'university or technical college' controversy was thoroughly exposed. 'It is clear,' said Professor P. M. S. Blackett, 'that the present large output of Soviet scientists and technologists has been brought about by a long-range plan initiated in the middle 1930s with the avowed object of

1. White Paper on *Technical Education*, 1956.

first equalling and then surpassing the technology of the west. Since in technology as in war, victory in the long run and on the average goes to the big battalions – of engineers and scientists – the Soviet Union seems likely eventually to achieve her aim if the west does not do something about it.'[1]

The massive developments in the U.S.S.R. and to a somewhat lesser degree in the U.S.A. created a sense of urgency here that had been conspicuously lacking hitherto. The Government acknowledged that the universities could only meet 'a fraction' of the need, and that therefore 'an increasing share must be taken by the technical colleges'. There was also a growing recognition of the urgent need for a better provision for the education of technicians. Can we, it was asked, continue to be content with a system of technical education that, in spite of the remarkable growth of part-time day release, is still mainly a night school education, attended by students at the end of their day's work? And as regards day release, it was noted that the readiness of employers to co-operate varied greatly. While the engineering, ship-building, and electrical goods industries released 90 per cent of their boys under eighteen, in some other large industries the percentage was relatively small.

In March 1956 the Government outlined a new policy for Technical Education and, although long experience of hope deferred begets caution, it was now possible to anticipate with some confidence a period of expansion, reconstruction, and reform.[2] There is an immense task to be accomplished before we can hope to secure an adequate system of technical education, but there has been substantial progress since the policy of advance was decided upon, and in the light of the Robbins Report it is now possible to get some idea of the shape of things to come.

We can expect a big increase in the number of students in higher education: the Robbins plans provide for 560,000 by

1. The second of his Lees Knowles lectures, as reported in *The Times*, 3 March 1956.
2. The new policy is outlined in the White Paper *Technical Education*.

1980 as against 216,000 in 1963. Many more will proceed to post-graduate studies and technological research: 30 per cent instead of the present 20. We shall have a chain of technological universities. There will be the five S.I.S.T.E.R.s (Imperial College, Manchester College of Science and Technology, one of the colleges of advanced technology, the University of Strathclyde, and one new foundation): and there will also be the other former Colleges of Advanced Technology awarding as universities their first and higher degrees.

We may expect, too, a substantial increase in the number of 'sandwich courses', and important changes in the system of grants and awards to students at universities and technical colleges.[1] Instead of the former National Council for Technological Awards there will be a National Council for Academic Awards empowered to grant degrees to students, especially those in regional and area colleges. Among girls of eighteen only one in five is pursuing any form of further education. We may expect, therefore, a campaign to correct this tendency of girls to stop their education when they leave school. There is likely to be a considerable expansion of colleges of further education and other technical institutions, and a great effort to secure a large increase in the number of young workers released by industry for part-time day study.

The demand for technicians – it is estimated that for every technologist five or six technicians are needed – may have some interesting repercussions on the curriculum of the secondary modern school, and there is certainly much to be said for a close and co-operative liaison between these schools and the technical colleges and farm institutes.[2] But the most formidable task of all will be to find teachers of the right calibre and with suitable qualifications for an advance on

1. See *Grants to Students*, Anderson Committee report (H.M.S.O., 1960).
2. For an interesting exposition of the case for an easier pathway from the secondary modern school to the technical college, see Address by Dr E. Williams, Principal of Hendon Technical College, reported in *The Times Educational Supplement*, 2 March 1956.

such a wide front. Many more will be required, but it is not only a question of numbers but even more, bearing in mind the influence of teacher upon student, is it one of finding men and women with a high sense of vocation.[1]

The Balance of the Curriculum

William Temple used to say – and with great emphasis – that the greatest educational issue of our time is the proper balance of the curriculum. A pupil's environment, he once declared, 'exists at three levels – the sub-human, studied in the Natural Sciences; the human, studied in the Humanities; and the super-human, studied in Divinity. The school must provide for all three.' The growing pressure on the schools to produce more and more potential technologists and technicians has given this issue an immediate and inescapable urgency. If we interpret the demands of our technocrats too narrowly, we shall endanger the quality of our citizenship by producing too many people unduly specialized in their branch of technology or their particular technical craft. And if we do that, we shall fail completely in our duty to make education a preparation for life.

The Central Advisory Council for Education (England) considered some aspects of this problem when, under the chairmanship of Sir Geoffrey Crowther, it drew up what is generally known as the Crowther Report. While given wide terms of reference by the Minister of Education in regard to the education of boys and girls between the ages of fifteen and eighteen, it was asked by him 'in particular to consider the balance at various levels of general and specialized studies between these ages'. One of the most constructive sections of the report deals with the balance of studies in 'The Sixth Form'. While the Council endorsed the principle of specialization at this stage, it was clearly unhappy about some of the ways in which it was operating. It noted, for

1. See *The Supply and Training of Teachers for Technical Colleges*, report of Willis Jackson Committee (H.M.S.O., 1957).

instance, that science syllabuses make considerably heavier demands than they used to do, and their radical revision was urged. The Council's enquiries, also, led them to the conclusion that the combination of subjects offered by pupils in the Arts' Sixth is often unsatisfactory because it does not form a coherent whole.

Seeking an appropriate counterpart to specialized study, the Council observed that between one-quarter and one-third of the school week is normally given to non-specialized subjects. Referring to this as 'minority-time', the Council found that, although of vital importance, it is often neglected or wasted. It urged, therefore, that 'minority-time' should be used for two main purposes, which it distinguished as 'common' and 'complementary'. The 'common' elements, it recommended, should be taken by arts and science specialists together; and it summarized them as religious education and all that goes to the formation of moral standards: art and music: and physical education. The 'complementary' elements, it advised, should be designed to ensure the 'literacy' of science specialists and the 'numeracy' of arts specialists. In coining these two terms it seems likely that the Council has made a permanent addition to our rich store of educational jargon, for they are already circulating as familiar currency. 'Literacy' in this context is defined as: 'not only the ability to use the mother-tongue as an adequate means of communication for adult purposes, but also the development of moral, aesthetic, and social judgement'. While 'Numeracy' is described as 'not only the ability to reason quantitatively, but also some understanding of scientific method and some acquaintance with the achievement of science'.

To discharge their wider reference Sir Geoffrey Crowther and his colleagues had to tackle some highly controversial issues. Of these the most prickly was the contentious problem already alluded to briefly in Chapter Three above, namely what recommendations to make about two important, unfulfilled provisions of the Education Act, 1944 – the raising of the school leaving age to sixteen, and the creation of county colleges for compulsory part-time education to eighteen. Which of these two big reforms should come first, that was the crux of the question. The upshot of the Council's deliberations was a recommendation that both of these projects 'should be reaffirmed as objectives of national policy': but as regards timing, the school leaving age proposal was given priority and, as already noted, the raising of the school leaving age to sixteen is now planned for 1970.

One of the most interesting sections in the report deals with the education of the intelligent young worker, 'neglected educational territory'. In this group, the Council maintains, lies the richest vein of untapped human resources, and it contends forcibly that more care should be taken over the development of these young people 'if this country is to keep a place among the nations that are in the van of spiritual and material progress'. One lesson to be learnt from this and other reports is that education is profoundly affected by factors that are not strictly educational – e.g. health, housing, mass media, and the determination of priorities. It is, therefore, essential for it to have an influential spokesman with an overall knowledge of its problems in places where national policy is decided. Plato appreciated the need for an outstanding Minister long ago, urging that care should be taken to see that the Minister responsible for education is 'of all the citizens in every way the best'. The Robbins Report brought this issue into the limelight by recommending that there should be a Minister responsible for universities and other autonomous, state-supported, institutions as well as the Minister vested with powers over schools and other institutions as defined in the 1944 Act. This question – one Minister or two – was warmly debated in Parliament and wisely, so most people thought, it was decided that there should be a single Minister (Secretary of State for Education and Science) responsible over the whole educational field with two Ministers of State to assist him.

BOOKS FOR FURTHER READING

CHAPTER ONE

Conant, J. B. *Education in a Divided World*. London, Oxford Univ. Press, 1948.

Hadow Report. *Education of the Adolescent*. London, H.M.S.O., 1926.

Hughes, A. G. *Education and the Democratic Ideal*. London, Longmans, 1951.

Jacks, M. L. *Modern Trends in Education*. London, Melrose, 1952.

James Eric (Lord James of Rusholme). *An Essay on the Content of Education*. London, Harrap, 1949.

Jefferys, M. V. C. *Glaucon: An Inquiry into the Aims of Education*. London, Pitman, 1950.

Livingstone, R. *On Education: The Future in Education, and Education for a World Adrift*. London, Cambridge Univ. Press, 1954.

National Union of Teachers. *The Curriculum of the Secondary School* (report of a Consultative Committee). London, Evans, 1952.

Niblett, W. R. *Education and the Modern Mind*. London, Faber, 1954.

Norwood, C. *The English Tradition in Education*. London, Murray, 1929.

Nunn, T. Percy. *Education: its Data and First Principles*, 3rd edition. London, Edward Arnold, 1945.

Peterson, A. D. C. *A Hundred Years of Education*. London, Duckworth, 1952.

Scottish Advisory Council for Education. *Report on Primary Schools* (1946): *Report on Secondary Schools* (1947). Edinburgh, H.M.S.O.

Spens Report. *Secondary Education*. London, H.M.S.O., 1938.

Vaizey, J. *Education for Tomorrow*, Harmondsworth, Penguin Books, 1962.

Whitehead, A. N. *The Aims of Education and Other Essays*. London, Williams & Norgate, 1929.

CHAPTER TWO

Adams, John, *The Evolution of Educational Theory*. London, Macmillan, 1912.

Bantock, G. H. *Freedom and Authority in Education*. London, Faber, 1952.

Catty, N. *The Theory and Practice of Education*. London, Methuen, revised edition, 1954.

Curtis, S. J., and Boultwood, M. E. A. *A Short History of Educational Ideas*. London, University Tutorial Press, 1953.

Daniel, M. V. *Activity in the Primary School*. Oxford, Blackwell, 1947.

Gardner, D. E. M. *Education under Eight*. London, Longmans, 1949. *The Education of Young Children*. London, Methuen, 1956.

Gesell, A. *The Child from Five to Ten*. London, Hamish Hamilton, 1946.

Greenough, A., and Crofts, F. A. *Theory and Practice in the New Secondary School*. London, Univ. of London Press, 1949.

Judges, A. V. (edited by). *Pioneers of English Education*. London, Faber, 1952.

Nettleship, L. *The Theory of Education in Plato's Republic*. London, Oxford Univ. Press, 1935.

Panton, J. H. *Modern Teaching Practice and Technique*. London, 1944.

Peel, E. A. *The Psychological Basis of Education*. Edinburgh, Oliver and Boyd, 1956.

Ross, J. S. *Groundwork of Educational Theory*. London, Harrap, 1942.

Rusk, R. R. *The Doctrines of the Great Educators*. London, Macmillan, Revised Edition, 1954.

Stott, C. A. *School Libraries*. London, Cambridge Univ. Press, revised edition, 1955.

Sturt, M. and Oakden, E. C. *Modern Psychology and Education*. London, Kegan Paul, Revised Edition, 1937.

CHAPTER THREE

Atkinson, M. *The Junior School Community*. London, Longmans, 1949.

Brew, J. Macalister. *In the Service of Youth*. London, Faber, 1943.

Dobinson, C. H. (edited by). *Education in a Changing World*. London, Oxford Univ. Press, 1951.

Fleming, C. M. *The Social Psychology of Education*. London, Routledge and Kegan Paul, 1944.

Gardner, D. E. M. *The Children's Play Centre*. London, Methuen, 1937.

Gaunt, H. C. A. *School: a Book for Parents*. London, Herbert Jenkins, 1953.

Highfield, M. E., and Pinsent, A. *A Survey of Rewards and Punishments in Schools*. London, Newnes (for National Foundation for Educational Research), 1952.

Isaacs, Susan. *The Nursery Years: the Mind of the Child from Birth to Six Years*. London, Routledge, 1929.

James, H. E. O., and others. *Periods of Stress in the Primary School*. London, National Association for Mental Health, 1956.

Jephcott, P. (edited by), *Some Young People*. London, Allen and Unwin, 1954.

Jordan, G. W., and Fisher, E. M. *Self-Portrait of Youth*. London, Heinemann, 1955.

King George's Jubilee Trust. *Citizens of Tomorrow*. London, Odhams, 1955.

Kuenstler, P. (edited by). *Social Group Work in Great Britain*. London, Faber, 1954.

Ministry of Education Pamphlet, No. 16. *Citizens Growing Up*. London, H.M.S.O., 1949.

Newsom, J. H. *The Child at School*. Harmondsworth, Penguin Books, 1950.

Reeves, M. *Growing up in a Modern Society*. London, Univ. of London Press, 1946.

Reports of Central Advisory Council (England) on *School and Life* (1947) and on *Out of School* (1948). London, H.M.S.O.

Report of Committee on *The Youth Service in England and Wales* (Albemarle Report), London, H.M.S.O., 1960.

Valentine, C. W. *Parents and children, a first book on the psychology of child development and training*. London, Methuen, 1953.

Chapter Four

Banks, O. *Parity and Prestige in English Secondary Education*. London, Routledge & Kegan Paul, 1955.

Central Advisory Council for Education (England). *Half Our Future* (Newsom Report), London, H.M.S.O., 1963.

Clarke, F. *Education and Social Change*. London, Sheldon Press, 1943.

Conant, J. B. *Education and Liberty*. Cambridge, U.S.A., Harvard Univ. Press, 1953.

Dempster, J. J. B. *Selection for Secondary Education, a Survey*. London, Methuen, 1954.

Dent, H. C. *Secondary Education for All, Origins and Development in England*. London, Routledge & Kegan Paul, 1949.

Eliot, T. S. *The Idea of a Christian Society*. London, Faber, 1939.

Hemming, J. *The Teaching of Social Studies in Secondary Schools*. London, Longmans, 1949.

James, Eric (Lord James of Rusholme). *Education and Leadership*. London, Harrap, 1951.

Judges, A. V. (edited by). *Looking Forward in Education*. London, Faber, 1955.

Mannheim, K. *Diagnosis of our Time*. London, Routledge & Kegan Paul, 1940.

Ottaway, A. K. C. *Education and Society, an Introduction to the Sociology of Education* (valuable also for its bibliography). London, Routledge & Kegan Paul, 1953.

Russell, Bertrand. *Education and the Social Order*. London, Allen and Unwin, 1932.

Simon, B. *Ingelligence Testing and the Comprehensive School*. London, Lawrence and Wishart, 1955.

Wootton, B. (Lady Wootton of Abinger). *Freedom under Planning*. London, Allen and Unwin, 1945.

CHAPTER FIVE

Alexander, W. P. *Education in England. The National System – How it works*. London, Newnes, 2nd ed., 1964.

Baron, George. *A Bibliographical Guide to the English Educational System*. London, Athlone Press, 2nd ed., 1964.

Curtis, S. J. *Education in Britain since 1900*. London, Dakers, 1952.

Dent, H. C. *The Education Act, 1944* (8th edition), London, Univ. of London Press, 1960; *The Educational System of England and Wales*, London, Univ. of London Press, 1961.

Leese, J. *Personalities and Power in English Education*. Leeds, E. J. Arnold, 1950.

Lowndes, G. A. N. *The Silent Social Revolution*. London, Oxford Univ. Press, 1937.

Richmond, W. K. *Education in England*. Harmondsworth, Penguin Books, 1945.

For the history of education see Curtis, S. J. *History of Education in Great Britain* (London, Univ. Tutorial Press, 3rd edition, 1953); or Barnard, H. C. *A Short History of English Education, 1760–1944* (London, Univ. of London Press, 1947).

CHAPTER SIX

Dent, H. C. *To be a Teacher*. London, Univ. of London Press, 1947.

Edmonds, E. L. *The School·Inspector*. London, Routledge & Kegan Paul, 1962.

Gurrey, P. *Education and the Training of Teachers*. London, Longmans, 1963.

Highet, G. *The Art of Teaching*. London, Methuen, 1951.

Kandel, I. L. *The New Era in Education*. London, Harrap, 1955.

McNair Report on Supply, Recruitment, and Training of Teachers and Youth Leaders, London, H.M.S.O., 1944.

Rich, R. W. *The Teacher in a Planned Society*. London, Univ. of London Press, 1950.

Richardson, C. A., and others. *The Education of Teachers in England, France, and the U.S.A*. Paris, UNESCO, 1953.

Selincourt, A. de. *The Schoolmaster*. London, Lehmann, 1951.

Simpson, J. H. *Schoolmaster's Harvest*. London, Faber, 1954.
Wilson, P. *Views and Prospects from Curzon Street*. Oxford, Blackwell, 1961.

Chapter Seven

Barker, Ernest. *Age and Youth*. London, Oxford Univ. Press, 1955.
Castle, E. B. *People in School*. London, Heinemann, 1953.
Fleming Report on the Public Schools and the General Educational System. London, H.M.S.O., 1944.
Hughes, Donald. *The Public Schools and the Future*. London, Cambridge Univ. Press, 1942.
Institute of Christian Education. *Religious Education in Schools*. S.P.C.K., 1954.
Leeson, S. *Christian Education*. London, Longmans, 1947.
Moberley, W. *The Crisis in the University*. London, S.C.M., 1949.
Wolfenden, J. F. *The Public Schools To-day, a study in Boarding School Education*. London, Univ. of London Press, 1949.

Chapter Eight

Argles, M. *South Kensington to Robbins*. London, Longmans, 1964.
Brown, J. A. C. *The Social Psychology of Industry*. Harmondsworth, Penguin Books, 1954.
Central Advisory Council for Education (England), *15 to 18*, Vols. I, II (Crowther Report). London, H.M.S.O., 1960.
Collier, K. G. *The Science of Humanity*. London, Nelson, 1950.
Committee on Higher Education. *Higher Education* (Robbins Report). London, H.M.S.O., 1963.
Dent, H. C. *Part-time Education in Great Britain*. London, Turnstile Press, 1949.
Dobinson, C. H. *Technical Education for Adolescents*. London, Harrap, 1951.
Edwards, Reese. *The Secondary Technical School*. London, Univ. of London Press, 1960.
Lewis, M. M. *Language in Society*. London, Nelson, 1947.
Mayo, Elton. *The Social Problems of an Industrial Civilization*. London, Routledge & Kegan Paul, 1949.
Venables, P. F. R. *Technical Education*. London, Bell, 1955.
Wheeler, O. A. *The Adventure of Youth*. London, Univ. of London Press, 1945.

INDEX

Abrams, Mark, 102
Academic Freedom, 120, 158–70, 181
Activity, 23–4, 57
Acts, Elementary Education (1870), 13, 97, 102, 133, 136, 140, 190, 192–3; Welsh Intermediate (1889), 125, 209; Board of Education (1899), 136, 139–40; Education (1902), 133–4, 135–6, 143, 156; Physical Training and Recreation (1937), 88; Education (1918), 81, 98, 119, 152; Education (1944), 14, 16, 19–20, 25, 28, 38, 56, 77, 81, 93, 97, 98, 102–3, 104, 107, 119, 124, 126, 134, 135, 136–40, 158, 180, 190–1, 192, 195, 196, 198, 210, 214, 217; Education (Scotland) (1945), 125; Local Government (1958), 92, 93
Adams, Sir John, 43, 44, 152
Adler, A., 45
Adolescence, 26, 39, 49, 80–2, 84
Adult community, responsibility of, 74, 83–4
Adult education, 16–19, 147, 180, 186, 214, 229
Affection, need of, 64–7
Agreed syllabuses, 190–2
Agriculture, 218
Aims, 25, 28–31, 57, 58
Albemarle Report, 85
Alexander, W. P., 109–10, 147
Allocation to secondary schools, 106–7
Aristotle, 11, 16, 29
Army Bureau of Current Affairs, 16
Arnold, Matthew, 33, 59, 125, 176, 194–5
Arnold, Thomas, 24, 41, 57–8, 101, 208
Art, colleges of, 156
Arts Council, 16, 214

Asquith, H. H. (1st Earl of Oxford and Asquith), 168
Associations of local authorities, 147
Attitude to work, 215–16

Bacon, Francis, 111, 208
Baden Powell (1st Baron), 101
Bagehot, W., 207
Ballard, P. B., 47
Banks, Olive, 105, 204
Barker, Sir Ernest, 16, 18, 130–1, 204, 205
Barker, Sir Ross, 137
B.B.C., 16, 27, 32, 69, 77, 100, 101
Beale, Dorothea, 24, 173
Beales, A. C. F., 190 n
Bell, Andrew, 13, 34
Beloe Report, 57 n
Benedict, Ruth, 49
Bentham, Jeremy, 175
Bevan, Aneurin, 199–200
Blackett, P. M. S., 224
Boyle, Sir E., 178
Bryce Commission, 136, 209–10
Buchan, John (1st Lord Tweedsmuir), 86
Burnham Committee, 153, 177–9
Burt, Sir Cyril, 47
Buss, Frances M., 24, 101, 173, 205
Butler, R. A., 19, 20, 38, 81, 106, 119, 124, 156, 180, 195, 200, 217

Carlyle, A. J., 128
Catty, N., 49–50
Central Advisory Council for Education (England), 72, 74, 81, 115, 179, 227–8
Central Advisory Council for Education (Wales), 126, 179
Chairmen of Education Committees, 145–6
Change of residence, effect of, 65